TO THE CHURCH OF ENGLAND

by

GARETH BENNETT
1929–1987

EDES CHRISTI
in Academia Oxoniensi

TO
THE CHURCH OF ENGLAND

Essays and Papers
and
The Preface to Crockford's Clerical Directory
1987/1988

by

GARETH BENNETT
Lately Fellow of New College, Oxford

edited
and with an Introductory Memoir

by

Geoffrey Rowell
Fellow and Chaplain of Keble College, Oxford

CHURCHMAN PUBLISHING

TO THE CHURCH OF ENGLAND
was first published in 1988 by
CHURCHMAN PUBLISHING LIMITED
117 Broomfield Avenue
Worthing
West Sussex BN14 7SF

Publisher: E. Peter Smith
Represented in Australia, Canada, India, Ireland,
New Zealand and the United States

Distributed to the Book Trade by
BAILEY BOOK DISTRIBUTION LIMITED
Warner House, Wear Bay Road, Folkestone Kent CT19 6PH

ISBN 1 85093 1100

All Rights Reserved Worldwide

Printed in Great Britain at the University Printing House, Oxford

CONTENTS

Contents

FOREWORD

The papers collected in this volume represent three areas of Garry Bennett's scholarship and concern—church history and historical theology (and in particular the Anglican tradition), contemporary issues in the church, and examples of his teaching sermons. The historical papers are for the most part not technical academic articles replete with learned footnotes, but represent rather the distillation of his scholarship for general audiences. Written with characteristic vigour and clarity they will be valued both for their exposition of important themes and personalities in English church history and as models of historical writing. Garry Bennett would have vigorously dissented from the trend noted by Robert Morgan, in an article surveying recent work in theology (*Theology*, July 1988, Lambeth Conference issue), that sociology had replaced history as the natural handmaid of theology.

The study of Martin Luther was a commemorative lecture to mark the five hundredth anniversary of the Reformer's birth in 1983. The lecture on Bishop Ken was written to mark the three hundredth anniversary of Ken's enthronement as Bishop of Bath and Wells and was delivered by Dr Bennett in the Quire of Wells Cathedral in September, 1985. The paper on Archbishop Tenison was given as a lecture to the Friends of Lambeth Palace Library.

Some of the papers on contemporary issues in the church were originally prepared for church commissions and working parties of which he was a member, particularly the Faith and Order Advisory Group and the Board for Mission and Unity. It has not always been easy to locate the original context of the papers included here and both editor and publisher would wish to apologise should there have been any inadvertent breach of copyright.

Opinions will vary concerning the re-printing of the *Crockford's* preface. The decision to include it in this collection reflects a conviction that (i) it was a carefully pondered analysis; (ii) that the impression most people got of its content was distorted by the selectivity of reporting in the media; (iii) that it needs to be judged as a whole and seen in the context of Garry Bennett's other writings; and (iv) that greater availability is in an Anglican tradition of 'open government.' No one is required to agree with every aspect of the analysis, but many will want to reflect upon it with the help of the other papers in this volume.

Dr Bennett left much unpublished academic work, and it is hoped that it will be possible to publish this in the future—in particular his Birkbeck Lectures on the Restoration Church. In accordance with the provisions of Dr Bennett's will the royalties from this volume will be used to support the work of Pusey House, Oxford.

Keble College,   GEOFFREY ROWELL
OXFORD

Gareth Vaughan Bennett (1929–1987)

An introductory memoir
by Geoffrey Rowell

The publication of the edition of *Crockford's Clerical Directory* for 1987/88 with a preface critical of many aspects of contemporary Anglicanism provoked an unprecedented attempt by the media to uncover the identity of the author of what was by long tradition an anonymous evaluation of the state of the Church. When, just over a week later, Dr Gareth Bennett was found dead in his car, apparently having taken his own life, and was subsequently named as the author of the preface, the name of one known largely within the worlds of historical scholarship and the Church of England became momentarily a household word. The papers in this volume—historical, contemporary and devotional—are published both for their intrinsic value, and as a memorial to a scholar-priest who was steeped in the Anglican tradition and was deeply concerned for the future of the church he loved.

By way of introduction it seemed appropriate to preface this collection with a short memoir of Gareth Bennett, though, as he would himself have been the first to admit, the lives of academics are not in general marked by dramatic incident or stirring events. The patient analysis required of the historian as he investigates the past may lead, as Garry Bennett's own work did, to a reinterpretation and new evaluation of a particular historical character or period; it will rarely be on a par with the events so studied.

*   *   *

Gareth Vaughan Bennett was born on 8 November 1929, at Westcliff-on-Sea in Essex. His birthday was, as he later liked to point out, the feast of the saints, martyrs and doctors of the Church of England. His parents were in their late twenties and belonged to a modest middle-class background. His father and grandfather both worked as clerks in the City, Walter Bennett working for the same shipping firm for over forty years until his retirement. His son remembered him as 'a vigorous, witty but vulnerable man'. His mother's family, the Vaughans, had owned a military outfitters at Camberley in Surrey.

Garry was an only child and in retrospect believed his childhood to have been over-protected. 'I was never allowed out with other children, and I used to sit at the window watching other boys (probably rather older than I) walking by in gangs or groups. I recall, even now, envying them their freedom and independence.' His only close companion was his cousin, who lived a few streets away. He was first sent to a private day school called 'The Priors' and then transferred to another, Haddon Court College, 'run by a genial fraud who had once been a PT instructor, and was intent on deep breathing.' For holidays the family went for a number of years to Blankenberge in Belgium. Although both his parents had been confirmed it was not a church-going family, and Garry only recalled two visits to the Prittlewell Sunday School and family talk heavily critical of the church and churchgoers. (His father had been brought up in a fundamentalist, Evangelical tradition, and had fallen away from regular churchgoing, not having found any of the local churches to his taste.) Moving to yet a third private school at the time of the Munich crisis, he became a voracious reader. 'This is what filled my rather solitary life. But I did not read any of the books which the real middle-class read: Beatrix Potter and A. A. Milne I never knew. The *Magnet* and the *Gem* and Percy F. Westerman were my mainstay.' Miss Higgins, the headmistress of this third school, was a devout Baptist, who sometimes took her pupils to her church and more often talked to them in school about it.

In May 1940 he was evacuated with his school to Chesham Bois. During this time, through his mother's insistence that he should go to Anglican services and not to Baptist ones, he went with another boy to Mattins in the village church and found that he enjoyed it. Not long after, his parents having moved to Cheam, he was taken away from Miss Higgins' school and did not go to school for nine months. In December they had to move to a cousin's house at East Horsley, where they remained until 1943. Through his mother's persistence he gained a place at the Royal Grammar School at Guildford, where he remained until the family moved back again to Southend after Easter 1943, when he was sent to Southend High School for Boys. Only then did he have the opportunity to show his academic ability, and read not only novels but theological and philosophical works from the local library. It was at this time that he encountered the Vicar of Prittlewell, Archdeacon Gowing, who suggested that he should be prepared for confirmation, and from that time he began attending church regularly, not only being confirmed but becoming a server and, together with his cousin, teaching in the Sunday School. The Prittlewell tradition was not Anglo-Catholic but 'middle Anglican'. Garry commented on this time:

Though (the vicar) was not a great intellectual, he was interested in history, and wrote a good small book on the church and a life of his father-in-law, the first bishop of Chelmsford. I recall all the mornings when I went off to church, getting up by myself and walking the mile up to St. Mary's. My parents were not at all pleased by my new-found religion, nor by the arrival of a series of curates who came to talk and stayed to tea and supper. Prittlewell was a great training-parish for young priests, and I learned a good deal of theology from them. Gradually I began to work myself with what may be called the 'Catholic' position of the Church of England. Oddly enough I read some of the easier works of Karl

Barth at this time and I was immensely impressed by his idea of God being God, but much of my thinking was about church-history. I read Newman's *Apologia* and had a mild attack of Roman fever. It was only mild because most of the Roman Catholics whom I knew at that time were positively unpleasant. Their ignorance of, and contempt for, other Christians would now be thought incredible. . . . Occasionally I went to St. Alban's, Westcliff-on-Sea, and discovered there a more congenial form of religion. It was all pre-Vatican II and not really well-attended, but there were a number of masters from the school who went regularly, notably the Senior History master, George Smith, whom I liked and admired, and who was always particularly courteous and kind. To see this substantial man with a distinguished war record, serving and acting as M.C. at the Mass was deeply moving to me.

The next challenge was university entrance—in particular Cambridge, on which Garry had set his sights, though with only a lukewarm reaction from his school. After rejections from a number of colleges he was called for interview and awarded a place at Christ's for 1949 with a year's break before the place could be taken up. Having secured the necessary passes in the Higher School Certificate, he was then summoned to a National Service medical and was 'half shocked, half relieved, to find myself classed Grade III: unfit for service.' Unexpectedly, in early October 1948 he was told that a place for that year had become available at Christ's.

Garry Bennett went up to a Cambridge largely populated by undergraduates much older than himself—many had been in the war and others had completed National Service between school and university. The work he found a shock, noting that 'the public school Scholars had been taught History very well, and knew books, authors and theories of which I was totally ignorant.' He was tutored by Anthony Steel and J. H. Plumb, whom he remembered describing him 'as having a mind historically "tabula rasa".' He was sensitive to the perceived social gap between himself and his public school contemporaries, as well as the academic one, but

4

demonstrated his ability with a top 2.1 in Prelims. He was also able to find a niche as a cox for one of the College Eights.

Religiously he continued to develop. It was a time in Cambridge when college chapels were well attended, and he went regularly morning and evening on Sundays and often on weekdays as well. Ian Ramsey, later to be Nolloth Professor of the Philosophy of the Christian Religion at Oxford and then bishop of Durham, was chaplain. He found him 'fussily kind' and recognised the brilliance of his mind, but did not know him well. When Ramsey gave up as chaplain his successor was an Irishman, J. S. Brown. Garry found him 'shy, humorous and unassuming' but believed that he proved to be one of the best college chaplains in Cambridge. 'He had virtually open house, and was used and abused by many of us . . . John Brown was a great gift to me, and the only senior member whom I really knew at all well in my time at Cambridge.' Outside Christ's he went initially to Christian Union meetings and sermons, but found the theology not to his taste and the people somewhat assertive and boring. Worship at the Little St. Mary's High Mass on Sundays spoke more deeply to him.

His second year in Cambridge brought him a 2.1 in the first part of the History Tripos and in the following vacation he went with a friend to stay in a rectory in Guernsey taken temporarily by a locum priest, R. H. Wornoll, a training college lecturer. Wornoll was an excellent preacher, whose sermons introduced the young history undergraduate 'to a wholly new set of ideas on the eucharist and its meaning'. Back at Cambridge his work improved and he was even encouraged by his tutor to think of the ultimate undergraduate accolade, the starred first. As his special subject he studied 'Church, State and Society, 1685 to 1718' and was lectured by Norman Sykes. In November he celebrated his twenty-first birthday, and, as a present from his father, was initiated as Freemason. (In later years he was to leave the

Craft.) Fearing that in Finals he would repeat his 2.1's, he applied to take an archives administration diploma at University College, London. Ordination nagged as a possibility but had not yet crystallised into a definite sense of vocation. In the event he gained the coveted starred First in History, and, thanks to college scholarships, was able to return to Cambridge to begin research with Norman Sykes, the Dixie Professor of Ecclesiastical History, later to be Dean of Winchester. The subject was White Kennett, Bishop of Peterborough from 1718 to 1728. Sykes he found 'businesslike, friendly, but not over helpful as a supervisor', though 'genuinely sympathetic' when in his third year of research, with his thesis all but completed, he was passed over for a research fellowship at Christ's. In May 1954 he was examined for his Ph.D. and was awarded it when only twenty-four and not yet qualified to take his MA. Encouraged by Sykes he put in for a number of academic jobs outside Cambridge and was appointed to a three-year lectureship in History at King's College, London. Looking back many years later on his Cambridge years he commented:

It is sometimes said that today Oxford and Cambridge colleges have lost much of the old sense of community and that the relationship between tutors and pupils is not what it was. My own experience is that this is just not true. The fellows of Christ's between 1948 and 1954 were, for the most part, self-centred and ill-mannered. There was practically no contact between tutors and pupils, apart from a few mass entertainments put on by the Master or a tutor spending his entertainment allowance. There was a great deal of rivalry and jockeying for position in college, and some nasty personal feuds. C. P. Snow's *The Masters* is said to be a kind of portrait of Christ's. From my underdog vantage-point it seemed quite accurate.

As an Assistant Lecturer at King's College, London, he found he had to take on a heavy teaching load in far from ideal conditions and some uneasy relations with colleagues. But he acknowledged a debt even to some of those with whom he disagreed, such as a Marxist historian who introduced him to a kind of history he had not encountered at Cambridge, so that he could go so far as to claim that he adopted a kind of Marxist approach as his own. He found a congenial colleague in Hubert Tayssandier, a French lecturer. 'His combination of wit, information and a genuine radicalism was a great stimulus to my own mind, which was in danger of settling down into mere orthodoxy. His dry views of religion and religious people . . . were wholly refreshing.' During this time the foundations of a wide-ranging historical knowledge were laid as he strove to meet the requirements of lecture courses in wholly unfamiliar areas of history. He lived first at his parents' home in Southend and commuted to London, and latterly found lodgings over a restaurant in Earl's Court. In 1955 Cambridge awarded him the Thirlwall prize for his thesis with a grant towards its publication. *White Kennett* was published by S.P.C.K. in 1957.

The Thirlwall award gave rise to hopes that he might return to Cambridge, but he was now seriously considering ordination. Norman Sykes encouraged him, not, Garry believed, 'on very religious grounds, but because he had a strong sense of the need for learned clergymen'.

He did not think of it as a particularly serious step. My mind was very much more old-fashionedly sacerdotal, and I worried a great deal about whether I was really up to it spiritually.

His vicar and the Bishop of Chelmsford encouraged him, but it was the Dean of King's, Eric Abbott, who was the determining influence. 'He was decisive in his view. Whatever doubts I had, he was clear that ordination was the right thing.' He was accepted for training and, on the advice of the Bishop of Chelmsford, undertook to spend three Long Vacation terms at Westcott House. In the first of these he was appreciative of the friendship of Simon

Barrington-Ward (now Bishop of Coventry). 'He was a great support, and his charm and simple piety were a good foil to my rather trenchant views on faith and order.'

The Principal, Ken Carey, did not know what to make of me at all. I found him very intense and uneasy, and he spent much effort trying to pull me down a peg or two. He kept on about his own Third in History at Oxford as if to reprove me for having got a First; he wholly refused to laugh at my jokes; and kept on asking me if I made my confession. Since he refused to allow me to tell him jokes; I refused to tell him my sins.

Irritated by the theological college pressure for all to be 'eager, sweetness and light' he sought Sykes' advice. He wisely counselled that the theological college hot-house should not be taken too seriously, he should get ordained and there would then be plenty of openings. Robert Runcie, then Vice-Principal, he also found a source of strength at this time.

He was the one member of the staff who actually seemed to think that it was a good thing that I was an academic, and we had a number of humorous conversations . . . He thought that all priests should have a secular side to them, and a false or intense piety was an enemy to real religion. He took a kind of benevolent oversight of me which was more that of equal to equal than I deserved. He was always cheering me up by asking my advice on this or that theological problem. I became quite devoted to him, and my diary is full of references to his kindness. He had intelligence, wit and style. But I can scarcely have realised that I was laying the foundation of a friendship with a future Archbishop of Canterbury.

White Kennett was finished in September of that year and he returned to King's for his second academic year. It was 1956 and the year of the Suez crisis, which provoked considerable political discussion in the college. As a result his political views veered considerably to the left, and he remembered taking part in a demonstration in Whitehall against the Government's Suez policy. In the Long

Vacation there followed a second term at Westcott, which he found much more enjoyable and did some intense reading in theology. He was ordained by the Bishop of Chelmsford at the Michaelmas ordination, and served a title as part-time curate of his home parish of Prittlewell combined with his King's lecturership. The illness of his vicar meant that he was much needed there and as a consequence did not return to Westcott for the Long Vacation term in his deacon's year as had been planned. He was ordained priest in September, 1957, celebrating the Eucharist for the first time at Prittlewell with his cousin serving and his parents present. A characteristic card from Eric Abbott prayed that his special vocation as a teaching priest would work out *ad majorem Dei gloriam*.

Back at King's he was able to move from the Earl's Court lodging to a room at St. Luke's Vicarage in Chelsea, where he enjoyed the company of the vicar, Ross Hook (later Bishop of Bradford) and his wife, Ruth. He responded to the suggestion of Clifford Dugmore, Professor of Ecclesiastical History at King's, that he should write on the early eighteenth-century Tory High Churchman, Bishop Francis Atterbury—a work which he thought would be brief but which became his major work of historical re-assessment *The Tory Crisis in Church and State*. The almost total incapacity of Archdeacon Gowing, the Vicar of Prittlewell, meant that a heavy burden of parochial work fell on the non-stipendiary, part-time curate.

In 1959 New College, Oxford, advertised for a Dean of Divinity in succession to Christopher Woodforde, who had been appointed Dean of Wells. After what he found a formidable interview and the uncomfortable experience of a damp bed in a college guest-room he was elected on 25 June as Fellow and Chaplain. On moving to New College in October 1959 he did not find the Chapel inheritance altogether easy.

There were no servers, readers or ordinands. Apart from a simple eight o'clock said service on Sunday and a shortened form of Mattins each morning at 8 a.m. there were no services but choral Evensong . . . There were no official chapel functions and no terminal card. The chapel congregation simply did not exist as such, though some went off to St. Aldate's, St. Ebbe's or Pusey House.

He was sensitive to the barbed comments of self-conscious non-Christians and to what he perceived as the superciliousness of some of the wealthier members of the College. 'There were times when I felt very solitary and as though there really were no loyal churchmen.' Gradually a congregation was built up, through invitations to freshmen, Sunday communion breakfasts, and a Wednesday late-night Eucharist followed by an 'At Home'. College retreats began and termly corporate communions, which could attract seventy or more communicants. Some of the pattern worked out at New College has subsequently been followed in other Oxford College Chapel communities.

Both his pastoral ministry and his tutorial expertise have been warmly remembered by former undergraduates and research students alike. Jeremy Harvey, now Head-master of Bishop Fox's School, Taunton, writes of the time when he was an undergraduate at New College and Garry had first arrived as Chaplain.

I was at New College from 1959–62. Garry asked me to serve for him in Chapel . . . He taught me for a Term or two though that had less impact than his actions and kindness . . . He would take me out for Sunday Lunch at Burford, and I often ended up talking with a group in his rooms. Garry showed me friendship, gave me his acceptance, was himself, and knew how not to intrude . . .

It is hard to envisage New College without Garry and a Garry not at New College. He probably did more for me than I realise (and that could be said for many, I suspect), and not least he let me find my own level and niche and interests.

I have thought about him—and the College—often since his death. He gave us so much.

10

In 1961 his father retired and in the same year he was appointed to one of the Wiccamical prebends on the foundation of Bishop Robert Sherburne in Chichester cathedral to which New College had the nomination. He also lost his academic mentor, Norman Sykes, who died suddenly that year as Dean of Winchester. Garry co-edited and contributed to a volume of essays, planned originally as a *Festschrift* for Sykes but in the event being published as a memorial volume.

In the summer of 1963 he had his first experience of the Anglican church in the third world, being invited to Zanzibar and Tanganyika by Herbert Sydenham, an old member of New College. After Zanzibar he went on to Dar-es-Salaam, Korogwe, Mkomaindo and to Masasi, where he stayed with the bishop, Trevor Huddleston. During his time in East Africa he lectured to ordinands and clergy schools, and addressed the University of East Africa in the presence of President Nyerere. The journey was, he felt, a good experience, but he noted the weakness in the kind of Anglicanism he found there, and encountered much confusion and discontent in the church.

As well as his work as chaplain and history tutor at New College, Garry served as Librarian from 1963. In 1968 he took his turn as Sub-Warden and in 1973–4 served as Junior Proctor of the University, when he found himself in office at a time of student troubles. He was also responsible for looking after the parishes in the gift of the College, work which he undertook most conscientiously. Following his proctorial year he went to South Carolina as Visiting Professor of History.

In 1975 he was elected as the University proctor on the General Synod and found himself in a new situation. At first he found this frustrating, having the experience of being passed over for better known members when he stood to speak and had a carefully prepared contribution to make. In 1977, his mother having sold her house in Southend the previous year, joined him in Oxford, where

11

he had bought a house in New Marston. She made her home with him there until her death in 1981—a loss he felt keenly. In 1979, having been chaplain of New College for twenty years he decided to give up his chaplaincy work, feeling that it needed a younger man. He remained as history tutor and gave what assistance he could at St. Michael's, New Marston, and also Pusey House, of which he had become a governor in 1977. In the Synod his initial frustration abated as his quality as a speaker was appreciated, and his historical and theological input recognised. A typical comment was that by Rosemary Hartill, the BBC's Religious Affairs Correspondent on a speech he made in the November 1985 Synod on suffragan bishops.

The clarity of Dr Bennett's contribution was a bright light in a rather dim debate. For he tried to go back to first principles and *then* to work out practically what should be done to change current practice. (*In Perspective*, BBC publications, 1988, p. 109)

When he spoke in July 1980 about the covenanting proposals with the Free Churches he spoke, as always, out of his historian's knowledge.

Perhaps one historian who spends all his time with Anglican history and doctrine may say what he thinks to be the middle Anglican way, the distinctive Anglican position, and why he thinks that is inconsistent with these proposals. I believe that the Anglican view of ministry is one of a firm, even one might say uncompromising, adherence to the historic ministry of the Church but combined with a most generous and openhearted attitude towards ministries in Churches which do not possess it, a tradition with openhearted liberality. Anglican writers from the Reformation era onwards have argued for the historic episcopal order, not as a kind of talisman, not as a sort of institutional magic, but as something completely bound up with their doctrine of the Church. . . . I know of no Anglican writer in the 16th or 17th centuries of standing who treats episcopacy as a mere convenience, a mere option, within Church order.

In November 1982 he argued cogently for a theological and practical re-assessment of the diaconate, before any decision was taken in the matter of women deacons. The General Synod, he warned, had fallen into 'a way of formulating changes before working out theologically or pastorally what those changes ought to be'. Had his advice been heeded present difficulties in the placing of an increasing number of women deacons might have been mitigated. In November 1984 he spoke on the ordination of women, reflecting on the evaluation of tradition in this connection.

There is dead tradition and there is living tradition. Catholicism is certainly not antiquarianism. I cannot think that it is an authentic Christian argument to say that there can never be any changes. In scripture there are often latent meanings and truths which emerge in response to new challenges and as there is under God living scripture so there is living tradition. There can be discovery and development within a tradition, the very purpose of which is to preserve the basic message of the gospel and the basic character of Christian communion in a world that continually changes. The problem is to distinguish true development from what is merely contemporary fashion. In the end, it would seem—a Church historian has to say this—that orthodoxy and catholic order always come through but often in the past distortions have extraordinarily prevailed and indeed been supported by most of the most powerful minds and persuasive voices of the age. In Church history, it has to be said, the popular majorities have a way of being very consistently wrong.

Six months later, speaking in the debate on the nature of Christian belief, he was critical of the subjectivity and moralising of a theology which seemed to him a contemporary version of liberal protestantism. He reminded the Synod that 'the first Christian preaching was of divine acts which went quite against all human expectation, which negated ordinary ways of thought. What God had done was wholly beyond reason, though reason might find it consistent with the other things

13

which God had done. It was shocking and unlooked for but full of hope.'

Christian doctrine is a reflection on that in awe and wonder and a working out of its implications. The Christian community emerged. The Scriptures were written. Christology was developed. All to express this thing which God had done and which made all the difference to men. That is why the traditional Christian creeds are basically recitals of events in the form of an offering of praise.

In one of his last speeches to Synod, in February 1987 on the Bishops report concerning the ordination of women, he concluded by commenting that the Archbishop had presented the proposals in that report as a way to preserve coherence. He did not agree. 'What he has shown is that the issue of the ordination of women actually cannot live with comprehensiveness. It is not like differences in theological opinion or liturgical practice, it involves the very structures of unity, and the difficulties will grow greater as time goes on, for I am convinced that you cannot ordain women as priests unless you also ordain them as bishops.'

Not only did he become a respected speaker in the Synod he was also involved in the work of important church commissions—the Doctrine Commission, the Faith and Order Advisory Group and the Board for Mission and Unity. Latterly he was elected to the Standing Committee of the Synod and the important Policy Sub-Committee, and finally in 1987 was elected to the Crown Appointments Commission.

Academically he continued to be productive. His study of Francis Atterbury, *The Tory Crisis in Church and State 1688–1730* was published in 1975, and he subsequently produced some distinguished chapters for the eighteenth-century volume of the *History of Oxford University* as well as many articles and papers, some of which are collected in this book. His standing as an historian was recognised by his being granted leave by Cambridge to supplicate for his Doctor of Letters in 1987. His studies of the eighteenth-century church made him familiar with the satirical squibs and polemic characteristic of the period, such as the following, published anonymously in 1710.

View here the POURTRAIT of a Factious Priest,
Who (spight of Proverbs) dares defile his Nest:
And where he shou'd defend the Church's Cause,
Basely deserts her, and arraigns her Laws.
Such, and no better is the Man that dares
With his Superiors to wage litigious Wars:
And to malignant Answers set his Hand,
To Sermons publish'd by Supreme Command.

Unhappy Church, by such Usurpers sway'd,
How is thy Native Purity decay'd?
How are thy Prelates changed from what they were
When Laud and Sancroft fill'd the Sacred Chair?
When for establish'd Faith they shou'd contend,
Meekness and Christian charity pretend;
But with a blind enthusiastick Rage,
For Schism and Toleration they engage;
With strange Delight and Vehemence espouse
Occasional Conformists shameful Cause . . .

Perhaps the historian's knowledge of the prevalence of such satire and polemic in the past needs to be borne in mind in any assessment of the fateful *Crockford's* Preface, the commission to write which he accepted with the intention of bringing clearly to light what he saw as a critical situation within both the Church of England and the Anglican Communion as a whole. Sharper the criticism may have been but in principle he was doing no more than his predecessors as authors of the *Crockford's* Preface had done in their critiques of Anglican policy, personalities and attitudes. His diary reveals that the preface was pondered over many months and that he wrestled hard to find appropriate expression for his analysis. Trying to write it amid the pressure of other commitments and endeavouring to get it right caused him some anxiety as to whether he would be able to finish it as he wished by the time it was needed. As it happened, although the Preface is dated Ascensiontide 1987, and was originally commissioned for a deadline at the end of May, the text was not in fact completed and delivered until early July, just two weeks before he learnt that he had been elected to membership of the Crown Appointments Commission.

He knew that the preface would cause controversy. He recognised that to discuss publicly issues of power and patronage in the church was to break a strong church convention. He hoped what he had written would provoke serious debate about important issues. He suspected that his identity might be guessed (but not known for sure because of the contract of anonymity under which the preface was written). But he had no conception that in 1987 the usual guessing game of cathedral closes, theological colleges, Oxbridge common rooms and the church bureaucracy would be magnified by a distorting press—for parts of which the November Synod discussions on issues of sexual morality had made church questions topical and controversial—into a national 'whodunnit.'

The Saturday before publication he had a restless night —but that was the consequence of a large architect's bill for a proposed extension to his house. There is no indication in his diary that he had any sense of impending doom. The press interest once the preface was published, and incessant telephone calls asking whether he was the author, precipitated him into a situation of public denial he had not foreseen, and were compounded by the not wholly unexpected sharp comments from churchmen. It is possible that 'inspired guesses' reported to him by journalists as emanating from church sources, were received by him as statements of fact meaning that he was likely to face public humiliation and exposure on the basis of a selective reading of the preface. The last entry in his diary simply reads: 'A reporter from the *Mail* rang up to offer me £5000 if I was the author and wished to go public with them. He said it was rumoured that an announcement was to be made in the next 48 hours.' Nonetheless he drove to Cambridge that Friday evening to represent New College at a Feast at King's College. On the Saturday, December 5th, the *Mail* published an article strongly suggesting that he was the author. There is no doubt that he felt himself under considerable pressure, Whether in the end the final tragic catalyst was the fortuitous death of his much-loved cat, which he discovered on his return home in an over-wrought state, we shall never know.

It would be unjust for his sharp mind (combined at times it must be said with a sharp tongue) to have no memorial apart from the public record of the dramatic and sad ending on a grey December day in 1987. He had preached earlier that year a Lenten address in Liverpool Parish Church (an address re-printed as part of this collection) that if he only had one sermon to preach, it would of course have to be about the love and free mercy of God to sinners, for that is the essence of the Gospel of Christ. It is in the context of that Gospel that these essays are presented in memory of a scholar-priest who knew his need of that mercy, and for whom that same mercy is asked.

HISTORICAL

Martin Luther: The Impact of The Reformer on Religious Thought

In his last years Martin Luther was a wonderful storyteller, rich in memories about his youth, his early career and his struggles as a reformer. Most of what we know about his early religious development is derived from these later recollections. At Wittenberg in the 1540s he lived as a kind of patriarch; and students, foreign Protestants and tourists came to sit at his feet and hang on his every word. Even at the dinner-table they noted down his talk to preserve each gem for posterity. And he, amid wretched illnesses and many anxieties, loved this eager young audience: he enjoyed good German phrases; and he loved to make a theological point with some pungent illustration of how things were in the days of the Papists before the gospel had been preached. There were stories of the futile goings-on of the scholastics before curriculum-reform had come to Wittenberg, of 'monkery' in the cloisters, and of his own 'breakthrough' to understanding in the tower-room of the Augustinian friars. But the fact is that passing time and emerging patterns of apologetic made much of what he said unreliable evidence; and he was always very bad at dates. If we relied on Luther himself we should be celebrating the five-hundredth anniversary of his birth not in 1983 but in 1984. He always said that he was born in 1484 but when his humanistically trained biographer, Philip Melanchthon, came to check the facts he discovered that the great man had got it wrong. Luther's mother, as is the way with very old ladies, could tell the exact day and hour—it was the eve of St. Martin's day at 11 at night—but for the

21

life of her she could not remember what year. It was Luther's businesslike brother Jacob who fixed it definitely for 1483. Indeed modern scholars have come to recognize that the reformer himself is a very unsure guide to the chronology of his own early development. Things happened so quickly, ideas and themes overlapped, and doctrines became firmed up in the course of controversy. In 1545 he admitted as much when he described his early works as 'a crude and inchoate muddle which now I myself cannot easily put in order'.

So, in spite of all the facile popular accounts, it is actually quite difficult to discover the man who made such a dramatic impact upon the German religious scene between 1517 and 1521. There will always have to be an interpretative reconstruction of the way he came to a distinctive Reformation theology, and the scholarly task is to keep the theory as close to the known evidence as possible. One thing of which we can be glad is that there now seems some let-up in the attempt to provide an explanation of Luther's theology in psycho-analytical terms. The fact is that there is insufficient evidence for his feeling of terror and inadequacy before his father or for his need for a sudden release from sexual frustration or sluggish bowel-movements. Modern research has come to confine its interests to Luther as an exceptionally gifted professional theologian, one who brought a powerful, constructive minds to the religious questions of his own day. This is not, of course, to say that his interests were purely academic. At the heart of his greatness as a theologian was his understanding of theology as a practical science: that its end is not a mere satisfaction of the mind but pastoral counsel for those who stand *coram Deo*, in the presence of God. Right theology was important only as it led on to right repentance, right praying and right living.

But what *was* the character of the world of late-medieval theology into which Luther came as a theological student at Wittenberg and Erfurt in 1508–11 and as professor at Wittenberg from 1512? In recent years there has been a number of perceptive studies of leading theologians who were his immediate predecessors and contemporaries, and in particular important figures like Gabriel Biel, Johannes Steinbach and Johann von Staupitz. In their persons we see how false was all that Erasmian satire on medieval universities and theological faculties, and indeed how unfair the later Luther was. So far from living in ivory towers, disputing arid and speculative points of divinity, they were all men who combined professional theology with popular preaching and pastoral care. Universities were expanding in numbers and new ones being founded. Among the theologians there was a vigorous debate about justification: that is how sinful men are restored to a right relationship with God. It was, after all, the chief and absorbing topic of medieval theology. Let us be clear. No medieval theologian thought that a man could earn justification by his own works or unaided efforts. For them Augustine held a pre-eminent place among the Fathers, and to assert justification by works was to fall into the error of that Pelagianism which he had so vehemently denounced. All insisted that justification was the work of God and depended on his free gift of grace. The question which they debated was a more difficult one. How does this work of grace consist with the freedom of man? For most medieval theologians reason and a power to choose were essential to the humanity of man. So, to what extent did a man have to meet God's gracious initiative with a free act of response, involving mind as well as heart? On this the theologians were divided, but the mainstream attempted to find some *via media* which avoided the downgrading of sinners into a tool of the will of God; they tried to hold together both the saving power of God *and* some way by which men could appropriate grace and make it their own.

There were, however, theologians who adopted positions at either end of the spectrum. On the side of those who stressed man's need to respond was the great

Tübingen professor, Gabriel Biel, who exercised so great
an influence on the young Luther through his teachers at
Erfurt. Biel was not just an academic; he was superior of
an experimental community of the Brethren of the
Common Life and a famous preacher with a large student
audience. His sermons still have the power to move, and
clearly he preached to convert. He urged the young to
take their condition seriously, turn to a gracious God,
and take upon them the following and the imitation of
Christ. He stressed continually the graciousness of God
and his acceptance of those who turned to him. And he
offered a special consolation. Though men have no works
in them which could earn their salvation, and do not have
within them a true love for God, yet he in his mercy will
look upon their efforts at the human level and accept
them *as though* they had been done in true repentance
and love for God. This was called a merit *de congruo*. In
Biel's sermons it comes over as the assurance of the mercy
of God who would accept an inadequate offering and
give a grace which really allowed men to grow into a true
likeness of Christ. But such a formula had already been
severely criticized as no better than Pelagianism by the proponents of a more radical late-medieval Augustinianism.
Gregory of Rimini, a fourteenth century member of
Luther's own order, had offered a doctrine of the total
incapacity of sinful man. For him man was helpless until
God acts towards him, and reveals to him that he has
been chosen before the very beginning of the world. It
was knowledge of this predestinating love which gave
hope. At Wittenberg, when Luther went there first in
1508, there was a course of study in the *via Gregorii*, and
it is of some importance that he began his study of
theology as the tide began to flow for an Augustinian
revival. When the complete works of Augustine were
published by Johannes Amerbach of Basel between 1490
and 1506 this publishing event provided the essential
texts. For a while at the beginning of the sixteenth
century the kind of theology which Biel represented was

24

on the defensive. Even his editor, Johannes Steinbach, withdrew tactically from many of his master's positions.

It was, then, at such a time of theological turmoil that Luther began his career as a theologian. Since 1505 he had been a monk in a rigorist order of Augustinian friars, and it now seems to be generally agreed that he was a most zealous member of it, attempting minutely to obey his rule and find in it a way of spiritual progress. At first all went well but by the time that he began a serious and professional study of theology at Wittenberg in the winter of 1508–9 he was clearly in a confused and troubled state. At the new university in Saxony he had to combine two tasks: to lecture in the faculty of Arts on Aristotle's *Nichomachean Ethics* and begin study in the faculty of Theology for his first degrees there. He was miserably overworked and his mind was divided between lecturing on Aristotle, whom he came to detest, and doing theology in the course of which he came more and more to admire Augustine. Aristotle seemed to him to be speaking of goodness as a quality of men's actions, Augustine of a goodness which is given by God. Luther's letters, annotations and lecture-notes from this time, and after his return to Erfurt, show his mind agonizing on the old question of how far a man can co-operate with grace and play any part in his thus coming to justification.

When in 1511 he went again to Wittenberg he was clearly in a kind of confusion and in search of a theological position, and his intellectual problem spilled over into the confessional. Here he found himself under the spiritual direction of an outstanding man, Johann von Staupitz, vicar-general of the Saxon congregation of his order and professor of biblical theology at Wittenberg. Recent research reveals something of the contemporary stature of Staupitz: an aristocrat who walked easily with rulers but was head of a German order dedicated to poverty, a professor who was also an influential popular preacher and sensitive confessor. As a theologian he was himself deeply influenced by the Augustinian revival, but he firmly resisted any understanding of Augustine which seemed wholly to eliminate a human response and an appropriation of grace. In Advent 1516 he preached at Nuremberg a famous course of sermons which were received there as a veritable evangelical experience, and can be regarded as the beginning of the Reform in that city. He spoke movingly of the predestinating will of God to justify an individual which precedes all human works. Christ, he said, turned to look on Peter before Peter turned to look at Christ. But for Staupitz knowledge of this justification came as an inner, mystical experience, as stirrings of love for God. Within the heart there would be struggle and confusion: on the one hand a growing sense of sin and falling short; but on the other hand a growing assurance of acceptance and consolation. Grace working within builds up a confidence in God's justification. We must never presume on it or take pride in it, but humbly grow into its meaning for us.

In later years Luther was to attribute his Reformation theology to Staupitz: *Ich habe all mein ding von Doktor Staupitz*. But in fact this kind of moderate Augustinianism was insufficient for him. It required a man to be too subjective, to look within himself to discern signs of his justification in his stirrings of love for God. Luther found that he could not *feel* anything, and he looked for some more objective assurance. For Staupitz all these doubts appeared nothing more than an attack of the scruples which so often afflicted young monks, and his inability to understand led Luther to seek out other confessors. Even in the way in which he interpreted Staupitz's own theology Luther can be seen moving to a more radical version of Augustine: to the total incapacity of man, his utter reliance on grace, his sense of being without hope until raised up by some positive declaration of God towards him.

In 1512 Staupitz withdrew from Wittenberg leaving the twenty-nine year-old Luther to succeed him as a Doctor of Theology, Professor of Biblical Studies, monastery and town preacher, and in charge of all the local affairs of the order. The rest of the story, down to 1517, is of a theological faculty which quickly becomes known for its radical, anti-Pelagian Augustinianism. The new Professor Dr. Luther finds a solution to his own problems in formulating a doctrine of the total helplessness of sinful man. And if one may indulge in a choice among the options of Luther-research it would seem to be some-where at the end of 1514 or the beginning of 1515 that his mind became fixed in an apologetic pattern. Is this the time of the famous Tower-experience? In some of the older accounts this is portrayed as a veritable evangelical conversion. It seems more probable that it was a moment of academic illumination in an upper library-room as he wrestled with the preparation for a course of lectures on the Epistle to the Romans. He decided to treat the phrase *Iustitia Dei* in Romans 1.17 not as the active or punishing justice of God but as a passive righteousness which God bestows on sinful men without merit of their own. Certainly the actual lectures, delivered in 1515–16, can be seen as a most thorough-going exposition of anti-Pelagian Augustinianism. Between 1516 and 1520 Luther's reputation and teaching made Wittenberg the university with the largest number of matriculations in Germany. He was engaged in energetic curriculum-reform, throwing out the old scholastic lectures and introducing history and classical languages. By 1517 he was writing excitedly that 'Our theology and that of St. Augustine, by the grace of God, are making rapid progress in our university. Aristotle is continuing to fall from his throne, and his end is only a matter of time.'

It is clear that other universities and theologians thought that the Wittenberg professor had adopted an extremist stance in the grace-versus-freedom debate, but there was no official Church teaching on the subject at that time and the authority of Augustine was a weighty one. What changed the whole situation was the way in which in the year 1517 an academic debate suddenly

27

exploded into a popular and national issue with the power actually to precipitate a collapse of the old order of the Church. When in October Luther launched himself into an attack on Tetzel, the indulgence preacher, he was only doing something of which many, if not most, of his academic contemporaries would heartily approve. The whole mercenary carnival of popular religion, with its relics, pilgrimages, indulgences, and multiplication of requiem masses, was a regular object of criticism from dons as well as humanists. Indeed the Ninety-Five Theses of 31 October 1517 dealt with matters which any professional academic could regard as open for debate. What caused all the trouble was the line adopted by Luther's opponents: Eck, Cajetan, Wimpina and Murner. If the debate had actually been about the theology of justification it might soon have been lost to view amid all the technical categories of professional theology. But Eck and the rest chose deliberately to rest their case not on the usual authorities for such a debate, the Scriptures and the Fathers, but on the precedents of a papal authority to decide and settle all ecclesiastical practices. Their tactic was fatal: it led Luther, step by step and wholly unwillingly, to develop a new view of authority in religious matters: the new doctrine of Justification by Faith Alone. It is indeed from 1518 onwards that he shapes the distinctive theology which was to shatter the ecclesiastical unity of the nation, raise up a great Protestant movement, and change the course of European history.

As Luther worked this out down to his three great Reformation treatises of 1520, all came to centre in his master-concept of the Faith which comes by hearing the Word of God. For him this 'Word' is the whole activity of God towards men. It is God in his self-communication: in the Old Testament and the New, but pre-eminently in the Cross of Christ. This is revelation, a knowledge which cannot be discovered by philosophy or any kind of human learning. Indeed it defeats all the expectations of mankind. Men look only for the glory of God, but God speaks through the Cross in a place and event where no reasonable man would expect to find him. And in this way he humbles all our self-confidence. True religion is being taken captive by the Word of God which creates faith in those who hear it. This religion of pure revelation with so negative a view of human reason was deeply unacceptable to many of the members of Luther's order assembled at Heidelberg in 1518. If the younger brethren and some visitors were enthusiastic, the older men drew back, including Staupitz himself.

We can understand this new idea of the proclaimed Word of God when we realise that it has a twofold action: it is Law and Gospel; it is Bad News as well as Good News; it produces despair before it gives faith. On the one hand, it speaks as *Law*: it proclaims that God is righteous and commands righteousness. There is set before men the terrifying goodness of the Ten Commandments and the Beatitudes, the life of Christ and his perfect obedience upon the Cross. All this is, in a sense, Bad News. Who can attain to such a righteousness? Luther recalled his own distress as a monk at finding such terrible demands even in the gospels. Such a Word could create only despair in mortal men, as the Law crushed in them all pride and pretence at human achievement. This Luther called 'God's strange work'. But when a man was thus in despair then, and only then, was he ready to hear the Word of God as *Gospel*. Now, on the other hand, the Word proclaimed that God is gracious, and he will give a righteousness which men have neither sought nor deserved. He will clothe them round with the righteousness of Christ and, though they are and remain sinners, account them among the justified. This, in Luther's phrase, was 'God's proper work'. Faith, then, was a despairing man's trust in this promise of God in his Word. It was a new relationship of dependence on God for what he chooses to give. A Christian is simply one who has been given this faith; the Church is simply the assembly of those who have it.

None can doubt the power of this concept of Justification. It was preached throughout Germany as a liberation from the intolerable burden of pious practices, from superstition, and from priestly power and institutions. It brought into existence evangelical communities which thought of themselves as brought into existence by the pure Word of God. Yet it is also important to realise that there were many Christians, including competent theologians and humanists as well as defenders of the Roman Curia, who could not accept its basic characteristics. There was, first, its deep-seated pessimism about human nature. Sinful man was *'incurvatus in se'*, turned in upon himself; he had lost all his natural goodness and all natural knowledge of God. Man's will was in bondage to *concupiscentia*, a radical self-love which made him incapable of turning to God or loving him. In this thoroughgoing account of the effect of sin Luther set himself directly against a more moderate Christian tradition which maintained a higher estimate of human capacity, even when clouded and wounded by sin: a tradition which thought of grace as coming to cleanse and perfect human nature rather than replace it. And then, secondly, it is clear that Lutheran teaching assigns to man an essentially *passive* role in his justification. In no sense does man choose God. Faith is not a conclusion after weighing the evidence; it is not intellectual consent or conviction; it is not 'a decision for Christ'. It is literally an offer which cannot be refused. The new relationship is one which God has created; it takes no account of human choice or participation. Of course, here again, Luther has chosen to set himself against that middle-way Christian tradition which has tried to hold together both God's saving action *and* man's free response of mind and heart. And then, thirdly, there is Luther's account of the special kind of righteousness which the justified man has. He makes it clear that the justified do not *become* righteous; rather they are *declared or accounted* to be such. In other words a man is given the *formal status* of a justified person but actually he remains the sinner that he was. Luther described this new double status as *simul justus et peccator*: 'at one and the same time justified and a sinner.' Man is set free from the fear of wrath, set free to love, but he is not thereby changed in his inner character. Perhaps it is in this notion of an 'alien' or 'imputed' righteousness that Luther distanced himself most definitely from the mainstream of the medieval theological tradi- tion, which had almost unanimously thought of grace as actually changing a man, giving him love with faith and beginning his growth into a personal holiness of life. This is surely the point at issue in Luther's great controversy of 1525 with Erasmus over the freedom or bondage of the will.

We have acknowledged the power of Luther's doctrine. His picture of a human crisis of despair resolved by God's decisive address to an individual has spoken to many who feel the power of sin and their own utter incapacity. It has been the way into faith characteristic of individuals who need to pass through an experience of conflict and resolution before they can think of themselves as real Christians, though it has been said that Lutheran doctrine solved many of the doubts and uncertainties of late- medieval religion by replacing them with one new and terrible uncertainty: whether one was indeed of the number of the Elect and whether one could be assured of election in oneself or in others. That was to be a problem which above all troubled and confused the subsequent history of the Protestant movement. Nor has the doctrine proved so helpful with those whose way into faith has been that of a progressive discovery of truth, and who find in the historic Christian community a place of authoritative teaching and of spiritual resources for a personal growth in faith and love. Perhaps there are different roads to travel and they need not be mutually exclusive. Certainly the Council of Trent in its famous decree on Justification in 1547 did not set itself against a doctrine of justification by faith. Read it carefully and, discounting the scholastic idiom of the time, it may be taken as a clear statement that no man can justify himself, that the initiative in justification is God's, and that grace is always paramount. What the decree tries to do is to steer a middle course between the extremes. Thus Gabriel Biel is implicitly criticised for having tipped the scale too far in the direction of human effort and merit and Luther is criticised for a doctrine which stresses too much the passivity of man.

Dogmatic theologians always have to be careful not to overstate a case. Within each great Christian doctrine there is a paradox which guards a mystery, a balance which must not be forced down on one side or the other. The danger is that a doctrine which is overstated cannot live with other doctrines which may have their own essential place in Christian teaching. One thing can be said with confidence about Martin Luther: he was no systematic theologian. His mind worked in short, passionate bursts and he had biblical insights which even today illuminate the meaning of Scripture and warn against false religion. He remains one of the greatest writers of biblical commentaries. But there is a tendency with him for one doctrine, vehemently asserted, to set aside other doctrines which also have their place in an understanding of salvation in Christ. It is only too apparent that Luther's version of Justification by Faith can be used with destructive force. Its view of man can lead to a pessimistic account of natural human capacities and of the possibilities for men which exist in this world. Its view of the Church as a pilgrim company passing through a vale of tears, sustained only by their faith, can lead to a certain failure to perceive its corporate and dynamic qualities. Luther, as we know, had a distinctly cool view of all ecclesiastical institutions, and it was other Protestants, and notably John Calvin, who had to develop a distinctively Reformed ecclesiology.

Luther's importance for his own age lay in his witness to the power of the Word to speak directly to individuals and raise them to faith in God's promise in Christ. The only true Treasure of the Church, as he said in 1517, is the Gospel. When that is forgotten it would seem that the Christian community is in real trouble, and when Luther proclaimed it to those who lived amid the complexities of a worldly and over-institutionalised Church, it could only come as a message of pure liberation. Clearly, it was not easy in the early-sixteenth century to hold this urgent evangelical priority together with a view of the Church as a historic, ordered society, which is itself sustained by grace, teaches with authority, and maintains Christians in unity with one another. Yet today in the ecumenical movement there is a growing conviction that these seeming opposites actually complement one another. Perhaps what our modern discussions need is an understanding of the greatness of Luther which retains what was for him the heart of the matter, which is God's gracious acceptance of sinners, but does not commit us to particular versions of his teaching which still have the power to divide us.

Archbishop Laud
and Episcopacy

William Laud, Archbishop of Canterbury from 1633 to 1645, is still a controversial figure. To many modern historians he is a kind of bogeyman, and they see him as the prime cause of that breakdown in the unity of English religion which led to the great Civil War. Others would see him as an Anglican martyr in the defense of the Catholic order of the Church of England, and with them the adjective 'Laudian' is the equivalent of Anglo-Catholic ecclesiastical orthodoxy. I want to suggest in this paper that this is not necessarily so. Laud was not primarily a theologian and we do not have from him any sustained or considered scholarly account of episcopacy. Like all archbishops he was concerned with administration, discipline and ecclesiastical politics; and on the whole he made a bad job of them. He was a sad little man, emotional and tactless in a situation of great delicacy and danger; and his lonely imprisonment, rigged trial and cruel execution ought not to make him into a theologically symbolic figure. Indeed the place of episcopacy in the Anglican understanding of the Church is not necessarily bound up with his opinions or politics. The most that Laud did was to reflect rather crudely an impressive Anglican theological achievement which lasted from the sixteenth to the mid-seventeenth centuries, and which made English scholars Christendom's acknowledged experts on the history of the Church in the first five centuries of the Christian era. In the process they developed a highly characteristic ecclesiology or theology of the nature of the Church. And what is strange, and not a little wonderful to modern Anglicans, is that that ecclesiology appears to have come into its own in the modern era and to be the basis of a series of ecumenical texts. The World Council of Churches *Lima* statement on ministry and the ARCIC *Final Report* are so congenial to Anglicans because their theological method and their terms of reference are much more like traditional Anglican positions than they are of traditional Roman or Reformed ones. So what I want to do in this lecture is to describe and analyse this Anglican ecclesiology as it developed from the Reformation to the mid-seventeenth century.

At once we have to say that the late-medieval Church had very unclear notions of the office and work of a bishop. Only in the Eastern Orthodox churches was there some echo of an earlier view of episcopacy, and in Greece and Asia Minor bishops remained what they had been since at least the seventh century. Dioceses were small, often a single town or an island; the bishop was accessible and retained his function as the celebrant of the ordinary liturgy of his people; and the whole Church was conceived of as a communion of episcopally-led local communities. But even in orthodoxy the picture became confused. By the 12th century, as the Slav peoples were evangelized, vast dioceses replaced the smaller ones of the Mediterranean world, and a Metropolitan of Novgorod was head of a large secular state. Already a pattern was emerging in which Christian bishops were magnates and lords rather than teachers and pastors. By the 12th century in the West a new theory of the nature of the Church had come to replace the earlier one. Now it was thought of as a spiritual monarchy with the Pope as king and all other church officers deriving their authority from him as subordinates in the hierarchy. The age saw an impressive growth in legal science and relationships within the Church were conceived of in jurisdictional terms. Thus the Pope was lawgiver and judge while the local bishop was an inferior magistrate appointed from above. It was then very difficult for the Reformers of the 16th century to see bishops as local pastors or preachers.

In England dioceses were of immense size. That of Lincoln stretched from the Humber to the Thames and the whole province of York had only three dioceses. Bishops were immersed in secular affairs, acting as royal ministers and diplomats. Visits to the dioceses were rare and most episcopal functions were performed by specially consecrated auxiliaries. While Mass could be celebrated with elaborate pontifical ceremonial, it was virtually unknown for a bishop to go more than occasionally to his cathedral. The great medieval churches were virtually never the centre of an active episcopal ministry.

It was common to all the Reformers that they wished to end this semi-secularized prelacy. Luther, Zwingli and Calvin were concerned to establish a preaching ministry in which the Word of God should be given free course, and yet their reformation seemed on all sides opposed by prelates and the papal church. Luther in particular responded by setting out a view of ministry which contrasted sharply with medieval practice. For him the Church was found wherever the Word of God was preached and the sacraments rightly administered. A Christian minister was defined not by his legal status or formal commission but by his function in setting forth the gospel. For him the great German dioceses were irrelevant and he could have no respect for bishops like his own, Albert of Brandenburg, a semi-secular prince who at the age of 23 had accumulated the archbishoprics of Magdeburg and Mainz, the latter the primatial see of Germany. Luther was not without a reverence for traditional ways, and he was prepared to accept a reformed episcopate as an expedient form of church-administration, but he firmly denied that any particular form of ministry was necessary for the life of a true church. His mind was formed by the texts and studies of the late-medieval university, and he seems to have had little close knowledge of the patristic period. Where Lutheran bishops existed they were superintendent ministers and primarily administrators. For the most part (except in Sweden) they were not in the historic episcopal succession.

It was with John Calvin, however, that there was a vigorous attempt to discover what episcopacy could mean among Protestants. His famous book, *The Institutes of the Christian Religion* in the edition of 1559, is a vigorous attempt to get behind papalism and medieval prelacy to set out a scriptural and primitive pattern of episcopacy. Calvin argued that scripture set out that there should be four permanent orders of ministry in the Church: pastors, teachers, elders and deacons. And these were to constitute a collegiate ministry within the context of a single city, combining preaching, doctrine, discipline and pastoral care. Clearly much depended on Calvin's highly individual scriptural exegesis but the powerful appeal of Calvinism lay not just in its doctrinal system but in its recovery of the idea of a local church with an ordered but genuinely pastoral ministry. Indeed Calvinists claimed insistently that their form of ministry was *the* scriptural one, and that their pastor, surrounded by his elders, was the equivalent of a bishop in the early Church before medieval corruption had created popery and prelacy.

The question was obviously a critical one for Anglicans as they came to reflect upon their own Reformation. Two provinces of the Western Church, Canterbury and York, had rejected the papal jurisdiction and declared their independence as a national church. In 1559 it was not entirely clear on what theory of the nature of the Church they had done this. There was a strong party which had been affected by continental Protestant ideas, and they were the most articulate and learned. But there were many with a more traditional ecclesiology who retained conservative ideas about continuity with the traditional system of church-order, the sacraments and theological formulation. What kept them all together within the one Church of England was not so much a view of the nature of the Church as a theology of kingship and religious

nationalism. Over against the claims for a papal supremacy the English Reformers appealed to those biblical
texts which indicated a right and duty in a 'godly prince'
to reform and settle the affairs of a national church.
Indeed the Elizabethan Settlement was itself an affirmation of this Royal Supremacy in ecclesiastical causes. The
danger was that Elizabeth's bishops were going to be
freed from being papal subordinate officers to being royal
agents and magistrates. Indeed much of the medieval past
remained in the reformed Church of England. The
bishops were Protestant in theology and shorn of much of
their medieval trappings but they were still recognizably
prelates. It became a matter of urgent necessity for the
apologists for the settlement to find some theological
rationale for Anglicanism which was not merely Erastian
or a clinging to elements of medieval usage.

The first defenders of the Anglican Settlement felt this
question keenly; they found themselves attacked on two
fronts: by 'Papists' who accused the bishops of being
nothing more than royal officials, lacking any continuity
with the historic Catholic episcopate, and by so-called
'Puritans' who demanded that the Genevan system should
be introduced as being based on Scripture and conformable to the usage of the reformed churches abroad. It was
in this uncomfortable position that a series of great
Anglican scholars attempted by theological and historical
research to develop a new view of the nature of the
Church and its unity and the place of an episcopal
ministry within it. Was the Church a monarchy in which
all depended on one religious sovereign from whom all
jurisdiction was derived as from Christ himself? Was it a
series of local congregations joined only by a presumption
that all good Christians would agree in the interpretation
of Scripture?

The first considerable Anglican to tackle the question
of Anglican credentials was John Jewel (1522–71),
Bishop of Salisbury, who ought to be acknowledged as
one of the teaching Fathers of the Church of England. He

was in many ways a convinced Protestant. The Church
was, for him, the community gathered by the preaching
of the Word of God; the sacraments were themselves
gospel-ordinances which drew men and women into faith
and held them in a holy society which existed by grace
alone. Jewel did not believe that men were saved by
adopting any particular ecclesiastical system or practice
but by faith in the God who had raised Christ from the
dead. But he was Catholic-minded enough to be aware of
the Church as a living organism, continuous from the first
age, having long experience in the spiritual life, having a
corporate wisdom, and a common external structure
which expressed its inner nature. Jewel was the most
learned patristic scholar of his day and his knowledge of
the first five centuries was unrivalled. His method was to
get behind the disputes and deadlocks of his own day by
appealing to the ecclesiology of the era of the great
Fathers and Councils. As a good Protestant he did not
think that the patristic writings were of an authority
equal to that of Scripture: they were sometimes in
disagreement; they were often allegorical and fanciful;
they reflected overmuch the philosophy of their own day.
But he was concerned to discern the patristic understanding of the nature of the Church, and he saw it as
essentially a communion of episcopally-led communities
or local churches. Each was the church in a single city
with its immediate surroundings; each was under the
presidency of a minister called the bishop who acted in
collegiality with his presbyters. By the end of the second
century this was a universally accepted pattern. The
bishop was not a secular lord, though he sometimes had
experience in secular affairs; he was teacher, preacher,
pastor and liturgist. He existed in the community, was
chosen by it and identified with it. By the end of the
second century it was coming to be held that a
community's continuity with the apostolic past was
expressed in the succession of its bishops in office. Clearly
there was much diversity in ceremonial, liturgy and

devotional practice but there was unity in essentials by the agreement of the bishops in the 'catholica'. Jewel saw that unity had been continually imperilled by new ideas; he saw the churches often in error and corruption but brought back to right doctrine by councils of bishops reaffirming the tradition in scripture and in the Church's past reflection on Scripture. Thus Jewel was a Protestant with a difference. He thought that the Roman system was corrupt and tyrannous by the standard of what he called 'Antiquity', the belief and practice of the Early Church, but he also thought that Protestant claims to an individual and contemporary interpretation of Scripture would lead to confusion, division and sectarianism. He claimed that the only way to preserve the insights of the Reformation from Popery or the sects was to place doctrine and pastoral case within the context of a reformed and episcopally-ordered church. He claimed that essential identity of the Anglican episcopate with that of the Primitive Church and declared that the doctrine of the Church of England was neither more nor less than that which the Councils of the Early Church had declared to be conformable with Scripture. It would be easy to multiply quotations from his great book, *The Apology of the Church of England*, published in Latin and English in 1564, or his even more impressive *Defence of the Apology* of 1567. I have just one quotation from the latter: 'we have departed from that church which these men call catholic ... and which we ourselves did evidently see with our eyes to have gone from the holy fathers, and from the apostles, and from Christ his own self, and from the primitive and catholic church; and we are come, as near as we possibly could, to the church of the apostles and of the old catholic bishops and fathers, which church we know hath hitherunto been sound and perfect'. When accused by his adversary, Thomas Harding, of being a royal official and not a catholic bishop, he replied: 'we succeed the bishops that have been before our days. We are elected, consecrate, confirmed and admitted, as they were'. In short, Jewel, for all his Protestant theology, for all his dislike of Popish ceremonies, had a vision of the Church as a communion of communions, in which each church was represented by its bishop and the unity of the whole was essentially conciliar in character. There would be in the whole Church a constant struggle to remain faithful to the apostolic tradition but there would also be a *semper reformanda* principle as the Church through its bishops sought to do away with corruption and accretions and make a priority for the gospel.

It is clear that a theory like Jewel's put Anglicans in some dilemma concerning the status of the reformed churches abroad which had abandoned an order of bishops. Obviously many in the Elizabethan Church felt great sympathy with fellow-Protestants and felt that a common understanding of the gospel was more important than differences of church-order. Jewel's own solution was to develop a theory of the 'emergency' situation. Everywhere on the continent prelates had conspired to thwart reformed preaching, and the reformers had had to decide between gospel and strict episcopal succession. For Jewel succession in itself was nothing: a man did not become a true bishop because a bishop decided to ordain him. The real succession lay in being bishop of a recognizable local community, itself in succession from apostolic times, and being accepted as such by other rightly believing communities. But if presented with the choice of right preaching or strict succession in ordination there was no doubt which a local or national church would decide. So Jewel was prepared to accept the ministers duly ordained in those foreign churches which had been forced to abandon episcopacy. So, though Jewel was clear that the pattern of a single bishop with his presbyters in a local church was that which accorded with Scripture and primitive practice, he never said that it was absolutely necessary.

Jewel's method of apologetic was followed by the

Anglican writers who came after him, and in particular by Whitgift, Hooker and Bancroft who found themselves in controversy with Elizabethan and Jacobean 'Puritan' writers. John Whitgift in his answer to the *Admonition to Parliament* of 1572 made short work of the assertion that the Genevan system was the only one prescribed in holy writ. This could be only a modern exegetical opinion, and against it he produced instance after instance of episcopal government in the first five centuries; he asked whether a continual practice and a universal consent did not constitute the true interpretation of a disputed scriptural text. England had not abandoned episcopacy because she had had no reason to do so. It had godly and orthodox bishops, and there had been no kind of emergency to make her depart from primitive practice. As to the ministers of the foreign reformed churches he would make no judgement. It was this silence which has wrought some confusion in the minds of modern English church historians. My old teacher, Professor Norman Sykes wrote in 1956 a book entitled *Old Priest New Presbyter*, and this has become very influential in certain ecumenical quarters. He argued that Anglicans had consistently recognized the orders of those ordained in the foreign churches and, even though they had not been episcopally ordained, had received them into the ministry of the Church of England; only after 1622 was this liberal practice ended. In fact Sykes's argument is supported by only eight instances, and A. J. Mason, in his monumental book, *The Church of England and Episcopacy* (1914) had already shown that each was doubtful in its evidence. Even so, eight examples scarcely make a doctrine when the overwhelming practice was of episcopal ordination. And it is interesting that one of the eight was Hadrian Saravia, a Dutchman who came to England to reside permanently in 1587 and was beneficed. The fact is that we just do not know whether Saravia was ever ordained in the English Church. What we do know is that in 1590 he published a book *De Diversis Gradibus Ministrorum*

Evangelii which is a most thoroughgoing argument for the necessity of bishops in a rightly ordered church and an angry dismissal of presbyterian claims to a parity of ministers.

No church in Christendom devoted so much time and scholarly effort to investigating the early history of the Christian ministry as Anglicans in the reigns of James I and Charles I. In the course of all this research men like Lancelot Andrewes and Joseph Hall sharpened up the argument, and I suspect changed its direction. Jewel and Hooker had a theological argument for episcopacy; it was part of their doctrine of the Church. The bishop, surrounded by his presbyters, teaching his people from his chair and celebrating the liturgy was a sign and symbol of the catholicity of the local community; he represented its continuity in time and its unity with other churches. His succession in office was a sign of the apostolic succession of the community itself. His participation in councils with other bishops was the unifying principle of the whole. Andrewes and the writers who came after him tended to lose this ecclesiological vision and to become increasingly concerned with a purely historical demonstration that such and such had occurred in the patristic age. The argument moved from a consideration of the nature of the Church to a study of the details of church-order in the first four or five centuries. The difference lay between looking to the patristic age for *principles* which might be embodied in the very different circumstances of a later age and looking to the past as a fixed model to be copied in detail.

It was this latter approach which was characteristic of William Laud himself. I have said that his opinions are not particularly profound. In his correspondence with a much greater scholar, Bishop Joseph Hall, the author of *Episcopacy by Divine Right* (1637) we see him in typical archiepiscopal fashion trying to sharpen up the argument and get it firmly on the basis of historically demonstrable evidence. Hall, in spite of the title of his book, had advanced the proposition that episcopacy had gradually emerged in the early Church as the Christian community had been guided into an order which protected the tradition of faith. Laud wanted it to be *divino jure*, that is specifically instituted by Christ. Hall admitted that there might be instances in which bishops were a threat to sound doctrine; Laud would have none of it. His diary for 17 January 1626 records him pressing upon Charles I this divine right view, and he was adamant that foreign refugees in England should conform to the established church. It was this rejection of the foreign reformed churches which was principally alleged against him at his trial. For his opponents it was to raise church-order to being a thing-in-itself rather than the context for right believing and right praying.

Laud was executed in 1645 and his death saw the virtual collapse of the Anglican church-order which he had so energetically defended. Episcopacy was abolished and the diocesan framework discarded. The deprived bishops lived quietly in retirement and, though they ordained deacons and priests, they did nothing to consecrate successors to themselves, and in 1660 when Charles II was restored there were only nine elderly men to continue the succession. It was in such unpropitious circumstances, when the Church of England seemed lost, that the defence of episcopacy came into the hands of a formidable and precisely learned group of men, of whom Henry Hammond, Herbert Thorndike and John Bramhall were the most notable. It was perhaps to be expected that such writers, deprived and exiled, and acutely conscious of the ruin of their Church should develop a severely polemical style but their contribution to the clarification of the character of the Early Church was outstanding. Much depended on the work which lay behind all they did: James Ussher's *Polycarpi et Ignatii Epistolae*, published in 1644. Single-handed Ussher solved a critical problem which had been disputed by Roman Catholic and Protestant divines since the 16th century. During the

Middle Ages the seven letters of Ignatius of Antioch, who was martyred about 110, had suffered additions and interpolations designed to make them accord with medieval theories of papal power. Learned opinion varied between Roman scholars who accepted the whole as genuine and Reformed divines who rejected the whole as spurious. The real point at issue was the episcopal church-government in local communities which was so clearly described in the texts. Ussher with marvellous critical skill virtually settled the Greek text and the result was a grievous blow to both the papal and presbyterian positions. The high-flown papal and sacerdotal language disappeared and what was left was a testimony to the existence and authority of the early bishop as the key to understanding the order of the Church in sub-Apostolic times. The scholars of the Interregnum had the evidence to claim that, of all the churches, the Church of England had been closest to the primitive pattern. Henry Hammond in particular published books and pamphlets which were of critical importance in ruining the self-confidence of the presbyterian party and in creating a body of opinion among clergy and laity which regarded episcopacy as the *sine qua non* of a rightly ordered church. Indeed the Act of Uniformity of 1662, which imposed a firm episcopalian order on the ministry of the restored church, was due not just to politics but to a considerable scholarly achievement. Since that time it has been consistent Anglican practice that none shall minister in the Church of England who has not been episcopally ordained.

For some of our ecumenical partners this insistence remains difficult to grasp and it seems like a reflection on the validity and effectiveness of their own ministries; they believe that they have been as blessed and fruitful as any episcopally-ordered ministry. We have to admit that a certain type of Anglo-Catholic has been insensitively dismissive of great ecclesiastical communions which have kept up a tradition of orthodox belief, have an ordered way of transmitting ministerial commission, and who use the sacraments of the gospel. But it is interesting that both the *Lima* Ministry text and the ARCIC *Final Report* return to a theme which has traditionally been an Anglican one: that the role of the bishop in the local church and of the college of bishops in the universal church is the best outward expression of the inner nature of the Christian community—and it may become the way by which that unity of Christians after which we all long may be symbolized and effected.

The Royal Supremacy:
A Theological Assessment

Central to the English Reformation was the assertion of a
Royal Supremacy in ecclesiastical affairs. It would be a
mistake, however, to regard this as mere Erastianism, a
subordination of the Church to the interests and policies
of the State. The sixteenth-century theory emerged out of
a theological debate which went back at least to the
twelfth century. Indeed, even before the Reformation
conflict began, a scholarly controversy about the nature
of the Church and its relation to secular rulers was one of
the chief concerns of university faculties of theology. At
the beginning of the sixteenth century it could not be said
that any particular theory had established itself decisively,
and the defenders of the Henrician and Elizabethan
settlements had ample medieval arguments upon which to
draw.

Medieval thought did not, in general, readily accept the
notion of a single omnicompetent authority in human
affairs. It was held that within any particular human
society different authorities would exist side-by-side, each
having its own credentials, purpose and special sphere of
competence. The wellbeing of a nation or a city was
thought to consist in holding all these legitimate authorities
in balance, so that each did its work without encroaching
upon the function of another. There was thus an
authority in the civil ruler, another in the ancient laws
and customs of the people, and another in the ecclesiastical hierarchy. Medieval cities were obvious examples of
this co-existence of various types of authority. Though
they claimed independence as communes and ordered
much of their ecclesiastical life they yet admitted within
the walls the jurisdictions of kings and feudal lords and

they recognised that the final word in doctrine, liturgy and the administration of the sacraments lay with the bishop as representative of the Catholic church. The great disputes of medieval politics were not so much about sovereignty as about the lines of demarcation between the various authorities. And it was thought the peculiar work of national assemblies of 'estates', usually with a strong ecclesiastical component, to resolve such disputes and re-establish harmony.

Such a basic concept consorted uneasily with the idea of a universal papal monarchy as this was developed by the canonists and the great lawyer-popes of the twelfth and thirteenth centuries. At a time when many secular rulers were attempting to control and exploit the resources of the Church in their own dominions, the papal theorists employed the precepts of Roman law to assert the existence of an ecclesiastical kingdom or empire which had the Pope as its sovereign lawgiver and supreme magistrate with the bishops as subordinate magistrates and the ordinary clergy as *ministri*. Within this universal monarchy the Supreme Pontiff claimed jurisdiction in all causes and over all ecclesiastical persons and property, and the right to the appointment of all his inferior officers. The result was an increasing centralisation of the Church's administration and its judicial system; and a series of jurisdictional disputes with secular rulers. At its fullest extent papal theory claimed a superiority of the Pope over the Emperor and other kings on the analogy that the concerns of the soul were of greater importance to mankind than those of the body, and that the ecclesiastical jurisdiction had precedence over all others. It was clearly difficult for princes to accept such papal claims, not least because in most European lands civil and ecclesiastical persons, administrations and courts were inextricably linked. In England, for example, the church courts dealt with matters which affected legal succession and property.

There were, then, not lacking powerful voices which

sought to deny or set limits upon this idea of a universal papal monarchy. William of Ockham (c1285–1347), one of the keenest medieval minds, sought in his *The Powers of Emperors and Popes* to confine the competence of the Pope to matters purely spiritual and pastoral. God had instituted kingship to exercise temporal jurisdiction, punish evildoers and keep the peace. The church was not a kingdom in this sense but the community of the faithful within a particular kingdom, and it was the ministry of the Pope and the bishops to build up this church in its spiritual characteristics. If he usurped the role of a secular prince it was the duty and right of a general council to bring his office back to its true function. Such an argument was developed further by Jean Gerson (1363–1429), perhaps the most eloquent of those 'conciliarists' who sought to set the office and ministry of a Pope within the context of a council of bishops. He too tried to define the distinction between the spiritual and secular. The Pope was undoubtedly the head of that hierarchy which spoke with authority in spiritual matters and all things which concerned the 'mystical body'. But ordinary secular princes had their God-given role and function: temporal government was 'naturally established' and regulated by natural law; a ruler was ordained for the good of his people; if he did not forward their welfare and promote justice he too could be called to account by the assembly of his people. The problem with fifteenth-century Popes was that they had confused the spiritual and temporal, and thereby diminished their real authority. If they acted as earthly princes they would be regarded and treated as such. Gerson claimed, then, to be a supporter of papal authority, rightly understood and distinguished from secular dominion.

Even before the Reformation English writers tended to reflect this conciliarist view of the relationship of the secular and ecclesiastical jurisdictions. In England the Roman code of law did not operate and the claims of the Papacy and the canon lawyers seemed most in conflict with the provisions of the 'common law' and acts of Parliament. A series of legal writers from Sir John Fortescue (1394–1470) to Christopher St. German (c1460–1540) had attacked the church courts on the grounds that they had mixed the civil with the spiritual and denied the king his right to do justice to all his subjects. St. German, in particular, argued that all coercive power and legal sanctions were inherently secular in character; he would limit the spirituality to giving advice in doctrinal and liturgical matters and acting as assessors when religious causes came before the king's courts.

It was clearly this English conciliarist and legal tradition which lay behind the great series of acts which established the Henrician reformation in the 1530s. The election of bishops by cathedral chapters, the ancient convocations of Canterbury and York, the system of church courts remained but were now to operate under royal control. This new 'headship' of the Church was conceived of in jurisdictional rather than sacramental terms and, as such, was not a simple replacement of papal power by royal power. The theory was that the king was uniting under himself the administration, judicatures and legislatures of his kingdom. It refused to accept that the Church was a separate *regnum*; it was that part of the body politic 'which is called the spirituality'. In ecclesiastical affairs there will still be the same institutions and the same law; the king will not ordain bishops though he will choose who shall be ordained; he will not sit in the church courts personally but act through those learned in ecclesiastical law; he will not decide doctrine but will see that convocation does not meet or proceed to make canons without his consent.

The theological debate about the meaning of this set of enactments began when the legislation was enforced. The opposition of Reginald Pole, John Fisher and Thomas More has usually been described as 'conservative' but it is important to realise that each took seriously the argument about the different spheres of the sacred and secular and the rights of a national ruler within his own dominions even in ecclesiastical matters. Reginald Pole's *A Defence of Ecclesiastical Unity* (1539) went a great way in admitting that a national *regnum* had its God-given justification and purpose, and that there were many matters of church organisation and property and even of worship which were best dealt with locally, but the Church was universal and a gift of God to all humanity: there were some matters in which the local church was a very poor judge and in which its knowledge was limited. Pole cites numerous authorities to show that a universal ministry is committed to the Pope who is by his Petrine commission much more than a local bishop. Thus the King of England cannot be Head of the Church of England because it is part of a universal whole. Thomas More's position is more complex. As a common-lawyer he was prepared to go to the very limit in conceding the power of the King-in-Parliament to be obeyed in any matters which could be described as temporal. He was willing to acknowledge that an act of Parliament made Elizabeth heir to the throne though the Church had declared her illegitimate. He was prepared to see the properties of the Church confiscated and its administration re-arranged by statute. He saw no basic objection to the king's controlling the operation of the church courts. His sticking point lay in his belief that the Act of Supremacy destroyed the freedom of the English Church to choose to be part of the universal community of Christendom of which the Pope was head and centre of unity. More was deeply critical of the contemporary Papacy and its policies but he saw the Henrician headship as removing the possibility that the English Church might resist theological and moral error if this was forced on it by the secular power.

More's critique was undoubtedly taken seriously by later defenders of the Royal Supremacy. Stephen Gardiner (1483–1555) was to be one of the leading figures in the so-called Marian reaction of the mid-1550s but in 1535 he published one of the seminal defences of the title of 'Head of the Church'. His *Oration of True Obedience* was in many ways a canon lawyer's book. He accepted that in England there could be no real distinction between Church and State, and it was false to regard the Church with its officers, courts and convocations as a purely spiritual sphere; there was a strongly temporal and coercive character to it, and this was properly the king's concern. To distinguish the spiritual and temporal areas within the Church's jurisdiction Gardiner employed the canonists' distinction between the *potestas ordinis* and the *potestas jurisdictionis*. With the *potestas ordinis* the king did not interfere: he did not claim to be a bishop or a priest; doctrine, the ministry, the sacraments were those of universal Christian tradition and remained properly the concern of the bishops and the convocations. On such matters the king would listen to the authoritative voice of those to whom such matters as preaching, ordination and the celebration of mass belonged. But their authority would be moral and pastoral in character. Where coercive jurisdiction was involved the case was quite different, and the *potestas jurisdictionis* was to be exercised under the Royal Supremacy. Gardiner offered the suggestion that the distinction between the two *potestates* was seen in those matters which a bishop could only do personally and those which he could delegate to his chancellor. Gardiner thus sought to combine the idea of a single *regnum* under one supreme administration with a freedom in the bishops to hold to the doctrine and practice of the universal Church in those things which were essential to unity.

After Mary's reconciliation of the realm to the Roman see the Elizabethan Act of Supremacy of 1559 re-established, with minor variations, the Henrician form of the Supremacy. To avoid the controversial term 'Head of the Church' it was provided that henceforth the royal title should be 'Supreme Governor'. Almost from the beginning the Supremacy came under fierce attack from two different quarters. English Puritans such as Thomas Cartwright represented an extreme version of Calvin's doctrine of the Church as having Christ only as its head and lord; for them there could be no trespassing on the 'Crown rights of the Redeemer' and the courts and assemblies of the Church must be ruled by the Word of God alone. Cartwright argued for a complete separation of Church and State; the civil magistrate must put aside his symbols of office if he were to participate as a believer in the life of the Church; to accept arguments from state policy or to admit mere worldly power was spiritual treason. In similar style Roman Catholics maintained that the Church of England was now a creation of the State, where bishops were royal officials without continuity with the historic Catholic episcopate; the English had rejected the authority of the Pope who by unbroken tradition had responsibility for the unity of the whole Church and subordinated spiritual matters to mere secular and political authority in a single nation.

While John Jewel and John Whitgift provided a scholarly case for Anglican continuity in order and doctrine with the ancient and undivided Church, it was Richard Hooker who offered the most cogent theological defence of the Royal Supremacy. At the heart of *The Laws of Ecclesiastical Polity* is Hooker's insistence on the unity of human society. Both Puritans and Papists sought to make a separation between the realm of Christ and the realm of Caesar as if these were two societies. But in a Christian nation commonwealth and church must consist of the same persons: it is one realm with two 'accidents', civil and religious. A Christian polity *is* a Church, for the Church is not to be identified merely with its clergy or officers. As in the orthodox doctrine of the Person of Christ there is a *communicatio idiomatum*. The commonwealth is raised up to having a moral and sacred character and the Church is given the means to educate and form the life of the nation. To separate the Church from the commonwealth and make it a separate society is to make it a sect and confine its sphere too narrowly to the religious. Hooker thus sought to set the Royal Supremacy within the context of a society which is Christian in profession. Like Gardiner he did not see the Supremacy as being the will of one person. The supreme governorship was regulated by the moral and religious ends of the society. Not least it was confined by the 'laws' of ecclesiastical polity. These are the possession of the whole community and are well-known: they are the traditional creeds, sacraments and institutions of Christendom. In the bishops, convocations and the canonists the supreme governor has authoritative advisers who speak not only for the Christian people of England but for the whole Church of God. In effect Hooker sought to make the exercise of the supremacy constitutional and conciliar in character. As kings were limited by the laws, institutions and the moral sense of their people, so the supreme governor operated within the laws of ecclesiastical polity and the religious sense of the community. Against the accusation that Anglicans had submitted themselves to a merely secular authority Hooker raised an edifice of scripture, tradition and moral reason as the context within which the royal power was to be exercised.

Richard Hooker's judicious defence of the Royal Supremacy attained almost the status of an official Anglican *apologia* but the reality of the English situation differed markedly from the ideal. The Elizabethan Church was heavily subordinated to state policy, to its pastoral detriment and the endangering of its unity. Widespread abuses belied its claim to be 'reformed'; its properties and revenues were plundered by the Crown and influential laymen; and its bishops were denied liberty to remedy glaring defects. Professor Patrick Collinson has shown in his recent book *The Religion of Protestants* that the advent of James I marked in many ways the first real exercise in the Hookerian practice of the Royal Supremacy.

The king was genuinely interested in religious affairs; he appointed learned and active bishops and supported their endeavours; he worked for religious unity in England and among a wider Protestant community. Such a supreme governor fulfilled the conditions of Hooker's theory and quickly became the focus for Anglican hopes for comprehensive reform and a recovery of the Church's revenues. In the writings of Lancelot Andrewes and William Laud there is an almost mystical view of monarchy as God's representative to whom obedience is due as a religious duty, and this is combined with a new view of episcopacy as itself of divine institution. The magnificent achievement of Anglican scholars in patristic studies revealed the vital role which episcopacy played in the polity of the first four centuries of the Church, and the responsibility of the episcopate as a college for maintaining the tradition of faith. James I's famous dictum 'No Bishop—No King' was a theological statement, intended to set forth the ideal of a union within a national church of the local civil power and the representatives of the unchanging tradition of Catholic Christendom. The danger of the Laudian position and its stress on monarchy and episcopate was that it would be seen as a threat to entrenched constitutional rights and to Protestant ecclesiology. Such an enhanced notion of the Supremacy was clearly a major cause of the collapse of the monarchy and the episcopal system in the years from 1642 to 1660.

The era after the Restoration in 1660 saw the beginning of a progressive retreat from a high theology of the Royal Supremacy. For a while there was a revival of Hookerian theory: a new stress on the religious or 'divine-right' character of Monarchy and a conservative scholarship which attempted to show the adhesion of Anglicans to the patristic understanding of episcopacy. But in the Restoration period the union of crown and episcopate was insecure. Charles II was a man of doubtful religion and his successor, James II, was an avowed Roman Catholic. Archbishops like Gilbert Sheldon and

William Sancroft found themselves interpreting the Supremacy in terms of the English constitution, subordinate to parliamentary control and legal enactment. The petition of the Seven Bishops in 1688 was an important moment in the theory of the Supremacy in their firm assertion that its exercise had to be within the bounds set by positive law.

After the Revolution of 1688 the conditions basic to the Hookerian theory gradually fell away. The theory of the religious unity of church and nation was maintained but the passing of the Toleration Act of 1689 had the effect of allowing the existence of dissenting religious bodies. Kings and governments actively patronised Dissent and resisted any restoration of the Anglican religious monopoly; bishops were appointed for their political services; and legislation (like the appointment of bishops for the colonies) denied. For the first time there appeared among Anglican theologians a critique of the Supremacy which was cautious and hostile. This is shown pre-eminently in the famous Convocation controversy of 1697–1717. It was now characteristic of 'Low-Church' writers, like William Wake in his *The Authority of Christian Princes over their Ecclesiastical Synods Asserted* (1697), to argue for a high doctrine of royal power. Wake indeed deployed an arsenal of precedents from early church history but later writers like Benjamin Hoadly reduced the argument to the crude level of the need for civil rulers to restrain clerical pretensions and religious quarrels. It was the 'High-Church' writers, like Francis Atterbury, and Nonjurors like George Hickes who moved towards a theory of the basic and necessary independence of the Church when matters of doctrine or pastoral need were at stake. Atterbury's *The Rights, Powers and Privileges of an English Convocation* (1701) was a tortured attempt to prove that the Royal Supremacy could never prevent the Church from taking emergency action to protect its faith and order. In fact, his arguments were condemned by a meeting of the judges as inconsistent with the Act of Supremacy. The reality of the eighteenth-century Church was that it was subordinated to the secular power. The Royal Supremacy came to be exercised by politicians, who controlled all appointments and refused to allow the Convocations to do business after 1717. Parliamentary statute became the usual means of regulating ecclesiastical matters. It was this situation which was plainly recognised by William Warburton in 1736 when he published *The Alliance of Church and State*, the only theoretical account of the Supremacy to be published in the middle years of the century. In effect Warburton marks a complete break with Hooker. In the rationalist style of the age he treats both church and state as voluntary associations, entered into by consent for the achievement of certain defined purposes. He does not presume that they must consist of the same persons and he concedes that their interests and ends may differ. They agree to enter into a compact for their mutual advantage: the Church gives up its independent powers of appointment, legislature and judiciary, and receives in return endowment from the public property, legal privileges and public recognition. It was said at the time that Warburton had removed any possible theological justification for the Royal Supremacy and made its continuance purely pragmatic; that he had, in fact, made out a case for disestablishment as much as for continued establishment.

With the repeal of the Test and Corporation acts in 1828 and the passing of Catholic Emancipation in 1829 the formal identity of church and nation, the 'Protestant Constitution', came to an end. Though the monarch had still to be 'in communion' with the Church of England, Parliament now consisted of men of any denomination or none. Already there existed Anglican churches in Scotland and the United States of America which were wholly independent of the Royal Supremacy. It is clear that the situation presented thoughtful churchmen with a grave theoretical dilemma. Anglicans were now faced with serious problems, financial and pastoral, and fundamental reform was needed if the established church was not to be eclipsed by other religious bodies. The uncertainty of relying upon the assistance of Parliament or politicians led to a widespread demand for greater freedom and independence from state control. A Whig government's attempt in 1833 to pass legislation to abolish bishoprics in Ireland precipitated an Anglican crisis. John Keble and others in the Oxford Movement sought to reawaken a sense of the Church as a divine society whose doctrines, ministry and sacraments were of apostolic provenance; they were not prepared to tolerate any secular authority which impeded or frustrated the essential characteristics of the Church. While they valued the constitution of the Church of England the Tractarians had no place for the Royal Supremacy in their doctrine of the Church; it was a local and temporary arrangement in which one part of the Catholic church found itself involved. This is not to say that Tractarians were in favour of disestablishment, and in 1838 W. E. Gladstone's *The State in its Relation with the Church* put forward what became a classic moderate plea for the continuance of the establishment. It was, he argued, not so much privilege as an opportunity of service. It would be simpler for the Church of England to accept a status as a disestablished sect but this would be an enormous disservice to the moral and spiritual life of the nation. For the state formally to disavow its connection with, and support for, religion would be to remove Christian influence in public education, in public life and in the legislature. To acknowledge all denominations equally would be confused and unsatisfactory to everyone. But in return for allowing bishops in the House of Lords and the association of clergymen with schools, the armed forces and the work of government the state had to have some say in appointments and some negative over ecclesiastical policy. Gladstone pleaded for restraint on all sides: for the state to allow synods to meet and for reforms to take place; for Anglican radicals to realise the opportunities which establishment brought; and for nonconformists to realise the importance of a Christian witness in the state. And in a sense the Gladstonian solution was already being implemented, notably in the formation of the Ecclesiastical Commissioners, a body set up by statute to allow Anglicans to re-order their own affairs.

The modern situation is a refinement and extension of the Gladstonian compromise. There is no theological justification for the Royal Supremacy and the Establishment as it now exists other than the general one that Christians will often accept limitations and anomalies in order to be of service to the world. Yet the Hookerian argument no longer applies. The identity of church and nation has long ended. The state does not offer itself as Christian or profess Christian policies in a society which is increasingly multi-cultural and multi-confessional. If the Church of England still professes to minister to the nation at large, it in fact deals with a minority of the population. As the Anglican Communion has increased rapidly in the world the Royal Supremacy and the state connection appear an English eccentricity rather than a characteristic of Anglicanism.

Why, then, does the Royal Supremacy continue?

1. The mystique of the English monarchy remains, and a pre-occupation with the Queen and her family seems to increase rather than diminish. Walter Bagehot long ago pointed out the symbolic function of monarchy and its association with religion, morality and the national identity. Many Anglicans value greatly their association with the Queen and her presence on public church occasions. A renunciation of the supreme governorship, which is seen as responsibility without power, would seem ungracious in view of the conscientious way in which the Queen and her predecessors have fulfilled the role.

2. All sides admit the immense complexity of disestablishment. Even those tentative steps in ecclesiastical legislation which the General Synod undertakes involve it in the

intricate business of unravelling a complex of statute, case-law and property rights built up over centuries. To dismantle the Royal Supremacy would mean finding alternative procedures and machinery, which could be controversial. There is a natural reluctance on the part of governments or the General Synod to embark upon such an undertaking.

3. The Church of England has already achieved a large measure of independence to order its own affairs. Though the Queen remains supreme governor and Parliament in the last resort legislates for the Church, in fact the General Synod is the Church's legislative body and the function of Parliament is simply to approve or negative that legislation. Instances of church measures being negatived are rare and specialised. Appointments to diocesan bishoprics are, in effect, made by the Crown Appointments Commission of the General Synod which recommends names to the Prime Minister for nomination by the Queen to deans and chapters for election. It is invisaged that the appointments of deans and cathedral clergy will soon be made by a similar commission. It is possible that within a relatively short period the Church of England will have attained something approaching the Scottish situation of an established church with full freedom to order its own affairs.

Thomas Ken (1637–1711), Bishop of Bath and Wells

In 1885, the bicentenary year of Thomas Ken's consecration as Bishop of Bath and Wells, the cathedral saw what was perhaps its most splendid service of the century. Representatives of the diocese and of the whole Anglican Communion came together to dedicate a memorial window and honour the memory of a man who seemed a saint exactly suited to the mind of the nineteenth century. He was one of the famous Seven Bishops who had resisted James II in his endeavour to force Popery on the nation; and for Anglo-Catholics in particular he was an exemplar of the spirituality of the Caroline age: an ascetic, a poet, a loving pastor and, at the last, a confessor who suffered for his beliefs. Thus John Keble planned to publish his works, Isaac Williams made him the subject of an epic poem, and in Tract 75 John Henry Newman invited the Church of England to resume the canonization of saints by adding Thomas Ken's name to the Kalendar. The Fellows of New College, Oxford, actually took Newman at his word, and when they reconstructed the great reredos of their chapel to represent the orders of the *Te Deum* a statue of Ken was numbered among those of the saints. When in 1888 E. H. Plumptre, Dean of Wells, wrote a two-volume biography it had a hushed air as of a man treading holy ground. But how does it seem today? Modern historical writing has a cooler tone than nineteenth-century hagiography. Is there any sense in which Ken turns out to be a man for our age as well?

His earliest years are not well recorded but there is the strong impression that even in his youth he was an old-fashioned figure. He was born in 1637, the son of a

London businessman or attorney. His mother died when he was four years old, his father when he was fourteen, and he was brought up by an elder sister and her husband. It was the kind of childhood, with the deaths of parents and siblings, which was common in the seventeenth century. But in Ken's case it brought him into the guardianship of a remarkable man, none other than Izaak Walton, the author of *The Compleat Angler*. Walton was well into his fifties when he took over the guidance of a sensitive and intelligent boy, and he formed a bridge with the great Anglican writers and preachers of a past generation. He had been the friend of John Donne, George Herbert and Sir Henry Wotton, and he was to write their lives; his great library was filled with volumes of Caroline divinity and editions of the works of the Fathers of the Early Church. Walton's own style has the mannered charm of the earlier part of the century and in particular a love of fancy and poetic imagery which sometimes conceals, sometimes reveals deep emotion. In the days of the Cromwellian regime, when it seemed that the Anglican system had been dismantled for ever, the Walton family kept up the old ways and went to secret services at which the Book of Common Prayer was used. Their heroes were divines like George Morley or Robert Sanderson who wrote in defence of the old divinity and church-order. It is clear that Walton was an affectionate man with distinctive views, and the young Ken became devoted to him as to a father. But for all the warmth and rare learning his was a world of the past, imbued with a spirit of resistance to change, anger and impatience with innovations, and a sense of belonging to a faithful remnant in a degenerate world. Thus Ken's early career seems to have been that of a young man never quite at ease among his contemporaries. He became a Scholar of Winchester in 1652 and a junior Fellow of New College in 1657. We hear briefly of his attending musical evenings in Oxford and going to Prayer Book services. Yet his uncompromising churchmanship made his circle of friends small and all of them, like his contemporary at New College, Francis Turner, showed by their subsequent careers that they shared his opinions.

For such a man the Restoration of Charles II and the re-establishment of the Church of England by 1662 was a relief and a release. By 1663 he had been ordained and had left Oxford to become domestic chaplain to George Morley, now Bishop of Winchester. Plumptre makes much of Ken's experience as a parish priest at Little Easton in Essex and Brighstone on the Isle of Wight but a letter of August 1663 makes it clear that he did not reside for any length of time at either of them. His home henceforth was at Winchester or at Chelsea where Morley had his London house. In the next few years he is found writing and doing business on behalf of his master. Of course, thereby he found himself thrust into the very centre of the world of ecclesiastical politics. Morley was one of the most influential bishops of the Restoration era and after 1663 close to Gilbert Sheldon, the Archbishop of Canterbury. He had been in exile with the king and the Earl of Clarendon, and always remained close to James, Duke of York, and his first wife, Anne Hyde, Clarendon's daughter. Domestic chaplains have a way of being thrust into great affairs beyond their years, and Ken found himself caught up in the inner working of high politics. It was a position which he shared with his friend, Francis Turner, who became chaplain and confidant to the Duke of York, accompanying him to sea and on his progresses round the country.

To understand Ken's subsequent career, then, it is necessary to look briefly at the situation of the Church in the years immediately after the Restoration. Everywhere in their visitations the bishops found a church which had virtually collapsed. Cathedrals were in ruins, parish churches in disrepair, and ministers were demoralised and desperately poor. Worst of all in strict Anglican eyes was the disappearance of many of the distinctive features of the old church. It was not just the years in which the

Prayer Book had been disused but the fact that in over half the parishes the celebration of the Holy Communion had altogether ceased. It was, too, a tragedy that many learned and experienced Presbyterian ministers had refused to conform to the Act of Uniformity of 1662, while some who did and even sought episcopal ordination were timeservers and negligent. In 1663 Sheldon, on becoming archbishop, had a parish-by-parish survey of Canterbury diocese compiled, and it was depressing that so few of his clergy could be noted as satisfactory. Bishops like Sheldon and Morley were painfully aware that they had to reform and reinvigorate the Church, recoup its finances, and raise the standards of education and preaching of the clergy. Sheldon himself was more a man of business than of learning or spirituality but he was aware that there had to be something more than administration and politics. He was concerned to encourage academics like John Fell and John Pearson to develop a new scholarly apologia for Anglicanism. But more important was to create a sense of devotion and of spiritual power which could impress itself on the younger clergy and be communicated to the parishes.

Thus gradually we see around the archbishop and Bishop Morley the creation of a group with a distinctive form of churchmanship with strong roots in the Caroline past. They have a character which is ascetic and almost monastic; they are concerned with the spiritual direction of individual souls; and there is a new kind of fervour and radicalism in their religious life. They are, for the most part, unmarried. Their leader is clearly William Sancroft, Dean of St. Paul's, but they include men like Francis Turner, Robert Frampton and John Lake. But it is Ken himself who quickly became the best known of the group and the most popular preacher. We possess in the diary of Lady Warwick the reaction of one devout woman to his sermons in Chelsea Old Church in the winter of 1667–8 when he was in attendance on Morley during what was a particularly difficult parliamentary session. His sermons on the Holy Communion moved 'her heart to long after the holy feast' and 'to weep bitterly', and again 'to bless God and have sweet communion with him'. When Ken preached on the text 'Sin no more', she was 'able to beg power against sin for the time to come'. We are here dealing with an intense and emotional spirituality, and it is about this time that he comes into prominence as a confessor and spiritual director both for clergy and laity. His own life was marked by a monastic rigour: he ate one meal a day; he gave away all his disposable possessions; he kept the 'hours' of the Church, rising in the middle of the night to pray. It is probably in these Winchester years that he wrote his well-known Morning and Evening Hymns with their echoes of the ancient hymns of the monastic offices. Down to 1684 he had no major preferment, remaining as Morley's chaplain and keeping close to old Izaak Walton who had come to live in the bishop's household.

Though we do not possess much correspondence from this time, it is possible to construct a picture of Ken's religious position. His library contained very little medieval or Reformation theology. For him the great age was that of the undivided Church of the first four centuries, and he continually interpreted Scripture in the light of the teaching of the great Fathers and Councils. Spiritually his affinity was with the Eastern Fathers, and his sermons are interspersed with quotations from their writings. The Church itself he sees as a divine society living down the ages its distinctive life of prayer and mission, its continuity characterised by a ministry, sacraments, liturgies and penitential discipline which have come down from the patristic era. He argues that the Church of England's doctrine, order and worship is closest to primitive practice of all the modern churches, and that both Rome and continental Protestantism have departed from it. Where he does draw on Rome it is in admiration for its rich tradition of spiritual teaching, its ascetic devotion and mystical theology; and his library was stocked with the spiritual classics of the Counter-Reformation. In his view of the world he is resolutely old-fashioned by the standards of the new science and mathematics of the age of reason which was just beginning. He believes in miracles and the existence of supernatural spirits, both holy and diabolic. Indeed his world is one in which man is surrounded by mysterious powers and forces; it is a kind of theatre in which God intervenes and in his providence changes the course of nations and individuals. The diarist Samuel Pepys records some interesting arguments which he had with Ken in the year 1683 when both of them accompanied the Earl of Dartmouth on a naval expedition to Tangier to dismantle the fortifications there. Pepys, the pragmatic adminis-trator and Fellow of the Royal Society, found Ken's sermons on board not at all to his taste being, as he wrote, 'full of the skill of a preacher but nothing of a natural philosopher, it being all forced meat'. The two spent the voyage in prolonged argument about the existence of spirits. It follows, then, that Ken would be resolutely hostile to advanced liberal divines like John Tillotson and Edward Stillingfleet who wished to refashion Christian preaching to fit in with the new ideas of reason and 'natural religion'. Tillotson's sermons which stressed morality rather than salvation and which were about prudential conduct and the rewards laid up in heaven for the well-disposed were *anathema* to him. These were the false teachings of 'Latitudinarian traditours'.

The Anglican plan to reform and revitalize the Church depended critically on the support of the government, and here lay their achilles heel. Archbishop Sheldon's rela-tions with Charles II were uniformly bad, and there was widespread suspicion throughout the reign that the king was a secret Roman Catholic and that all his policies were designed to secure the emancipation and public employment of Papists. Certainly Charles usually treated Anglican clergy with contempt and some of his episcopal appointments, like that of Thomas Wood to Lichfield in

1671, were scandalous. Strangely enough, it was always James, Duke of York, who seemed more sympathetic. Though by 1673 it was known that he was a practising Roman Catholic, he retained his Anglican friends and chaplains and kept up warm friendships with leading bishops and clergy. Men like Turner and Ken knew him well and admired him; they accepted his repeated assurances that as king he would support the Anglican cause. In fact, Charles II was always reasonably pleasant to Ken: he called him 'that little black fellow', joked about going to church to have Ken tell him about his sins, and would not take offence when the ascetic divine declined to have Nell Gwyn to stay in his lodgings when the court was at Winchester. But it was to James that Ken was really attached. In 1679 it was James who chose him to go to Holland to be domestic chaplain to his daughter Mary, after her marriage to William of Orange. The duke clearly approved of Ken's decisive intervention to see that Mary kept up Anglican worship in her own chapel and did not join in with the Dutch Reformed Church, though this led him into grave disfavour with William. It is clear, too, that Ken and James had much the same kind of religious mind. The diarist John Evelyn reports a conversation between the two at Winchester in 1685 in which they discussed miracles, spirits and portents apparently in complete agreement.

Thus in the last years of Charles II's reign the Sancroftian group threw itself fervently behind James. They were his earnest defenders against those Whigs who wished to exclude him from the throne and they looked to his accession to bring in a new age of church renewal. When Sancroft himself became archbishop in 1678 it opened up a heyday for the appointment of his friends to the episcopal bench: Turner, John Lake of Chichester, William Lloyd of Norwich, Thomas White of Peterborough and, at the end of 1684, Ken to the see of Bath and Wells. Perhaps he was the man who most clearly embodied the Sancroftian ideal of the episcopate. Unmarried, ascetically devout and a passionate preacher, he was also an experienced administrator through the long years as Morley's chaplain and man of business. And he was dedicated to a reform of the manners and ministrations of the clergy. The only doubt was whether such a deeply sensitive and private man was able to withstand the political shocks which were to descend upon him almost from the moment of his consecration on 25 January 1685.

The first of these crises happened within weeks when it became apparent that Charles II was dying. In view of all the doubt about the king's religion, much depended on what went on at his deathbed; and Ken, although the junior bishop, was chosen by his brethren to prepare Charles for death, receive his last profession, and grant him absolution. But from the Anglican point of view what passed was a disaster. The king failed to respond and soon James had the room cleared. When it was all over, the new king announced that his brother had been received into the Roman Church and had received the Last Rites from a Roman priest. It was scarcely a good omen for what was to follow but Sancroft and his allies still lived in hope that they could work with James. In the summer of 1685 they had a chance to demonstrate their loyalty and usefulness. In the West Country, and for the most part in Ken's own diocese, a rebellion broke out under the leadership of the late king's illegitimate son, the Duke of Monmouth. The peasantry of Somerset, the miners of the Mendips, and the Dissenting towndwellers of Taunton and Bridgewater rallied round Monmouth's standard. By 1 July Wells itself was in the hands of the rebels who stabled their horses in the cathedral, damaged the organ and terrorized the inhabitants of the precincts. But on 6 July the rebels were utterly defeated on Sedgemoor and Monmouth was taken. It fell to Ken to be one of the clergy who prepared him for his execution and accompanied him to the scaffold. What passed there seems important for Ken's later life and decisions. With

some vehemence they pressed upon the condemned man
the heinousness of the sin of rebellion, exhorting him that
if he died an Anglican (as he professed to do) he ought to
repent publicly of his wickedness in resisting his legitimate king. It was a doctrine which was soon to come
home to roost. But more immediately Ken's concern was
for his own diocese and his first visit to it in July was to
find it in chaos: his cathedral desecrated but, worse, the
prisons of Wells crowded with rebels and a ghastly series
of trials, executions and transportations in process at the
'Bloody Assize'. It seems that it was now that he made his
name in the diocese. He pleaded for the lives of many
prisoners, visited those incarcerated in Wells, Taunton
and Bridgewater, and organized food and medical
attention. There remain a number of letters of thanks for
his efforts.

An even greater crisis was to follow in the next year
1686. Against the hopes and expectations of his Anglican
friends, James II went back on all that he had promised to
them and reversed his policies. From the summer the
whole weight of government influence was turned against
the Church as the king searched around for allies who
would support him in establishing a general toleration
which would include Roman Catholics. Sancroft was
banished the Court, a series of second-rate timeservers
was appointed as bishops and finally in 1687 the king
issued a Declaration of Indulgence which at a blow
ruined any Anglican discipline over the morals or
religious duties of the people. Amid the collapse of their
world, it was difficult for the bishops to know what to do
but they decided to begin with a preaching campaign,
designed to warn the king and, if possible, get him to see
the danger of what he was doing. It is clear that this
attack from the pulpit was led by Bishop Ken. He alone
had the passionate oratory and his reputation for holiness
of life was well-known. Evelyn and others recorded the
immense crowds which came to his sermons. In Lent
1687 the Chapel Royal at Whitehall was packed to the

doors, with the Princess Anne and at least thirty of the greatest nobility present to hear him discourse on the Catholic truth which the Church of England taught and exhort them to stand fast in the face of Popish aggression. On Palm Sunday in St. Martin-in-the-Fields the church was so crowded that latecomers missed what Evelyn described as 'the wonderful eloquence of this admirable preacher'. And it was not just in London that Ken caused a sensation. On Ascension Day the bishop preached in Bath Abbey, again before the Princess Anne, and the scene is recorded for us by a Jesuit from the queen's household who was dispatched to take notes and write to refute what was said. In August the king himself came to Bath and took over the abbey for a service of 'touching for the King's Evil', at which he was attended only by Roman priests. The following Sunday Ken went again to Bath to preach and re-assure the people.

By the following year 1688 the situation was serious. James's campaign seemed to be succeeding and it looked as though his endeavours to pack a parliament might actually produce a majority. In a last effort to break the resistance of the clergy he decided to re-issue his declaration of indulgence of the previous year and instruct all incumbents in London and the provinces to read it out on two successive Sundays. Sancroft held anguished meetings at Lambeth and it was decided to refuse to obey. At Wells on the evening of 15 May Ken received an urgent summons to return to London. After two days hard riding he was at Lambeth and on the evening of 18 May he appended his signature to the famous document known as the Petition of the Seven Bishops. That evening six of them set out for Whitehall Palace. The archbishop was forbidden the Court but James received the rest, not suspecting anything amiss. Turner and Ken were personal friends. But on reading the petition he was thunderstruck. It asked him not to insist on the clergy's reading the declaration because it was illegal to set aside acts of Parliament duly passed. This

70

was indeed the direct disobedience which James had hoped to avoid, an act which could easily become a rallying-point for others. 'I did not expect this from your Church', he said, 'especially from some of you.' There followed an awkward scene in which James accused the bishops of rebellion and they equally energetically denied it. Back at Lambeth they circularized the dioceses urging that the clergy should not comply with the king's orders, and in London and the provinces there was virtually no reading of the declaration. For James it was an impossible situation. Either he capitulated or he sought to bring the bishops to heel. Disastrously for him he decided to prosecute the seven for seditious libel and, when they refused to give any sureties, he had no alternative but to remand them to the Tower of London. This is the scene which has become part of English historical memory. The bishops rode through the London streets to their prison with Ken sitting in the seat of honour beside the Primate. As they went, they were watched by vast anxious crowds who knelt to beg their blessing and even pressed forward to touch the hem of their garments. In the Tower they were visited by relays of peers, bishops and even Dissenting ministers. Their trial in Westminster Hall on 29 June was in many ways a formality. By this time James was a beaten man and only too ready to get the whole thing over with the least loss of face. But the acquittal set off delirious rejoicing throughout the country and the first popular defiance of the government.

The bishops had intended to do no more than warn James but the movement of resistance which they had begun now escalated in a way which they had not foreseen. Ken down in his diocese in the summer was alarmed at reports that a Dutch invasion force was making ready. In the autumn he was back in London to join with other bishops in pleading with James to reverse his policies before it was too late. But the king appeared now to be in a state of breakdown, talking endlessly and doing nothing. In mid-October Ken despaired and came back to Wells to wait and pray and prepare his clergy and people for what could only be disaster. When William invaded and his troops came near to Wells, Ken withdrew, sending via Sancroft a profession of his continued loyalty to James.

The outcome of the invasion and James's flight to France left Ken in great difficulties. At this point the old archbishop seems just to have collapsed; he would neither meet William nor go to Parliament. It was left to his younger brethren like Turner and Ken to fight for some way of preserving James's title by proposing that he remain king but that a regent should actually govern. When that failed and the throne was offered to William and Mary, men like Ken were faced with the problem of whether they could transfer their allegiance and swear new oaths. It is apparent that the bishop found this an agonizing decision. At the house of his friend, George Hooper, rector of Lambeth, he came one evening almost to the point of accepting the new regime. He had never (he said) carried the point of divine right and hereditary succession very high; unity and pastoral work were more important than such theory. He was extremely reluctant to be part of a formal schism and fearful that if he and others left the established church it would be abandoned to Latitudinarians who would abandon its Catholic order and dilute its doctrines. But there was the point of personal integrity and keeping faith. In spite of his errors James had been a kind friend, and the oaths sworn to him were sacred. And what of those words about loyalty spoken to Monmouth on the scaffold? Should a priest go back on words which he had pressed on a dying man? In the end for Ken it was a personal decision not to take the oaths rather than an affirmation of any high political or religious theory.

Of course, he did not go voluntarily from his diocese. Nonjurors were suspended from office on 1 August 1689 and deprived on 1 February following, but Ken stayed in Wells in the palace. It was acutely embarrassing for the government and not least for Queen Mary, whose chaplain he had once been. There were attempts at persuasion and expedients proposed. But in April 1691 it was decided that the see had to be filled and, after various refusals, Dr. Richard Kidder was nominated as the new bishop. When the news came, Ken went into the cathedral, took his place in the bishop's chair, and before witnesses asserted his right as the true and canonical Bishop of Bath and Wells. He then withdrew into retirement, at 54 still a reasonably young man.

In the years which followed he lived mostly at Longleat, the home of Viscount Weymouth, but there were visits to friends to act as spiritual director. Occasionally he preached by invitation in parish churches but he would not join in the state prayers. His position as a Nonjuror was a moderate one: he could not take the oaths himself but he would not blame those who felt they could, and he did not wish the separation to be a permanent one. Other Nonjurors thought that the whole Church of England had become apostate by adhering to a usurper. Such claims Ken rejected; he would join in no Jacobite plots and he would not take part in the consecration of a succession of Nonjuring bishops. When in 1704 his supplanter, Richard Kidder, was killed in the palace by the fall of a chimney-stack, Queen Anne let it be known that she would like to see Ken once again as bishop. Significantly he declined on the grounds of age and infirmity. When he learned that his friend George Hooper was to be nominated he urged him to accept and formally resigned his see. At the very end of his life he led a movement of moderate Nonjurors who declared their intention of rejoining the Church of England. He intended as a symbolic act to travel to Wells to make his communion, and it seems sad that illness and his death in 1711 prevented him, though Victorian poets and painters lingered over this scene of what might have been.

It is possible that Ken is not for us quite the saint that he was for our Victorian fathers. An unkind critic might say that our own era is marked by a spirituality which is often trite and undemanding; we stress human satisfaction rather than self-sacrifice; we are concerned to make religion fit a science-based culture rather than question whether science is sufficient for all things; and we sometimes imagine that our faith is enhanced by discarding the experience and tradition of the past. Ken is a figure alien to all that. But he was a holy man with a radical love for God, and he regarded keeping to the faith as he understood it as more important than anything which the world had to offer; he was a faithful pastor and teacher in confusing and dispiriting times. If he is not a saint for our day, at least he has some important truths to teach it.

John Tillotson (1630–94), Dean and Archbishop of Canterbury: Portrait of a Liberal

Although John Tillotson was archbishop of Canterbury for only three and a half years he left the impress of his personality on the 18th century Church of England far more firmly than any of his successors. All this was not so much because of what he did in office but because he represented more than any other man the critical change which came over English religious life between 1660 and 1740. He was a one time Puritan who became, *par excellence*, the exponent of the ideas and personal style of the Age of Reason. Indeed if any man was father of the 18th century Church, aristocratic, urbane, latitudinarian, rational and unenthusiastic, it was he. When in 1751 Thomas Birch, secretary of the Royal Society, wrote his biography it was as of a man who was the very epitome of a divine of the age of Walpole and Newcastle, and who had abandoned the religion of an obscure and superstitious past and blended philosophy, science and religion into one set of rational and liberal beliefs. And yet to other 18th century thinkers Tillotson was thought malign rather than admirable. John Wesley believed that he had obscured and buried the authentic gospel, and created a religion based on mere morality and good works. Dr. Johnson thought that his sermons, so extravagant, admired by many, lacked warmth and force and real feeling, and failed to deal with sin and redemption. And to hundreds of ordinary parish-priests he was not so much a Father-in-God as a 'Latitudinarian traitor', a bishop wholly out of sympathy with their hopes and aspirations, and prepared to betray much of which they held dear. Their real enmity to him and his memory is shown by their willingness to believe such stories of him as that he had never been baptized. The legend of 'undipped John' remained as a powerful indication that no matter how attractive his ideas were to some, to ordinary clergy and churchpeople he remained an enigma and a threat.

To put this in perspective we have to examine the nature of Tillotson's liberalism, and to do this we must look at his origins and background. He was born in 1630 into a milieu wholly Puritan. His father, a Halifax clothier, was still alive in 1679 when the son was dean of Canterbury, and he remained a firm and orthodox Calvinist, unmoved by John's later opinions. It is remarkable how his whole youth was conceived within a traditional Puritan family. He went up to Cambridge in 1647 just when it had been purged of royalists, and his tutor and many of his contemporaries at Clare were men, all of whom were to be ejected for nonconformity after the Act of Uniformity of 1662. His tutor, David Clarkson, was not only ejected but became a vigorous nonconformist writer, in 1681 publishing his *No Evidence of Diocesan Episcopacy in Primitive Times* against Edward Stillingfleet. When in 1656 Tillotson left Cambridge it was to be chaplain to Edmund Prideaux, attorney-general to Oliver Cromwell. As late as September 1661 when a first sermon of his was published he seems still to have been a Presbyterian minister, and indeed he attended on the commissioners at the famous Savoy Conference in July 1661 in the capacity of an adviser to the Presbyterian group. Alone among his Cambridge college contemporaries he seems to have submitted to the new order. One may ask why?

The fact was that even before the Restoration in 1660 there was the beginning of a collapse of that view of the world in which Puritanism had flourished. To men of the early-17th century the world was a place of mystery, full of spirits, powers, and forces. Keith Thomas and others have shown the deep-seated belief in magic, white and black, where 'canning' men and women pitted their powers against witches. Indeed, even after the Restoration, preachers were unwilling to abandon their belief in the active forces of the devil lest with *that* loss of belief went a disbelief in miracles, divine grace, and providential intervention in human affairs. William Lamont has shown the contemporary belief in prophecy and apocalyptic. Even in William III's reign men as diverse as Richard Baxter, Bishop William Lloyd of St. Asaph, and Sir Isaac Newton wrestled with the meaning of prophecies in the Book of Revelation. Books were published with detailed illustrations of monstrous births, children with two heads, sheep born with one eye in the centre of the head, or ghosts of varying appearances: all to indicate some coming judgement or crisis. Puritanism was not an ordered, rational, liberal world-view: it was about a human existence which was uncertain, fearful and sinful; and it was about the awful power and intervention of God; his inscrutable providence in justifying men and women; his spirit at work to raise them up, and gather faithful communities, and elect nations in a world of crisis and the coming end of all things. This was the setting of the New Model Army of the Fifth Monarchymen. The religious assumptions of all this are clear: (1) Christian faith was conceived of essentially as something given by *authority*; it came from an authoritative past in the form of sacred scriptures and the dogmatic formulations of the early church. Arguments were won or lost by a claim to a more accurate exegesis of proof-texts or a closer conformity to the pattern of the early church. The essence of the theological endeavour was attention to a body of authoritative teaching. (2) Secondly, Christianity was thought of in terms of *Revelation*: it was a series of saving events, knowledge of which was *revealed* to men. And it centred in Christ as saviour and judge. (3) And, thirdly, there was an all-pervading belief in *Providence*:

the immediate intervention of God in the world to order and alter the course of events. But in the 1650s new teachings, a new world-view, grew up *from within Puritanism*. It was as though Calvinists themselves grew weary of endless religious conflicts and bitterness, of the violence and assertions of the sects, and of the distraction of order and social harmony which the Revolution had produced. It was a movement which was eventually to lead to the virtual collapse and disappearance of English Presbyterianism, and in the 18th century it became English Unitarianism. One of the early indications of a change was at Cambridge with attractive groups of men who were to exercise a powerful influence over young dons like Tillotson and his contemporaries, Edward Stillingfleet and Simon Patrick. These Cambridge Platonists, as they were called, introduced two emphases which were highly uncharacteristic of orthodox Calvinism: *on reason* and on men's natural capacity for morality. This *reason*, to the Platonists, was a kind of quasi-mystical theory, an inner faculty which was able to perceive the moral perfection of God, and to find that moral beauty so compelling that it flowed back into the personality and out into life. The Cambridge men, Henry More, Benjamin Whichcote, John Smith and Ralph Cudworth, were gentle, devout and eirenic. All the accounts stress the immense influence they were to have on a whole generation of English clergy, of whom Tillotson was to become the most eminent.

But the real making of John Tillotson was not so much in Cambridge but in London, and from about 1660 until his death he was basically a resident in the city. At first he was an associate of Presbyterians like Newton, Bates and Calamy, and his first published sermon in September 1661 was preached for Bates. But with the Act of Uniformity he separated himself from his old friends, presumably was episcopally ordained, and quickly came under the influence which was to prove much more powerful and enduring, even than his Cambridge mentors. It was that of a much neglected Restoration divine, Dr. John Wilkins, who became rector of St. Laurence Jewry in 1662. Tillotson became Lecturer or stipendiary preacher in the church at about the same time; he was later to act as editor of Wilkins's published writings, and in particular to publish in 1672 his *Of the Principles and Duties of Natural Religion*: in my view one of the seminal works of the Restoration era, and without which it is impossible to understand the new liberal theology and preaching which became so common in the early 18th century. Wilkins was an early scientist, not a brilliant one or really an experimentalist but at Wadham College as a don in the last years of the Protectorate he had been the presiding genius of a society or club which had met to discuss natural phenomena. He was an early member of the Royal Society. Wilkins's early book *The Discovery of a New World in the Moon* (1638) is not so much a description of scientific discoveries as the recommendation of a new approach to religion, based on human reason and a close study of the natural order. Wilkins's whole approach has something in common with St. Thomas Aquinas. He believes that a careful dispassionate study of natural phenomena will establish certain principles which are of the utmost importance for religion: (1) that everything is endowed with a natural principle by which it seeks its own perfection or well-being; (2) that the world has been given an ascending order of existence: from the inanimate, to the vegetable, to animals, and finally to man who alone possesses *reason* the highest principle of life. Such principles are not capable of mathematical demonstration, but probability and common-sense show them to be true. They lie at the heart of any reasonable approach to the business of living. And so he goes on to argue for what he calls a 'natural religion'. Quite apart from all the traditional, scriptural, authoritative accounts of religion there is an account written in the hearts and minds of men, accessible to the calm, deliberate, rational mind. And it can be improved upon to yield *three* basic notions: (1) the divine existence; (2) the moral order of the universe; and that (3) religion, worship and piety must always be in harmony with this natural morality which reason affirmed. His account of man and his well-being is significant. Natural morality and religion will always point a man to what are his own best interests. There can be no real conflict between an individual's duty and his interest: 'nothing is properly his duty, but what is really his interest'. It is this prudential view of religion, as a combination of natural ideas of morality and common sense, without dogma or traditional authority, which came to be so immensely popular and satisfying to cultured men of the Restoration period.

It is essentially as Wilkins's protégé and his colleague in a great London church that Tillotson made his reputation as a preacher. For a very short time he had been rector of Kirton in Suffolk, but although the living was a valuable one, worth over £200 a year, he resigned it in 1663. It is clear that among country people he was not a success, and the parish complained to the patron that in all his time Jesus Christ had not been preached among them. His sphere was London where he quickly cultivated a wide and admiring circle of businessmen, including his brother Joshua and Thomas Firmin. When he became preacher of Lincoln's Inn in 1663 he began a close association with London lawyers. As a preacher to this sophisticated urban congregation he acquired a quite extraordinary reputation, and it is of interest to look at the sermons which were so extravagantly admired in his own day. They were, first of all, a complete break with the style of the previous generation. He abandoned all the involved and artificial illustrations employed by both Catholic and Puritan preachers, and the whole apparatus of classical and patristic allusion; he rejected much of the common phraseology of theology and all its technical terms. Instead there was an ordered and systematic appeal to reason and the natural order, and an attempt to show that the Bible was only a 'republication' or confirmation of natural theology and the findings of the new science. His sermons stressed the order and design of the universe now being revealed, the natural moral order which was discoverable by reason and common-sense. God was not so much one who intervened in power but the great designer or architect of a beneficent order to which men should conform. The high point of each sermon's appeal was that men should employ an enlightened self-interest by conforming themselves to this morality. Piety, justice, charity and honesty were not just commanded; they could be shown to conduce to personal happiness and even to lead on to prosperity and a good reputation. The teachings of Christ and the scriptures were powerful illustrations of this basic truth. Controversial questions were eschewed. Disputed matters like election and predestination were ignored, but more: the person and work of Christ, the nature of salvation, the authority of scripture, the order of the church, the patristic writings, all these were underplayed. To a modern reader Tillotson's sermons seem cold and lifeless; there is complacency about his assumption that a good disposition and common-sense are the basic requirements in a Christian. But to men brought up amid the rant and rancour of the civil war, it was a relief to hear calm, ordered, prudential discourses, which assumed an ordered and coherent universe, and seemed to lead on to an ordered and well-managed society.

In a sense the preaching-style was paralleled by the man's personality. I suspect that nobody knew him well. But he was kind, well-mannered, considerate and willing to take time for letters and private discussions. He was the kind of clergyman who was liked by and consulted by important and well-born people; he had that combination of respectful attention and austere moral seriousness which aristocrats and royal persons seemed to find particularly impressive. He was discreet and sympathetic, but not obsequious and curiously detached from the whole business of clerical preferment and parties. As the years went by he began to build up substantial numbers of aristocratic friends, not least among some important Whig families like the Russells. We possess a series of letters between him and Lady Russell, and his style is calm, strangely remote, and yet not cold. His counsel was given and received, but it did not establish any real intimacy or dependence. Like some liberals he affected to be unpolitical, and to regard others as the plotters and intriguers; his own views were not a religious position but basic Christianity in the spirit of the gospel. It is not entirely unsurprising that other Anglicans and some dissenters found it hard simply to equate his version of Christianity with generosity, and that they found even irritating his air of unruffled moral assurance.

On a number of occasions in Charles II's reign he was engaged, mostly with his friends, Edward Stillingfleet and Edward Fowler, in schemes or negotiations for protestant reunion: that is for the settlement of the religious question by the comprehension of some Dissenters in the Established Church and the indulgence or toleration of those who could not be so included. The first attempt was in the winter of 1667–8 when he, Stillingfleet and Hezekiah Burton joined in discussions with Richard Baxter, Marton and Bates. It is possible to misunderstand these schemes of comprehension, and I think we cannot put them in context unless we see that there were two types of comprehension scheme. There was one type which was actually favoured by High Churchmen like Sancroft, Fell, Turner, Hickes and others; they desired Christian reunion because they wanted a united church in which they could exercise discipline: reform church attendance, control morals, and ensure that children were catechized and confirmed. They feared a divided religious situation for fear that this might lead to toleration and the making of religion a purely voluntary activity. They were thus willing to abolish the rates and subscriptions imposed on conformist clergy, and they were willing to make it relatively easy for Presbyterians and others to receive episcopal ordination: usually by some formula of conditional ordination with laying-on of hands. But it needs to be understood that Tillotson and his allies had a somewhat different view. Their type of comprehension involved not so much the coming together of two bodies with clear theologies and strong conceptions of church-order, but a meeting of liberal minds to promote a church with a new liberalized liturgy. It is this tendency of Tillotson to convert comprehension negotiations into a subtle attempt to reduce the dogmatic character of the church which alienated many churchmen from the whole concept of comprehension. It is important to remember that the negotiations were conducted with a relatively small section of the English dissenters, the London group of the Presbyterians, those who had already receded from, or were in process of receding from, their orthodox Calvinism. Already these men had abandoned typical Presbyterian church-order; their congregations were often groups who attached themselves to a particular minister, and many of the London congregations were wealthy and eminent businessmen. But, as against Baptists and those Congregationalists who retained an orthodox theology, the Presbyterians were a denomination which was declining in numbers and slowly dying. In 1674 and again in 1680 Tillotson and Stillingfleet attempted further negotiations, which foundered on the suspicions both of churchmen and dissenters.

During these years he remained primarily a London preacher without even a living, but gradually he found valuable preferments coming to him. In 1672 during the king's attempt at a general declaration of indulgence he was made Dean of Canterbury but his residentiaryship at St. Paul's, his most valuable preferment, came by the intervention of his highly-placed liberally minded friends. His visits down to Canterbury were few: to the audits and some chapter meetings but, it would appear, not always to fulfill periods of residence. Archbishop Sancroft made one or two critical comments on his dean's easygoing style, but the relationship between a firm, old-fashioned churchman of the Tory school and a Latitudinarian preacher with powerful Exclusionist-Whig connections was not particularly cordial.

It is clear that Tillotson's day came in 1688 when William of Orange arrived in London after the flight of James II. The Dean of Canterbury was one of the divines who waited on him immediately, and Gilbert Burnet who had come over with William suggested him as Clerk of the Closet to the new king and queen. Tillotson was brought into close, almost daily contact with William, and his peculiar talent with the highborn came into its own. The king had been exhibiting all kinds of irritation with Burnet's fussy, bossy, dominating and indiscreet manner but in Tillotson he found an Anglican divine whom he could like and admire, whose reticence, highmindedness, and liberal theology was entirely to his taste. By the autumn of 1689 the king had put himself wholly in the hands of his new favourite for ecclesiastical advice, and both had embarked on their cherished project for a comprehension. From September a stream of episcopal appointments began to flow to Tillotson's friends and associates: Stillingfleet and Patrick among them. With the king so closely behind him the Dean of Canterbury was confident of success in achieving comprehension. Toleration had been granted in the early summer of 1689, and this had contented most dissenters, but he and the king were intent on the admission of the Presbyterians into the established church. In September 1689 Tillotson composed a paper of what he called 'Probable concessions which will be made by the Church of England'. They were of the widest extent: a rewritten liturgy, a mere declaration from the clergy that they would conform to it, the admission of those ordained in the foreign Protestant churches to minister in the Church of England, and a supplementary ordination for English nonconformist ministers. In the autumn a royal commission of carefully picked Tillotsonians began the work of rewriting the Book of Common Prayer. There was an air of quiet confidence. Tillotson was in constant attendance on the king, he did not himself become a bishop at this time but merely exchanged his Deanery of Canterbury for that of St. Paul's, which was nearer and more convenient. He seemed to have been genuinely reluctant to assume too prominent a role, knowing the animosity which his religious views attracted, but when he kissed the king's hand for the deanery of St. Paul's William informed him that he was eventually to be Archbishop of Canterbury when Sancroft's deprivation left the see vacant. It was clear that the whole comprehension scheme would depend on the Convocation of Canterbury which was summoned to meet at the end of November. Royal, ministerial and episcopal pressure was brought to bear on the clergy, and the new appointments to bishoprics, deaneries and archdeaconries were carefully selected to be in favour of the scheme. But there was, as Burnet reports, a groundswell of anger at the grass-roots, and the proctorial elections were vigorously fought. On 21 November the first business of the Lower House was to elect a Prolocutor. Tillotson was proposed as the man who had the confidence of the king, and he was immediately voted down by 55 to 28 in favour of Dr. Jane of Oxford, a known opponent of the comprehension proposals. In the next few weeks the hostility of the clergy was such that William had no alternative but to prorogue the Convocation.

In 1691 Tillotson duly became Archbishop of Canterbury but his appointment was in some ways a sad moment for him and the established church. For all his qualities, he was an archbishop whom the ordinary clergy did not want. Gradually a gap opened up between the episcopate and the higher clergy on the one hand and the rank and file of the clergy on the other. Under royal and ministerial patronage the leadership of the Church became more and more adapted to the Tillotsonian

image: urbane, rationalising, moralistic, socially conservative. Cultured gentlemen as they were, pious, liberal
and reasonable, the 18th century episcopate was not
scandalous: they merely lacked a gospel which could be
conveyed with power to the people of a rural and
industrialising society. And that characteristic they shared
with old Dissent. Vital Christianity had to be found
elsewhere than among the bishops, deans, archdeacons
and gentlemen-rectors. It was in the Evangelical revival,
the Methodist movement, and eventually in the Tractarian
rediscovery of the church and the sacraments. In a sense
John Tillotson represents not a kind of Anglican tragedy,
but a lesson that when it comes to Christian faith, its
preaching and its practice, urbanity, wit, reason and
liberality are valuable but they are not all—and they are
not enough.

Rational Churchmen:
the Latitudinarians

The group of English churchmen who in the later 17th century carried or attracted the description 'Latitudinarians' present us with two distinct problems: who were they? and what is their character as a movement or phase in religious thought? Neither question is simple. The term 'Latitudinarian' is itself of uncertain meaning. It began as a term of contempt or abuse, and never quite lost this overtone. It was first heard during the Commonwealth period, and was used by orthodox Calvinists to describe those who dissented from their own theological system: it was used of the Cambridge group of divines who revived Platonism in the 1650s; and it was used in retrospect of the liberal theology of William Chillingworth. The term 'Latitudinarianism', unlovely as it was, indicated a 'man of a wide swallow'; and one Calvinist described it as 'the sink and sewer of all error and iniquity', because it seemed to represent the endeavour of all those who would try to restore a place to human reason in discovering the things of religion. 'Carnal reason', any reliance on human powers, seemed to encroach on the sovereign gift of grace by which alone a man was given knowledge of God's salvation. In 1662 Simon Patrick (for the initials 'S.P.' would indicate it was he) published a pamphlet *A Brief Account of the New Sect of Latitude-men*, and it is clear that his definition included all those who abhored the rigidities of systematic theology and the hold of Aristotle on the academic studies of the universities. It was a plea against Calvinism in theology *and* against Laudianism in ecclesiastical matters. In the early 18th century the definition was still uncertain. It came to be applied to men like Samuel Clarke and

Benjamin Hoadly, whose theology was of a thorough-going rationalism. Dr Clarke's work on the doctrine of the Trinity and Hoadly's discoveries on the nature of the Church's authority were far from that position which the Church of England had customarily held. When the men of the Oxford Movement looked back, the Latitudinarians whom they knew were true 18th century divines who despised tradition, were contemptuous of patristic scholarship, and who had delivered the Church into the hands of semi-pagan politicians. Writing in 1851 Bishop Samuel Wilberforce of Oxford declared himself dedicated to an Anglican divinity which avoided 'on the one hand a breezy Latitudinarianism and on the other the barren authoritarianism of the Church of Rome'.

The term then is wide, but it has customarily been used for a more inclusive group of Anglican divines. They were mostly London clergy who in the Restoration era carried a considerable reputation as preachers. Indeed John Tillotson's sermons are still taken to represent the most typical expression of the group's views. The new preaching was an immense change: a breach with the homiletic conventions of the immediate past. He abandoned the involved illustrations which both the Catholic and the Puritan traditions had employed. He rejected the almost mechanical iteration of terms and phrases. He substituted an appeal to reason and to common-sense, and attempted to show that the Bible was in accord with natural theology and with the findings of the new science. His sermons were unadorned and unhurried; they were a continual appeal to the common experience of his hearers, and they advocated an enlightened self-interest. Piety, justice, charity, honesty were not only enjoined in scripture, they conduced to happiness and reward. Tillotson was convinced that moral reformation, self-discipline, public charity were imperative after the confusions, angers, and destruction of the Civil Wars; and he eschewed all controversial questions. He advocates prudence as the needful virtue: as a practical reason confirmed by the gift of revelation: with which it is wholly in accord. It is this preaching which packed the pews of City churches. Simon Patrick, Edward Stillingfleet, Thomas Tenison (whose ministry at St Martin's-in-the-Fields was so popular), William Lloyd and Gilbert Burnet: these men, within a generation changed the preaching style and the mode of thought of English churchmen.

It is easy to think of them as Low Churchmen; as the spiritual counterpart of Whigs—over against the High Churchmen and their spiritual counterparts, the Tories. And the view of the Latitudinarians is part of a continuing English historico-political myth. The Latitudinarians (so the myth goes) were the spiritual successors of the Cambridge Platonists. They were Puritans who had lapsed into rationalism, and (though they conformed at the Restoration) they remained men fundamentally in opposition to that English High Church tradition which laid so much stress on patristic tradition and was zealous for church order. The Latitudinarians (we know) were for comprehension, a widening of the terms of communion of the Church of England. They wished to relax the oaths and declarations required of Anglican clergymen, and admit moderate dissenters into the ministry. In each of the years 1673–5 Tillotson and Stillingfleet were the spokesmen of a group of Anglicans who negotiated with the non-conformists on the terms of a comprehension bill. And this is taken to indicate that the Latitudinarians represented a Low-Church party over against High Churchmen like Sheldon or Sancroft. Again, after 1688 and the coming to the throne of William III, the Latitudinarian group was again earnest to promote a comprehension; and, even though this failed, they became the men whom (above all) William appointed to the episcopate. And the usual histories talk of the 'packing of the episcopal bench with "Whig Latitudinarians" '. The whole view has become a commonplace—but it is this picture of the Tillotson-Stillingfleet-Patrick group as a

Low-Church party which I want to question. There are certain obvious flaws. A belief in the role of reason in theological method is, of course, typical of Anglican divinity from Hooker through the Caroline divines down to 1660. Comprehension was by no means a Low Church contrivance: it was regularly proposed by those churchmen who wished to preserve the effectiveness of Anglican discipline over the nation. Clearly if there were a Toleration, and the various sects were all allowed a liberty, the Church's machinery of the enforcement of morals would fall to the ground. Comprehension was, indeed, a High Church device to counter proposals for a general toleration. It meant the reconstruction of a national Church by admitting moderate dissenters and then the effective prosecution of intransigent dissenters. Again, recent studies on the reign of William III have shown that his ecclesiastical régime was by no means a 'Whig' one. His first ministry was a Tory one; his ecclesiastical policy was taken from the Earl of Nottingham, a noted 'high' Anglican, and a man like Stillingfleet was actually rejected for the primacy in 1695 because he was thought too rigid a churchman. The time is clearly ripe for a re-appraisal of the Latitudinarians as being churchmen in a continuing Anglican tradition of divinity.

THE ROOTS OF LATITUDINARIANISM

We need then, first, to examine the roots of Restoration Latitudinarianism. It is a commonplace that the Latitudinarians were mostly Cambridge men, and that they learned much from Henry More, Benjamin Whichcote and Ralph Cudworth. G. R. Cragg and Bishop Henry McAdoo both stress the bonds of friendship which bound the older and the younger men. But they also stress the differences. The Platonists' view of reason was something involving the harmonious action of the personality; it was a faculty in man which allowed him to perceive the moral perfection of God, and to find that moral beauty so compelling that it flowed back into his personality and out into his life. There is a mystical quality about the Platonists, an exultation which the Latitudinarians cannot emulate. And in the last resort their view of reason is quite different: it belongs not to mysticism but to a longer tradition of practical divinity or casuistry, which is to be found in other seventeenth century divines.

Let us look, for example, at the work of a divine who has not usually been accounted a Latitudinarian. *Jeremy Taylor*, who became bishop of Down and Connor in 1660, has even acquired the reputation as being a rigid churchman. But if we examine his theological position, it is by no means different in kind or manner from that of Simon Patrick or Edward Stillingfleet. His work is marked by a consistent liberality. Like so many men of his generation he had been involved in a defensive battle against Calvinism, and he exhibits a desire to avoid commitment to any theological system or carefully formulated body of doctrine. While concerned to defend the 'fundamentals' of the Christian faith, he was yet prepared to admit a wide variety of teaching on things indifferent. In trying to keep a balance between the authority of scripture, the evidence of antiquity, and the claims of reason he conceived of himself as embarked on a search for truth which would make the things of the traditional past available to the needs of the contemporary world. Of course, this three-fold formula could mean little or nothing, and it will be helpful to examine what it meant in practice.

Taylor takes his stand on the primacy and unique authority of Holy Scripture. 'We are acquitted', he writes, 'by the testimony of the primitive fathers from any other necessity of believing than of such articles as are recorded in Scripture'. But he is well aware that the biblical writings do not exist in a vacuum; they require interpretation, and he is deeply hostile to the vagaries and excesses of exegesis which were common in his own day. He will not agree that every man is his own individual authority; nor does he think that the historic Church should be tested against the scriptural interpretation of any one man. Taylor is thus concerned to place exegesis in its proper context. And in his impressive work *The Liberty of Prophesying* (1647) he expounds the notion of a 'practical divinity'. The divine must do his work of exegesis within the community of the Church: he must be in contact with its pastoral care, its liturgical worship, and its spiritual discipline. The end of biblical study is not a satisfaction of the mind but a growth of moral personality. Not least by it the individual learns his place in the Christian community. Taylor began his career as a moral theologian and he continued to have a casuistic concern. The test of any interpretation of scripture was a practical and rational one: to examine whether it builds up the life of the Church and increases it in holiness and service.

Similarly Taylor has a practical and cautious approach to the Fathers. He denies utterly that they can ever be used as an appeal to an independent authority. He was vehemently critical of those who sought to piece together extracts from the patristic writings to support some private theory. After the critical work of a scholar like Jean Daillé this was impossible, and the evidence had to be used critically and in a reasonable way. He contended that a critical and discriminating use of the Fathers showed that they said nothing new. They themselves witnessed only to those scriptural truths which the Early Church had regarded as fundamental. In other words the Fathers had exercised a 'practical divinity', and pointed to those doctrines which were held as essential to the life of the first communities. This notion of there being a body of 'fundamentals', and the distinction between them and 'things indifferent', is very important to Taylor. Having marked out this area of 'fundamentals' to his own satisfaction, he then goes on to claim the widest possible liberty in the area of secondary or speculative matters upon which scripture affords no decisive direction. In this uncertain area the best judge is human reason: a practical comparison of things, offices and institutions to discover what is most spiritually effective. But he insists this is not an untutored reason. It is exercised by men whose spiritual formation is rooted in the community life of the historic church. When the question at issue is one of ecclesiastical order or the form of worship, then the only safe way is to follow the traditional pattern of the Church, while at the same time being careful that this pattern is constantly adapted to contemporary needs. He is concerned that there should be a constant rational appraisal by which the life and practice of the primitive church is compared with that of the present. But this is in no sense to be done in an antiquarian spirit, as if one were slavishly to copy the past. The real endeavour is that men, standing in a living tradition should by use of their reason attempt to make the treasures of the past available for the spiritual nourishment of the present. From all this may be seen the essentials of Taylor's method: (1) his belief in a *practical reasoning* on scripture and tradition by men nourished in the life of the Church; (2) his test, continually applied, of a growth in moral personality, and; (3) his readiness to use contemporary knowledge and insights to represent an ancient faith. Here, in effect, in a noted Caroline divine, are just the essential beliefs of the Latitudinarians.

THE NEW PHILOSOPHY

But, of course, Taylor and his contemporaries were primarily concerned with the controversy with Calvinism, and after 1660 this was no longer the main issue. The plea for a place for reason in divinity is an attack on overspeculative theology and the construction of theological systems. It is used to oppose doctrines such as predestination and election. But after 1660 Anglican apologists have to face a new problem: that of the new science. It was, of course, *not* an overt threat: many of the early members of the Royal Society were devout believers: but we need to stress how revolutionary was the *method* involved. The scientists collected evidence, and waited patiently on observed phenomena. They endeavoured to collect their specimens, and sort them into categories; and to arrange these occurrences in historical order, and see what common character or theme appeared. It was a sphere in which the microscope and telescope revealed a new world. They were confronted by a steadily augmented range of observed data about the physical universe, which made it necessary to reconsider the implications of many traditionally accepted ideas. It is not often that a generation is presented with a new heaven and a new earth, and the new philosophy had obvious implications for theological method. It challenged radically the Aristotelianism of the universities: a vast system of authoritative deduction based on traditional 'authorities'. 'Aristotle' to the new scientists was 'a dead hand', and the new inductive methods had to battle against entrenched authority which represented it as the enemy of hallowed antiquity.

It was awareness of the dangerous character of this gap which led many English churchmen to devote themselves to bridging it. And it is this endeavour which lies at the heart of the Latitudinarian movement. They tried to unite revelation and reason in a way which preserved the past while admitting the present. Herein perhaps lies something of their strength, while at the same time accounting for some of their obvious weaknesses.

Perhaps the most obvious figure among them to be considered here is that neglected writer, John Wilkins, whose *Of the Principles and Duties of Natural Religion* lay behind so many Latitudinarian sermons. Wilkins was himself a scientist: not a brilliant one, but a book like his *The Discovery of a New World* shows that he was able to take the conclusions of others and link them up into an intelligible whole. Many commentators have commented on the similarity of method between Wilkins and Aquinas, and the *Summa Theologica* is clearly a diffused influence behind the whole treatise on natural religion. Wilkins begins with an outline of the different kind of evidence by which knowledge of things is established. The assent which proceeds from acceptance of evidence is either of the nature of knowledge or certainty *or* of opinion and probability: according to the evidence. The difference would seem to be between mathematics or natural science. Evidence in natural science needs to be weighed, compared, ordered, and requires the exercise of human reason. Yet this reasonable survey will itself establish certain principles: (1) that everything is endowed with a natural principle by which it seeks its own perfection and well-being: (2) that there is in the created world an ascending order: the inanimate, the animate, the vegetable, the sensitive, animal and man. And the highest form has life, sense (and the supreme human characteristic) reason. He agrees that not all the principles of natural religion are capable of demonstration, and even these may be questioned. But experimental proof cannot be required in such matters, and we must go by which is the most probable and which can command assent. Such natural principles must lie at the heart of any reasonable approach to the business of living. And so he goes on to argue for the 'reasonableness and credibility of the principles of natural religion'. And he believes that these can be put under three heads: (1) the Divine existence (2) apprehension of the divine perfections (3) worship and obedience to the divine pattern of creation. All these arguments are (he freely admits) not demonstrable: 'of which the nature of the thing is not capable' but they are more probable than anything else. And he believes that there can be no contribution from the findings of natural science which will contradict these principles. Indeed 'the admirable continuance of natural things' points to their beauty, order, and fitness for their purpose, and their ceaseless urge to their own perfection. He turns the subject to man's nature and to the human body. Man also is 'necessarily inclined to seek his own well-being and happiness' and 'nothing properly is his duty, but what is really his interest'.

Thus in Wilkins we find a rather traditional basis for typical Latitudinarian positions: a belief in man's ability to discover a natural religion which is discovered in much the same way as the general theories which men have in natural sciences like botany, biology, or geology. And, secondly, a notion that prudence is a religious principle: and that rational self-interest is close to divine worship. Worship involves temporal as well as spiritual rewards.

Wilkins, of course, goes on to consider revealed religion; and at once we are struck by his remarkable conservatism. Having rooted religion in the reason and nature of mankind, he goes on to show that revelation adds an essential element: it shows us the true nature of happiness and the perfect end to which we all tend. There is nothing in revelation which is contrary to reason, though there may be much which is above and beyond it. This (alas!) involves him in an elaborate attempt to prove the reasonableness of the O.T., and to defend the historicity of the Mosaic history of creation which we may well find somewhat unhappy. But his account of Jesus as the sum of that perfection to which all humanity is directed is cogent and not unmoving. Wilkins was not himself a great preacher, and although he ended his life as bishop of Chester, he was primarily a scholar. His influence lay primarily with those preachers who read his works: and not least with his son-in-law, John Tillotson, who edited and published much of his material.

RATIONAL CHURCHMEN

Wilkins had thus provided a theoretical framework. He had exalted the power of reason to discover the principles of a natural religion; he had denied that reason could ever conflict with revelation rightly understood. And it was on this basis that the early scientists operated. Bishop Sprat, in his *History of the Royal Society* (1667) spoke for a body of bishops, churchmen and scientists who made the same plea that their work and experiments contributed to God's glory and to the discovery of human welfare.

But, of course, some difficult questions remained. What of the Fathers of the Early Church? What of church order and authority? It was with these and related questions which the younger Latitudinarians like Simon Patrick and Edward Stillingfleet dealt. And here again we see a combination of rationality with a reverence for scripture and antiquity. To some Wilkins's nature might have seemed to leave the way open to a wholly 'natural' view of religion, but the younger men build easily on the foundation laid by Jeremy Taylor. They re-vamp the early 17th century Anglican theological method to include scripture and tradition but with an even greater stress on reason than Taylor allows. Perhaps the most learned and distinguished writer of the school, Edward Stillingfleet, may be taken as an example. In his *Rational Account of the Grounds of the Protestant Religion*, first published c.1664 and subsequently revised, he shows a weighty patristic learning and defends the use of the Fathers energetically as an essential element in Anglican divinity. He knows all about the battle of the Ancients and Moderns, but will not become a partisan of either. Nothing which the patristic writers put forward need be accepted merely because it is old and is derived from some primitive era of the Church's life. He claims that in their own day the Fathers admitted the claims of reason and proceeded by way of rational inference. While he accepts that God's revelation, given in Scripture is authoritative, yet it still requires 'a rational assent'. Rational man has a right to determine what is revelation, and his faith in it must be the result of a 'rational and discursive act of mind'. He is certain that this was the position of the great Alexandrians, and he believes that the Fathers in general concur that there can never be a conflict between a true formulation of the apostolic tradition and the claim of men to exercise their own reason. Thus Stillingfleet and others of his cast of mind, believed that the continuing faith and order of the Church was itself a product of the interaction of scripture, tradition and reason. Its recommendation to a reasonable man was a practical one: that in the past and the present it conduced to that moral and spiritual guidance and formation, which men required. In other words they thought that reason did not abolish the authority either of scripture or tradition.

Archbishop Tenison and the Reshaping of The Church of England

Among the collections of the Lambeth Library the papers of Thomas Tenison, archbishop of Canterbury from 1694 to 1715, can claim a kind of pre-eminence. They provide the prime evidence for that profound alteration in the character and mission of the Church of England which took place in the era after the Revolution of 1688. Tenison is not usually counted among the great archbishops of Canterbury, and yet as historical research goes on it becomes increasingly clear that he was the key-figure in the devising of a new strategy for a situation in which it appeared that the influence of the Church had been diminished almost beyond recovery. His misfortune was that in promoting new methods he became a focus for the grievances of all those clergy and laity who grieved for a lost past rather than looked for a present opportunity. It is difficult now to rediscover the man behind the myth. The strident assertions of the newsmen and pamphleteers survive, accusing him of being a 'Whig Latitudinarian', the ally of politicians who sought to destroy the authority of Church and clergy. Even Jonathan Swift contributed his skilful talent to the work of vilification. In the Convocation of Canterbury Tenison came into direct confrontation with the predominant party in the Lower House, and he suffered the unprecedented indignity of having his primatial authority openly defied. Queen Anne, on her accession, virtually forbade him the Court, and he had to stand by while the Archbishop of York was admitted as her confessor and confidential adviser. Perhaps things might have been different if his personality had been more open and outgoing, but he was a deeply reserved and serious-minded man, whose depth of feeling and pastoral concern were often hidden from all but his closest friends. In an age of witty and expressive letter-writers he wrote terse notes in an almost illegible hand. Gossip, social scandal or personal revelation were wholly foreign to his nature, and his presence on public occasions was invariably severe. It was his opponents, like the mercurial Francis Atterbury, who appeared passionate and vital. And in his last years the miseries he suffered from repeated attacks of the gout led to his being confined at Lambeth as the prisoner of a clique of chaplains and advisers. Yet this is the man who, amid all his troubles, saw a new direction for the Church and pushed it firmly into something which begins to resemble its modern shape.

To understand the nature of the change it is necessary to recall the coercive character of Anglicanism in the age before the Glorious Revolution. The papers of William Sancroft, archbishop from 1677 to 1691, witness to an ecclesiastical policy based on an alliance of Church and State to enforce religious uniformity on the nation. The old primate lived frugally at Lambeth, rarely venturing away from home, dividing his time between chapel and an immense labour at his desk. His life was devoted to a single cause: that of making the traditional machinery of the Church work. His letters concern visitations, the ecclesiastical courts, the suppression of Dissent, and the enforcement of morals. He was well aware of the weaknesses behind the splendid façade of establishment, and what was most alarming of all: the almost complete indifference of the ordinary people to the distinctive features of Anglican churchmanship. The reports of his suffragans indicated only too clearly that a continual pressure had to be exerted on the laity to attend services, receive the sacrament once a year, and send their children to be catechized and confirmed. In such a situation the Dissenters were a continual threat to the monopoly claimed by the Established Church. Sancroft was not a cruel man but he was convinced that he had to call in the assistance of the state to prop up the influence of the clergy and to deter their rivals. The years from 1681 to 1686 were the high point of his strategy. Eager benches of county magistrates, working closely with bishops and parish clergy, enforced the penal laws against Nonconformists to the point where it seemed that their meeting-houses were almost suppressed except in the larger towns. The records of the church courts abound with cases of those who had neglected their religious duties: who had absented themselves from Sunday worship or the Easter sacrament or who had worked on Sundays or holydays. Other prosecutions were for fornication or adultery, begetting bastard children and profane swearing. By 1686 the combined efforts of magistrates and clergy had produced an impressive appearance of Anglican uniformity, even if its foundations were built upon the sand. Sancroft's scheme of things conceived of the Church as primarily a sphere of clerical authority and administration. He was unaffectedly devoted to Anglican worship and piety but the laity appear as listeners to sermons and attenders at the sacraments, unless it is as churchwardens enforcing these things on their neighbours. Much of the archbishop's voluminous correspondence, now in the Bodleian, is concerned with protecting clerical rights, raising clerical incomes, and seeing that clerical ministrations were available to all. It is the things for which this policy does not provide which are, to later consideration, most notable.

Clearly it was not easy to develop an alternative strategy when the existing episcopate was so dedicated to a coercive regime, but that the beginnings of one did exist is shown in the distinguished ministries of a group of London parish priests, of whom the most energetic was Thomas Tenison as vicar of St. Martin-in-the-Fields. Contemporaries of every shade of churchmanship united in the opinion that he was a parochial minister of extraordinary power and originality of approach. Indeed in 1687 the saintly Bishop Ken wrote of him: 'God prosper his Labours. He gives the Age so great an Example of a good parish priest that I cannot but have a particular Reverence for Him.' [Christ Church, Oxford, Wake Mss, 17, fo. 21: to William Wake, 12 August 1687]. Tenison had been appointed in 1680 after a worthy career at Cambridge and in a succession of country parishes, ending as upper minister of St. Peter Mancroft, Norwich; but at St. Martin's the man and the parish were uniquely matched. It was known at this time simply as 'the great cure'. It included not just the royal palaces and the fashionable new streets extending out to the west but also some of the vilest slums in the metropolis. With so much ostentatious wealth in evidence, the poor lived crowded into tenements and alleys amid squalor, stench and disease. The death-rate, and in particular the infant-mortality, was appalling. Tenison was undemonstrative by nature and his manner deliberate but passion touched him when he contemplated the face of his parish. The contrasts were stark. The well-to-do came to his church in great numbers. John Evelyn, the diarist and one of his greatest admirers, records that the vicar preached regularly to a congregation of over a thousand. On a Sacrament Sunday, when officer-holders had to qualify under the Test Acts by receiving Holy Communion, vast quantities of bread and wine were consumed. And yet all around were brothels, ginshops and gambling-houses, with crime, violence and savage criminal retribution. It was scarcely a situation in which ecclesiastical coercion had any meaningful role to play, and Tenison became a pioneer in extensive relief work combined with practical evangelism. His sermons, which Evelyn so much appreciated, were intensely practical: instant exhortations to fortunate laypeople to assist in the relief and Christian instruction of the poor and unchurched. His own income was large, as much as £1000 a year, and most of it was spent on employing curates and forwarding his charitable projects. But much of the work was done freely by groups or 'societies' of earnest laymen, and they provided most of the money required. One bitter November night in 1687 he sat by the bedside of Nell Gwyn as she lay dying in her lodgings in Pall Mall; and, perhaps troubled by the thought of many sins, she accepted his suggestion for a public bequest: not to the church but to one of his relief schemes, for 'clothes for the winter and such other necessaries as he shall think fit' for the poorest of his parishioners. It was specifically provided that it should be for all without distinction and that poor Roman Catholics were not to be excluded.

The essence of Tenison's parochial strategy, then, was to commit responsibility for evangelistic work to 'societies' of laymen, and it is clear that thereby he released a store of energy and earnest devotion which had previously been tapped only by the Nonconformist congregations. In London the members of the societies were the 'middling sort of people', businessmen, craftsmen and their apprentices. Some of the groups met for bible-study and prayer, but all regarded themselves, like Tenison himself, as dedicated to 'practical Christianity'. They provided food and clothes, and visited prisons and bridewells, but their prime aim lay in the Christian instruction of the unchurched. Much of their effort was directed towards the children of the parish. Thus in 1683 Tenison founded a small free school and five years later, after an energetic drive for subscriptions, enlarged it and settled it on a site next to the church. Here the children of the indigent could be fed, clothed and educated. When they were ready to leave, the charity would pay for them to be entered as apprentices. They were to be taught the elements of literacy and to cast accounts, but the whole education was to be on the strictest Anglican principles. The masters had to be regular communicants and bring their pupils regularly to church; the children had to learn the catechism and recite from the Bible and Prayer Book. The sight of these clean and neatly dressed scholars filling the galleries and sitting attentatively during service and sermon had the power to move churchpeople to tears, knowing as they did the squalor from which so many of the youngsters came. In similar manner Tenison founded in the parish a lending library to provide literature, both learned and devotional, for the clergy and others of the area who wished to study. In both his school and his library he was a pioneer but perhaps most of all in his use of the laity.

A model for an alternative strategy existed, but it was virtually impossible before 1688 for any Anglican clergyman, including Tenison himself, to accept the notion that the Church of England might become basically a voluntary body, working within the legal framework of the Establishment but attempting freely to engage the hearts, minds and allegiance of the English people. Thus James II's attempt to establish a complete Toleration and dismantle the whole apparatus of Anglican coercion came as a shattering blow. Tenison's immediate reaction in the face of this threat was an endeavour to preserve the old scheme of things by re-establishing Protestant unity, and so he became the leading exponent of the policy known as Comprehension, an alteration of the formularies and liturgy of the Church of England so that moderate Dissenting ministers and their congregations might be rejoined to the Established Church. It was hoped that thereby the national character of the Church might be recovered with only the more extreme sects left outside, and that some co-operation between government and Church in a national religious discipline might be preserved. Recent research makes it clear how important was Tenison's contribution to this project. His own relations with the London Dissenting ministers had always been cordial, and he was the natural go-between between them and a group of senior London incumbents. At Lambeth he continually pressed Archbishop Sancroft to support comprehension, and he was the secretary of a group which in the summer of 1688 and again at the beginning of 1689 tried to remodel the Book of Common Prayer. In the autumn of 1689 he was the executive member of King William III's Royal Commission for a Comprehension. The detailed work he put into the scheme cannot be doubted. Two interleaved prayer-books, now in the Lambeth Library as Mss. 886 and 2173, have copious annotations in his handwriting. The collapse of all this with the defeat of Comprehension by the lower clergy in the Convocation of 1689 was a veritable watershed in Tenison's thinking. In later years he even professed himself as glad that it had failed. Such a scheme would have been deeply divisive for the clergy, and it was never clear how many Dissenters it would have attracted. Henceforth he accepted that the Toleration Act of 1689 had introduced a new era in English history, and that for all practical purposes churchgoing had become voluntary and that other religious denominations had been given their freedom. What was required was a new initiative in mission, at home and overseas, a new plan for Christian education, and the creation of new agencies apart from the older structures of diocese, cathedral, parish and ecclesiastical court.

The direction of this new shaping of the Church's work was soon to fall to Tenison himself. In 1692 he was appointed Bishop of Lincoln and two years later, on the sudden death of Archbishop Tillotson, he found himself Archbishop of Canterbury. For the whole of his primacy he was to lead a Church in a state of shock and turmoil, as the full effects of the Toleration Act became known. Congregations slumped and numbers of communicants diminished remorselessly. Parish priests were faced with a new phenomenon: that of a Dissenting meeting-house, open for worship and competing with them for the allegiance of their flocks. For many clergy the past Stuart era of religious discipline became invested with the glow of a golden age, and they made ready with the encouragement of Tory politicians to agitate for a return to the conditions before 1685 and the onset of James II.

Against this involvement of churchmen in factious politics the new archbishop set his face like a flint. He seems to have accepted that the English people as a whole had opted for the widest possible interpretation of the Toleration, and that now little was to be gained from governments or politicians. He was possessed by a fear that too aggressive a role in politics might well, one day, produce a terrible reaction and a real oppression of the Church at the hands of its political enemies. Indeed his constant theme was that churchmen must devote themselves to practical religion. If there was any disciplining to be done, it was to be upon the clergy themselves: to eliminate non-residence, unauthorised pluralities and neglect of fabric and parsonage. Tenison's own example was undeniably impressive. He was the first archbishop since the Reformation actually to visit, ordain and confirm in person in the diocese. At his primary visitation in 1695 he confirmed 1200 in the cathedral on one occasion. Such energy and thoroughness was paralleled in other Williamite bishops as they attempted to draw their clergy's attention away from politics to a new evangelistic concern. Archbishop Sharp of York and Bishops Burnet, Stillingfleet, Patrick and Kidder journeyed out into remote parts of their dioceses which had scarcely ever before seen a confirmation service; episcopal visitations enquired into clerical negligence; and candidates for holy orders were examined with a quite unaccustomed rigour. By 1716 the rise in standards was perceptible.

Perhaps Tenison's most distinctive contribution, however, was the patronage which he gave to the new voluntary movement, which now grew up beside the older institutions of the Church. There came into existence a national network of 'societies' and their local correspondents, raising money for charity-schools, the distribution of Christian literature, and the support of foreign missions. Though the movement was usually under the patronage of bishops and clergy, and in no way in opposition to them, the work was planned, directed and financed by active Anglican laymen. Many of the secretaries and treasurers were not in orders but came from a business or commercial background. Men like John Chamberlayne or Henry Newman were the first examples of a new type of Christian leader, serving many committees, writing innumerable reports and appeals, and conducting an immense correspondence with helpers at home and overseas.

The first manifestation of the voluntary movement was, mercifully, not to become a permanent part of the life of the Church of England. In 1690 there had been founded in the city of London a 'Society for the Reformation of Manners', a body of laymen who took it upon themselves to suppress vice and profanity by bringing prosecutions before the civil magistrates. To the modern mind this smacks of gross narrowness and a pharisaical preoccupation with other men's sins, but one has to remember the degradation of life in Augustan London and the total collapse of the church courts as instruments of social control. Soon there was an extraordinary increase in the number of cases involving brothel-keepers, lewd stage-performances, profane swearing and sabbath-breaking. In 1691 Queen Mary had issued out a royal letter instructing the magistrates of Middlesex to lend their assistance, and Tenison as primate lent the movement his full support. In 1699 he sent a circular letter to all the bishops of his province commending the societies to their care and protection. By the end of Anne's reign they were a nationwide organisation, and visiting foreigners were remarking on the gloom of English Sundays, the nervousness of street-walkers and their customers, and the low voice in which profanities were uttered. Obviously the societies did not enjoy universal popularity. High Churchmen suspected them as not under proper clerical control and objected to the participation of Dissenters in them. By the 1730s, however, the Reformation societies seem to have exhausted themselves and fallen into disuse.

More successful, and certainly more lasting in their

effects, were the two great societies which were to change the face of the eighteenth-century Church. It was only to be expected that Tenison, as a pioneer-founder of a library and school, would be a firm supporter of Thomas Bray's 'Society for Promoting Christian Knowledge' which came into existence at the end of 1698. After 1695, when the Licensing Act expired, a flood of anti-clerical and heterodox literature poured forth on to the popular book-market, much of it openly deriding the basic tenets of Christian faith. A Blasphemy Act of 1697 proved a dead-letter from the start, and it became urgently necessary to provide not just serious books of apologetic but cheap tracts and, for the young, a basic religious knowledge. Indeed Thomas Bray began his extraordinary career by writing a simple teaching manual in response to Tenison's injunctions of 1695 urging the clergy to give priority to catechetical instruction. S.P.C.K. at first provided libraries for priests working in the colonies, but its chief work came to be in publishing, in setting up parochial lending libraries and, above all, in establishing a national network of charity schools. It was in education that the growth of the society's work revealed a truly urgent need and almost an eagerness of the laity to contribute. In the diocese of Lincoln alone over two hundred charity schools were in existence by 1714. Two of the new schools were founded by Tenison himself: at Lambeth and Croydon. His papers abound with S.P.C.K. projects. Each year he appointed the preacher of the charity school sermon; and amid a busy life he found time to peruse books before their publication. Indeed in 1711 he was the only reader to detect that a Dutch version of the Book of Common Prayer had had heretical sentiments inserted into it by the translator. The whole edition was solemnly cast into the fire in the kitchen of Lambeth Palace.

The society, however, with which he was most closely connected was that for the Propagation of the Gospel in Foreign Parts, and through it Tenison may claim to be the first archbishop with a vision of Anglicanism as a world-wide family of churches and dioceses. Until 1701 the spiritual condition of the English colonies was lamentable. The Bishop of London had been given their ecclesiastical oversight in 1634 but he had neither funds nor an administration to assist him. The Lambeth correspondence shows just how closely Tenison supported Bray from the beginning in his bid to establish an Anglican 'de propaganda fide', a chartered society to raise and hold funds, to plan missionary strategy, and to support churches, colleges and men overseas. The archbishop was mainly instrumental in obtaining the Royal Charter in June 1701, and thereafter he presided regularly at business meetings. His letters reveal a detailed interest in the West Indian islands and the mainland American colonies, and in particular his concern for the conversion of the Indian tribes. By his death in 1715 the scene had been transformed: the Church overseas had a firm home-base, money was available for work which could not be locally financed, and libraries, colleges and church-buildings were coming into existence. Tenison's chief aim was, however, continually frustrated: his wish to found bishoprics for the islands and continental America. As early as 1704 he had had the legal problems investigated and was grievously disappointed when a parliamentary bill to effect it lapsed with the death of Queen Anne. In his will he left the considerable sum of £1000 to be kept as an endowment for the bishoprics, should the politicians ever allow the project. In all, Tenison's papers provide a complete contrast with Sancroft's. Now the view is not just of a national Church and its political problems but that of a mother-Church with a sense of mission to distant sugar-islands, plantations spreading out into the wilderness, and to new races and peoples.

The period of Tenison's primacy was one of bitter and unceasing political faction, and yet this new Anglican strategy was in itself surprisingly uncontroversial. A few churchmen attacked the societies as innovations but few could deny that some new flexible administration was required outside the legally defined constitution. In fact, High and Low Churchmen, Whigs and Tories, were equally supporters of Christian literature, foreign missions and charity schools. That behind all the political turmoil a quiet spiritual revolution was taking place may well account for the archbishop's increasing impatience with political agitation among his clergy. The campaign in Parliament and Convocation to limit the Toleration and to restore the 'rights, powers and privileges' of the clerical order he regarded as a vain attempt to live in the past. His dogged resistance in Convocation and his use of the primatial authority to silence debate made him a deeply unpopular man. In essence he was not a deeply political animal but he found himself more and more drawn into alliance with those Whig politicians who themselves opposed the Tory campaigns. But the legend grew, fuelled by the caricatures of the journalists and pamphleteers, of a Whig archbishop, neglectful of his clergy's legitimate aspirations, and tyrannical in his use of power. Perhaps in the end his greatest cause of offending was that he lived rather longer than the Tory divines had expected. It turned out to be a race between him and Queen Anne as to which of them should succumb first to the gout. Tory candidates for the archbishopric waited in eager expectation but Lambeth Palace held out longer than Kensington Palace. Tenison survived to crown King George I, and to ensure that the Tory divines were denied their day. Stolid and prosaic he may have been but not without greatness. In the midst of all his troubles he had the heart of the matter in him, and a pastoral vision which made possible the reshaping of the Church's mission.

The Englishman's View
of the Clergy

In the Department of Prints and Drawings in the British
Library the largest collection is that devoted to the clergy
of the Church of England. Its only rivals in size are those
for Sportsmen and military men. And it is interesting to
discover that, apart from the routine official portraits of
bishops, deans and other eminent divines, most of the
drawings are caricatures. Some are wry but affectionate.
Many reflect religious differences and suspicions. There
are sour Puritans with enormous white bands, Laudians
with lace and frills, Puseyites concealing the Pope under
their vestments and Evangelicals threatening their congregations with hell fire. Methodism has its own box, and
the contents have been admirably catalogued under the
title of 'Methodism Derided'. Of course, there is social
comment. Vast obese 18th century rectors carrying off a
poor farmer's pig and goose; and, later on, silly-ass
parsons caught out in a social gaffe at an old ladies'
teaparty. *Punch* used to specialize in clerical jokes, from
the most famous one of all, 'The Curate's Egg' to
innumerable pompous bishops in railway carriages being
deflated by innocent sweet young things. Strangely there
is virtually nothing in the collection showing an ordinary
parish priest doing his ordinary pastoral work. It may be,
of course, that the ridiculous is always more memorable
than the serious but I suspect that the real reason is that
the English have always been uncertain about a clergyman's role in society, and they have taken refuge in
caricature to hide a certain unease.

The sociologists tell us that most of our present
attitudes and beliefs have a much longer history than we
realize. Most of our ideas have come down to us by a

111

long process of transmission. Families, villages, towns, universities and professions have long corporate memories. Parents impart their attitudes to their children, old tales are retold in family talk or in pubs or common-rooms; even infants at school have an amazing tradition of games, stories and beliefs. Who would immediately recognize that the jingle about Humpty Dumpty is derived from the siege of Gloucester during the Civil War, and that it was children's mockery at the failure of the royalist forces to breach the wall with a siege-engine? Or that phrases like 'Jack-in-the-Box' and 'Round Robin' are even older and derived from Protestant ridicule of the sacrament reserved in a pyx in the parish church? Impressions remain when their causes have passed into oblivion. And nowhere is this more true than with the clergy. They have been the profession always closest to ordinary people, and are the object of the longest corporate memory. Some years ago I visited one of the parishes of which New College is patron, because the vicar had resigned in despair at the unco-operative attitude of the people, and even his church folk. He could do nothing to please them. And this I found impossible to understand. He was a kind, sensible and godly man who had tried to attract young families and teenagers to church. When I spoke to the local people I could still get no nearer to understanding. It was only when I went to our college records that it all became clear. Great Horwood (as it was not inappropriately named) had been wholly owned by the college, which had been both landlord and titheowner. Successive vicars had been ex-Fellows who had acted as the college's local agent. The great vicarage, in which the present incumbent was living uncomfortably, had been built at the college's expense. In 1960, of course, all had changed. The land had long been sold to local farmers who were prosperous men, tithe had long been abolished, and the vicar was not an Oxford graduate. But the corporate memory remained, and took this form of an attitude of grudging which the people could not really explain, even to themselves.

Something of this uncertainty about the role of the clergy clearly dates from the great shock which English society sustained at the Reformation. Within a generation the priest's role in the local community was radically changed, and we now are coming to see how much the changes were forced from above rather than generated from below. The pre-Reformation clergy were mostly very poor, often ignorant men and much concerned with their rights and professional status. There was clearly much anti-clericalism, if one can judge from the records of the church courts. But most of it stemmed not from a *disregard* for their function but because they failed to provide it or were too mercenary in demanding payment for what they did. A priest was vital in a medieval community which invariably centred on its church. It is hard now to enter into the mental world of four hundred and fifty years ago. In the countryside most people were illiterate, and they thought in pictures rather than in theories. Their stories, customs and rituals were vital to their community existence. They did not require from their priest elaborate theology or explanations of scripture but an affirmation of their existing view of the world. They saw it as a place of conflict, danger and testing; it was full of powers and forces, good and malign. Devils, evil spirits and witchcraft abounded. If one's child was ill, or the cow ceased to give milk, or the crops failed, one looked for some agent which had caused it: some old woman living alone with her cat might be suspected; one might resort to some other 'cunning' man or woman to reverse the spell. And over against all these evil forces were the good ones, many of them within the charge of the Church: saints and angels came to one's aid, Our Lady had an immense power to heal and protect, and there was a great armoury of forces in the sacraments. The priest above all was the one who said mass for the community, bringing God among them, offering a sacrifice of propitiation for the sins of the living and the dead. Masses were said continually and for numerous reasons: for the intentions of the living and the repose of the souls of the dead. Above all the priest was the man who warded off the fear of death. Death was the close companion of medieval people. Most children died in their first year, a man who reached fifty would have lost not only both parents but his wife, most of his children, and probably most of his contemporaries. Epidemics could wipe out whole villages. And death was a terrible prospect. Medieval churches had 'doom' windows, depicting the souls in hell in eternal torment or the souls in purgatory enduring the cleansing fires. The priest was the one who could provide the ceremonies of grace and power. He blessed and cleansed with holy water; he confessed and absolved; he brought the last rites, and he said repeated requiem masses. In the 15th century, when the Black Death subsided, there was an enormous phase of church building. Even small villages built large choirs and naves, and many chapels and altars. Brotherhoods were set up to tend the altars, pay for the masses, and pray for the dead. Recent research has shown how much ordinary people shared in this cult: it was they who tended lights, cared for statues and roods, provided the labour to build and repair. A priest might be severely criticized but always for failing to do his work: being absent, refusing the sacraments, not taking part in accustomed ceremonies. The evidence is that in pre-Reformation England a priest was an essential member of a community of immensely traditional beliefs and customs. Obviously some of the younger, better-educated clergy of the 16th century objected strongly to this role assigned to them. Protestantism in England began not as a popular movement but as a reaction of some of the new university graduates to what seemed like the superstitious ignorance and demands of their flocks. But right down to the very break with Rome the older order was intact. Wills provided for requiems, the establishment of chantries, chapels and statues.

Modern research is unanimous in stressing what a terrible shock the Reformation was to ordinary English people and how suddenly it burst upon them. Protestants were an élite. They were to be found particularly among the educated laity: gentlemen, and professional people, who had been to the new grammar schools. But the real religious spearhead of the new movement was a new generation of clergymen. The universities were beginning to turn out men educated in humanistic scientific study and the new Protestant theology was particularly attractive to them. They were above all preachers rather than priests, and they attracted the attention of those who were relatively sophisticated, and especially the majority who were literate. The court, London, the larger towns, merchant communities, lawyers, were above all the places where they were heard gladly. Many gentlemen and their families became convinced Protestants. But the effect when the Reformation was imposed on ordinary villages was to destroy much of what had given the community coherence and identity. The statues, the lights, the altars, all so carefully tended, were destroyed. The guilds and brotherhoods of lay people were dissolved and their funds confiscated. The whole cult of the dead, of prayer and commemoration was suppressed. The mass with its mystery, colour, movement and song was abolished. A quarterly communion service took its place. However sound we may think the new Protestant teaching of justification by faith alone, no one can deny the cultural shock: nor the tradition of resentment which remained. The greatest problem was the relationship of people to the new Protestant minister. More often than we realise, he was a kind of vacant space. There was great difficulty in finding really competent and informed Protestant incumbents, and many fell into the position of neither doing the old ceremonies nor preaching the new gospel. In such cases there was often a simple loss of religious interest, shown most notably in a new problem of church repairs. People would not give money or labour to a church from which they had been in some manner excluded. It was when a minister was a convinced and uncompromising Protestant that trouble often broke out. He would be an educated man, because the Calvinist ideal of a minister was of a trained professional, spending many hours a day in his study and dedicated to preaching. He would be a married man with a wife and family, and concerned to buy books, furnish a house, educate his sons and marry his daughters above the peasantry. All this tended to provide not another family in the parish but a family with a place in the social hierarchy, in some way different from the lower orders. But it was above all the *preaching* stress of the convinced Protestant minister which created tension between minister and people. We tend to think that it is only modern congregations who show resistance to sermons, and like them short and simple; there is an idea that our forbears sat easily for an hour's close scriptural discourse. But there is plenty of evidence that Elizabethan congregations absolutely hated having to sit for so long, and did not understand what was being said. Perhaps in city churches, at university, even at court these professional discourses were admired, though even here some very able men tried to make them witty and poetic. But out in the parishes the air is suddenly full of complaint. Parishioners say they cannot hear or don't like their minister's voice or they don't like the pulpit. Ministers complain of restlessness, whispering, laughing barely suppressed, walking out before sermon or during it: but above all *sleeping*. Down to Hogarth's wonderful drawing called 'The Sleeping Congregation', there is a great series of descriptions or drawings of the English asleep in church. Even that fine Elizabethan preacher, John Aungier, reported that in his church 'some sleep from the beginning to the end, as if they came for no other purpose but to sleep'. He concluded one sermon by banging his Bible shut, and announcing to his newly awakened congregation: 'Hell was made for sermon-sleepers!' Perhaps he and his kind genuinely mistook the capacity of simple folk to concentrate for long on a single discourse, and to sit still as it went on. These were minds which learned by story, dramatic enactment and personal participation. Perhaps here is one of the roots of that rooted English distaste for theology, that dislike of parsons as men who talk unintelligible stuff six feet above a plain man's head.

The result was an erosion of religion as part of a strong popular culture. The clergy found themselves working with a kind of élite, a godly group of the articulate and better-educated: the gentry, professional people, business people and skilled artisans. The vicar or rector could find himself regarded as the property of a pious coterie to which simple folk could not, and would not, wish to aspire. And, in particular, a belief that the Lord's Supper was for special Christians not ordinary folk. It was all too easy for this to develop into an increasing indifference to the church and religion, and for the parson to be seen as a man who exhorted and disapproved. Doubtless there were many loving, saintly men who spent their lives happily among their rural flocks. George Herbert at Bemerton was obviously kind and sympathetic, a man of religious vision and depth. But too many clergy fell into a way of criticizing and seeking to suppress the ways and customs of the community. They were, for example, as educated men and good Protestants the deadly enemies of anything which smacked of magic or witchcraft. And there was much of that. 'Wise' or 'cunning' men and women continued to operate, cast spells, charm warts and find lost articles. Much of this was suppressed, and it became positively dangerous to act in a way which might be interpreted as witchcraft. But with the old practices had gone a sense of mystery and awe, even a sacramental notion, and these could easily be replaced by cynicism and materialism. And similarly the clergy fell into the way of attacking the pleasures, games and sports of the community. Sermons are full of inveighings against 'wakes and fairs, bull-baitings, cockfighting, ales, May games, piping and dancing', and especially if these were done in sermon-time. A result of all this is an important one for English religion: the loss of an association of the parish minister with a vigorous popular or working-class culture. The Anglican clergyman by 1700 did not have the character of a priest in contemporary Ireland, Poland, Italy or Greece. Religion did not express the aspirations or identity of ordinary people. Though rectors and vicars were often poor and their origins humble, they were not of the people in the sense that a priest in Ireland was among the Catholic peasantry.

The role into which many English clergy could so easily slip is well illustrated by the marvellous late-18th century diary of James Woodforde, rector of Weston Longville in Norfolk. I have an affection for him since I live in rooms which he once occupied as a Fellow of New College. He was clearly a good and kind man who loved country life. He had a good income from tithe and lived in the style of a minor country gentleman including the consumption of enormous meals, all recorded in succulent detail in his diary. He did his duty and was generous to anyone in need. He would sit up all night with a dying woman to comfort her husband, but he was equally prepared to box the ears of a young labourer who cheeked him. He gave the farmers a tithe 'frolic' (as he called it) and entertained the lonely old men of the parish at Christmas, but his only real friends were the gentry and certain other clergy, and this small group entertained each other regularly. His sermons are about duty and leading a good life, and about being grateful to God for one's benefits. In spite of pressure from the squire and the farmers the attendance at his services was modest rather than large. The labourers who came were singers and bellringers who made it clear what interested them. When he tried to change the tune of the metrical psalm they impudently ignored him and sang the old one. The Holy Communion, celebrated only four times a year, was attended by a pious group. When Woodforde died in 1803 he was clearly a respected country parson; it is impossible not to like so uncomplicated a figure. It is difficult to believe that his parishioners can have seen him as a figure of vital religion. Not to make too fine a point he was a figure produced by a system of social subordination, and he had neither a gospel to preach nor a sacramental system which involved his people.

It is clear, however, that, even in Woodforde's day, many Anglican clergy wanted their people to think of them as something more. And the more recent history of the churches has been marked by successive movements of reform and renewal, each in its way introducing a more vital role for the minister in the life of the community. One of the greatest of these movements was Methodism. Today it is like the rest of the denominations primarily a middle-class thing, but in its beginnings it was indubitably an Anglican attempt to recreate a poor man's religion and to create a new kind of poor minister. The genius of Wesley was that he saw in the new industrial England the emergence of new communities, and he understood that religious faith could give them coherence, hope and a sense of purpose. Certainly Wesley revived a dramatic preaching style but sermons were not at the heart of Methodism; it was its sense of community. Methodists had their 'class system': local groups under a leader. Their national leaders were Anglican priests but their local leaders were also the leaders of the local community: miners, weavers, iron-founders, pottery workers. They discovered talent in working-men, and let them be itinerant preachers or local preachers without too much formal education. John Wesley himself thought of them as lay helpers, and conceived of the movement finding a place within the Church of England. That vision was destroyed by the gap which existed between this new kind of ministry and the old of the Anglican clergy, even that between Wesley himself and his lay helpers. When the itinerant preachers became the ministers of Methodism, they were themselves on the way to being the clergymen which their founder had not wished them to be. But nevertheless early Methodism was able to create communities of working people with a ministry which came from among them. It provided opportunities of education with its schools, loans and even insurance; it had its own kind of respectability and Methodists were able to prosper in business and lift themselves from the ranks of the very poor. In Wales Methodists gave a coherence to new mining communities. The ministry was a hard and unrewarding thing in terms of economic reward; ministers were supposed to 'travel' from place to place. But the work provided a way by which a poor boy with the gift of speech could move into a position of leadership among his own people. And there are signs of the respect and dependence which early Methodist communities offered to these men.

Another movement for recovering a vital role for the minister was the Evangelical revival in the Church of England. Evangelicals, with their call for personal conversion to Christ and a life of strict obedience to his way of holiness became the most influential group in the early 19th century. Ministers such as Charles Simeon inaugurated a new style of seriousness in clergymen and a complete dedication to evangelism. They were closely associated with politicians, civil servants, lawyers and businessmen, and they were a moving force behind humanitarian movements. But the Evangelical clergy were very much from the traditional Anglican circles, and their real successes lay in the new areas of suburbia where communities were growing up without real coherence. Evangelicals were successful in retirement towns and watering-places, in London suburbs and in university towns. They had great influence in schools and among undergraduates. Their work in working-class areas is less clear. They were devoted to orphanages, rescue work with fallen women, the temperance movement, and to missions in slum areas: they were earnest in the denunciation of prostitutes, pornography and fornication.

A recent study of Evangelicals however finds that their real impact on the poor was small. The Evangelical vicar, with his staff of earnest, public schoolboy curates, was a cultural divide away from working-class people; and he gave the impression that to know him and his parishioners one had to learn a new middle class religious language. They did much to foster the notion of a clergyman as a man easily shocked, before whom one could not speak naturally, who was concerned not so much with you but with your conversion.

The Anglo-Catholic or (as it was sometimes called) Puseyite movement represented yet another attempt to find a new role for the clergy. In the face of the barreness of so much Anglican worship it attempted to recreate a sense of the living church, continuance in time, and making Christ present not just in a traditional teaching but in a sacramental system. The sense of being a priest, a man set apart by ordination, bearing the authority of the historic Christian community, making sacred things present for the people, gave a new sense of purpose to many clergy. And particularly to those who found themselves in the new parishes of industrial England. And then they came into contact with one church which seemed to have succeeded where others had conspicuously failed. No one can doubt the impact of the Roman ministry in the urban areas of nineteenth-century England. This devout, practising community of Irish labourers, strongly dependent on their clergy and treating them with an elaborate respect was indubitably a cause of self-reproach among Anglican clergy whose relationship to the working-classes was often so distant. As new parishes were founded and churches built in working-class districts the Anglican priest often adopted the style of his Roman counterpart. Often unmarried, living in clergy-houses, authoritative in manner, they attempted to produce a new ministry to the Anglican poor with an elaborate ceremonial which gave participation to many of the congregation. In Birmingham, Leeds and East London

there were heroic ministries, often deeply disapproved of
by the Anglican establishment. Such priests were not easy
to deal with. By the end of the 19th century many of
them were trained in new Anglo-Catholic theological
colleges associated with religious orders. Many were of
humble origins, who had moved up from servers and
acolytes, to seminary student, to Anglo-Catholic curate.
Such men were often profoundly hostile to Evangelical
and Liberal bishops, and themselves socialist in policies as
against the predominantly Tory attitude of the Evangelicals and the Church at large. The Anglo-Catholic slum
priest or his colleague in fashionable London or seaside
churches could be much loved and cherished by their
congregations. Their weakness was that they often did
not realise how strange their ways were to many
congregations brought up on centuries of indoctrination
against Popery. Sometimes their efforts in country
parishes to introduce new ornaments, vestments and
services, and especially auricular confession, led to deep
suspicion and strong resistance. One suspects that some
of the resistance to the ASB is not entirely on doctrinal or
aesthetic grounds but on a feeling that such services are
what the clergy want and intend to persuade the people
to adopt.

In one of his poems W. H. Auden speaks of the power
of 'ancestral voices', and it is impossible when any
English priest begins his ministry not to hear them
echoing. We are the heirs of a function in English life
which is very ancient indeed. And it is not just believers
who have a series of memories and attitudes but
unbelievers as well. Of course there will always be a kind
of unease about men's attitude to a minister of the
Gospel, a publicly professed Christian. It is the semi-
believer or fellow-traveller or occasional attender who
feels it most acutely. The priest's commitment is a
reproach to his weakness of belief, and his presence an
invitation to an involvement he does not wish. There is
a compulsive desire to fend off this threat by caricature,

criticism or the establishing of a strictly businesslike relationship. I have come to look at your roof, vicar, not to have you look at my soul: if that is understood I'll get the ladders out'. But an English clergyman, in his pastoral work, soon has to learn to live with a series of engrained visions of him and his work which he may find puzzling, unfair and irritating. Much clerical wit and even verse is still devoted to the odd ideas which people have of the clergy. Television often manages to project comic or theatrical stereotypes which are rooted in past situations. In fact today the Anglican ministry is drawn from a wider social range than ever before. With the collapse of the most obvious class-distinction, a priest and his family are likely to be much closer to their local population: in type of housing, income, and education of children. He is no longer immediately to be connected with conservative politics though he may well have moved into a new set of liberal but essentially middle-class values. MORI conducted a poll into popular attitudes to the Anglican clergy, and it came out surprisingly favourable. People thought doctors and nurses harder working and more useful but priests and ministers as much to be admired as dedicated people. There were, however, significant signs that the old images retain their power, and more than 40% in each case thought that they were (a) separated from ordinary people by social class, (b) offered a morality too impractical for ordinary people, (c) related to a churchgoing group and not to the whole community. It would seem that the dispelling of old images has some way to go, and perhaps we have some self-examination to do in the fulfilling of our ministry.

CHURCH, MINISTRY AND UNITY:
CONTEMPORARY STUDIES

Tradition and Change
in The Church

The issue of the ordination of women to the priesthood and episcopate is a difficult one because it cannot be considered merely in terms of human rights and sexual equality. What is admitted on all sides to be a proposal for innovation raises in an acute form the question of by what authority such a change could be brought about. And the problem is an especially severe one for Anglicans who are members of a Communion of independent churches with a notion of 'dispersed authority' which requires that attention shall be given to Scripture, Tradition and Reason in the process of making an authoritative decision. How therefore may we best understand and express the relationship between tradition and change in the Church?

SCRIPTURE

The Anglican formularies make it clear that the canonical scriptures of the Old and New Testaments are the primary source of authority. But an appeal to the authority of Scripture is no simple matter. The question of the ordination of women will not be solved by citing particular texts, for or against, or by declaring that the 'thrust' of Scripture is clearly on one side or the other. Scriptural exegesis, no matter how scholarly its technique, is conditioned by the mental world, assumptions and aims of the exegete. The best interpreters of Scripture are those who are most aware of their own intellectual, social and ecclesiastical setting. Thus modern exegetes recognise that there are 'two horizons' of scriptural interpretation:

the past as it was when the texts were written and the present world in which the scholar is doing his work and addressing his contemporaries. The modern subject of 'hermeneutics' is an attempt to foster in the mind of the exegete an awareness of the models, methods and beliefs he brings to his work. All this is intended to offset the main temptation of scriptural interpretation: the appropriation of texts to a modern purpose without allowing for the distance between the world of the writers of the past and our own day. When Scripture is used in the debate over the ordination of women it is important that both proponents and opponents realise the degree to which their convictions can determine their conclusions.

This is not to say that no authority is to be found in the Bible. What we need to determine is what kind of authority it is. What we now call the Bible, the canonical writings of the Old and New Testaments, were selected by the early Church on the basis of an understanding of what they contained. First-century Judaism had a wide body of religious literature and the early Christian communities made a choice of that which they believed witnessed to Christ and which helped them to interpret their experience of him and his Spirit in their common life. In particular they were concerned with Judaism's long-standing debate about the interaction of Law (or Torah) and Prophecy. For all Jewish thinkers Torah was the centre of their religion; it was what gave Israel its identity as a holy and obedient people. But the intensely religious spirit of Torah also generated a body of writings which sought to make it a way of love and renewal rather than a dead obedience. Prophecy was thus understood as a gift of God's spirit to restore and renew a people who had become alienated from the true meaning of Torah. A whole literature of rabbinic interpretation sought to make the provisions of the Law applicable to a changing society, while the prophetic and apocalyptic writings stressed that the reality of Israel's religion lay not in conformity to a code but by being renewed in the spirit for a new relationship with God. It is this latter theme of first-century Judaism which early Christianity took up and the New Testament writings may be regarded as an extension of, and commentary upon, it. The epistles, gospels and Apocalypse are the products of communities which preserved the memory of Jesus in the light of their experience of the Holy Spirit. The writings are thus the various communities' interpretation of the meaning of Jesus together with their understanding of the content of the message, the character of their discipleship, and how they were to deal with the disputes, difficulties and dangers which confronted them.

It is this witness to the first Christians' experience which gives Scripture its authority. It was in the light of their understanding of Christ that they established a canon of sacred writings, receiving some of the texts of Judaism and of primitive Christianity and rejecting others. Indeed it is arguable that it is this early perspective on Scripture which is authoritative for Christians rather than any original meaning of Old Testament texts. It is the work of the critical scholar to enter, as far as is possible, into the thought-world of early Christianity. His is essentially a historical quest; he can tell us what the writings meant within the context of the culture, society and conventions of the time in which they were written. It is quite another matter to expect him to provide authoritative guidance on modern questions such as the ordination of women in a Church which exists in a totally different environment and culture. The very character of modern academic New Testament scholarship makes it unfitted for this kind of task. It no longer regards itself as primarily directed to Christian apologetic and it has withdrawn from questions which seem to be about the modern Church rather than about the ancient communities. There are indeed many scholars who think that the mind-set of the ancient writers was so far removed from our own thinking and situation that it is impossible to bring it to bear on problems which the Early Church did not invisage. In particular biblical scholars have no real expertise in disentangling what is permanent in the teaching of the New Testament and what is merely an aspect of its cultural setting. Such a separation of content and form is against the whole thrust of New Testament scholarship as it is now practised. Thus its expertise may well provide insights into the original setting of the texts; it may well furnish perspectives and warn against anachronisms; but the opinions of the experts cannot be determinative of questions which concern the self-understanding, unity and mission of today's Church.

It would seem then that a modern question like that of the ordination of women must be decided by the modern Church on the basis of a contemporary understanding of its common life. This is not to claim that ecclesiastical authorities have some mysterious key to the meaning of scripture or tradition which is denied to competent scholars. The difference is rather one of context. Today's Church is heir to a long tradition of living in community, theological reflection and of turning worship and prayer into proclamation, mission and service. It wishes to remain true to its origins but it cannot aim simply to recreate the world of the New Testament. That was a time of formation, experiment and of the first attempts by Christians to articulate their experience of knowing Christ in the power of the Spirit. That process of interpretation continued and still continues in a substantially different cultural and social setting, and it is only those who are engaged in the worship, prayer, mission and sacrificial service of the modern Church who have the authority to make a response to new questions and challenges.

TRADITION

An appeal to the Tradition of the Church has always had an important place in Anglican thinking. From the

English Reformation onwards there has been a concern that there should be some controlling principle to scriptural interpretation lest it should degenerate into mere opinionation and cause discord and schism. Thus the earliest Anglican 'apologies' sought to deal with disputed questions by bringing to bear the test of 'antiquity', the theological formularies and the church-practice of the undivided Church of the first four centuries. This awareness of their being a tradition of faith transmitted within a continuing community dates from at least the second century and is arguably to be found in the writings of Paul. The classical exponent of the idea was Irenaeus of Lyons who conceived of there being a public ministry of teaching to be found in the great churches of apostolic foundation and committed to their successive bishops in office. Such a concept of a 'Catholic' tradition has had a powerful influence in forming the Church's notion of authority. In the case of Anglicans it has tended to take the form of reliance on a scholarly historical enquiry into the patristic precedents. With Roman Catholics it has been identified with the body of dogma and church-practice which has been formed under their own ecclesiastical authority. Protestants have always had a more cautious approach to any authority other than Scripture and a suspicion that much which passes for Tradition is a corruption of original Christianity but it can scarcely be doubted that the great Reformers had an intense adhesion to the orthodox formulations of the Early Church and recognised an authority in them.

When, however, modern debate turns on an appeal to 'Tradition' the matter is not quite as simple as some controversialists seem to imagine. Tradition requires a hermeneutic as much as Scripture. Those who take their stand on 'the unbroken tradition of the Church' need to be aware of their own standpoint and assumptions. It is indeed only too easy for the tradition in which people believe themselves to stand to be a myth which gives them a sense of security and a means of identification with other members of a particular Christian group. It is clear that Tradition is not some unified body of doctrine and practice which can be established by historical research. Scholars long ago disposed of the idea of a *consensus patrum*, and modern patristic studies tend to stress that there are different strands of tradition even within a particular era, and that theology and church-usage differ so much from one age to another that the disparities often seem more remarkable than the continuities. Yet, even with these cautions, Tradition is a concept with which the Church cannot dispense. It is clearly insufficient to say that Trinitarian doctrine, post-Nicene Christology and monoepiscopacy can be simply read off from Scripture, and even the reformers admitted an ecclesiastical authority in the great Councils to explicate Scripture and guard a particular interpretation of it. It seems apparent that at certain critical moments in Christian history the Church was presented with alternative possibilities of interpretation. Arius, it is now generally admitted, had an arguable case, so why did Athanasius win through? Why was the vision of the Church in the Pastoral epistles preferred to that of Marcion? There was clearly a process of reflection and decision in the face of challenge and controversy. And the process was not confined to the realm of ideas for it was impossible to separate a tradition of doctrine from the context of order, liturgy and spiritual discipline in which it was set.

The essential problem which the concept of Tradition presents to the theologian is that of identity amid change. What is it that remains permanent when so much is altered with the passage of time? This is not basically a question for the historian of doctrine but for the modern Church. We modern Christians cannot recreate the church-life of the second century or the thirteenth or the sixteenth. We are not antiquarians. It is noticeable that it is only those churches whose setting has remained largely unchanged, like some of the churches of eastern Christianity, which can adopt this 'fundamentalist' approach to Tradition. What other churches have had to recognise is that Tradition is a living and developing thing as the Christian community responds to changes in human culture and society by developing its theology, liturgy and community structures. If Tradition is a living thing it is the task of theologians, pastors and indeed ordinary Christians to reflect on what it is that the Tradition is intended to guard and preserve and what are the forms which may have to change if the heart of the matter is to retain its ancient meaning and power in a new situation. It has to be stressed that this is not primarily a question for academics. They can dispel misunderstandings of the past, discern what past priorities and visions were, and show what changes have occurred but the responsibility for deciding how the Tradition is to be embodied in the life of the modern Church lies with the Church itself. Tradition is not a code nor a set of binding precedents nor is it concerned with details. It is a series of formularies, structures, liturgies and usages, all of them provisional in form, by which the modern Church tries to remain true to its origins while living a life of witness and holiness in modern society.

Church history may, however, provide some indications of the way in which the Tradition has developed in the past. (a) Change must emerge out of a genuine crisis in which Gospel and Church are seen to be at stake. The challenge must be a radical one which calls in question the validity of an existing expression of the message or the community and demands a response. It must stem from a wide concern within the Christian community and not from some sectional or particular interest. (b) It must lead on to a process of reflection on the nature of Gospel and Church in order to renew their expression and must not have the character of a struggle for power among groups of sects. (c) Though it may initially involve controversy and division among Christians, there must emerge a process of convergence and reception. This may or may not happen. The real danger to the unity of the Church lies not in the existence of controversy but in a recalcitrant unwillingness on either side to accept the mind of the Church. (d) If a development is 'received' there needs to be some formulation of it by appropriate public authority so that it may be accepted as a norm to be acted upon.

What seems to have little evidence in Church history is the notion of 'creative discontinuity' which is favoured by some modern liberals. In particular there has been misuse of the term *kairos*, which refers properly to the Christ-event 'in the fulness of time' and not to changes in the Church's formularies or ecclesiastical discipline. When individuals or pressure-groups employ this kind of language, as when they claim to discern the working of the Holy Spirit in support of their cause, they are usually testifying to the force of their convictions rather than adding anything to a debate among Christians. The patristic writers, with their great stress on loyalty to a public tradition of teaching would regard advocates of a decisive break with the past as exhibiting one of the usual marks of heresy. It is, too, inaccurate to cite the Reformation as consecrating the notion that there are moments when there have to be decisive breaks with the Christian past. The mainstream reformers would have rejected unequivocally the accusation that they were innovators. Luther and Calvin wrote extensively against 'fanatics' who introduced new teaching on the basis of claims to inspiration by the Spirit. Each regarded himself as restoring a traditional biblical exegesis and patristic doctrine and order over against relatively recent abuses and deformation. Most modern scholars stress the conservative thrust of Reformation theology. The principle of *semper reformanda* implies not radical breaks with the past but a constant appraisal of the doctrine and practice of the Church to keep it true to its origins.

REASON

Though Anglicans acknowledge an authority in human reason, there appears in practice some uncertainty as to what this means. Certainly in the classical Anglican divines it did not mean an intention to judge the Christian message or community by the standards, conventions or customs of a particular period or society. It was not to set reason over against revelation. It was rather a principle which brought to any argument the test of theological coherence. Did it cohere with a proclamation of repentence and forgiveness? Did it cohere with man's natural sense of morality? Did it lead on to holiness, unity and service? Reason may indeed require Christians to reject and separate themselves from ideas and conduct which the world approves or condones. But it is inevitable that secular thinking will set the Church's agenda for debate, and social and cultural changes may well raise for Christians valid questions about whether their church-practice is based on some essential Christian principle or merely reflects the past practice of the secular society in which they have been set. Of course, the Church is a very ancient community and society itself. Its system of symbol, recital, liturgy and use of language is complex and has a place in the mind of believers which is not entirely accessible to an immediate rational assessment. Iconoclasts have the capacity to do damage beyond anything they intend or understand; and it is always dangerous to interfere with a people's religious system. It is far easier to destroy religious communities than to build them up, and there are many examples of supposedly rational persons who did violence in ancient societies by not understanding what gave them their identity.

AUTHORITATIVE DECISION-MAKING

The argument of this paper is, then, that a modern question like the ordination of women is not answered definitively by the expertise of biblical scholars or by historians of doctrine. Nor is it clear that pressure groups from particular backgrounds are especially well-equipped to declare what aspects of modern Western liberal thought are to be incorporated permanently into the Church's tradition. In the end these decisions must be made by the Church of today using its own judgement upon the Scriptures and the Tradition which are its inheritance, and gathering the mind of the Christian Church in all its diversity. There is, in the end, no escaping a doctrine of God's guidance of his Church when that has been sought by a community which has carefully informed itself, consulted the faithful and exercised through its councils and leaders the authority which the Lord has committed to it. What is clear is that this process of ecclesiastical decision-making is subject to certain constraints which some may find irksome indeed.

There is, first, the constraint of *patience*. It can be said of a true Catholicism that in the establishment of an authoritative decision it moves slowly but surely. A proposal must go through various stages at any one of which it may succeed or fail; and advocates and opponents must be sufficiently open to accept either possibility. The sequence of events would seem to be something like this. At first there will be a time when a proposal is merely tentative; it will be canvassed and discussed by private individuals and groups. Then there will be a stage in which it will come before the churches but will be regarded as an 'open question'. No-one should presume that it is already the mind of the Church, that its victory is inevitable, or that those who wish to retain the traditional practice of the Church are culpable as opponents of progress. There may then come a stage of 'provisional' acceptance in which the proposal is offered

136

to the local churches throughout the world without its being finally decided. This will be a time for the sharing of reflections and experiences. And finally in the light of a clear 'reception' by the faithful there will be an authoritative act by which the new development is incorporated into the tradition. Obviously such a process will seem to some intolerable slow and there will be moves to short-circuit it. Denominations of a sect-type will be able to make instant decisions. A papal *magisterium* may make a fairly rapid decision for or against and then have to live with the longer term mind of its own communion. Anglicans, by the very nature of their character as a family of independent churches, will be committed to the way of patience, consultation and reception.

A second restraint is that of *ecumenical commitment*. If Christians today existed in a state of complete division from each other the problem would be less severe. A church which regarded itself as complete in itself, founded on some principle which justified unilateral action in matters of faith and order, would be able to act as though it were the whole Catholic Church. It would confine itself to its own processes of consultation and decision, and thereby would confirm its isolation from other Christians. But a measure of a church's commitment to the ecumenical movement is not its attendance at conferences nor its joining in assent to ecumenical texts and statements but in its willingness to make sacrifice of its separate existence in pursuit of a common goal. The world's main Christian churches are slowly and painfully moving to the point where they can acknowledge each other as fellow-pilgrims, holding the apostolic faith and ready for visible unity. The Roman Catholic Church, while still holding that the Catholic Church 'subsists' in itself, clearly does accept the restraints of the ecumenical movement and it is altogether unlikely that there will be any further papal action in matters of faith or order which would compromise the agreement which has already been reached. It is inconsistent for Anglicans to engage in dialogue with Roman Catholics for the reconciliation of ministries while taking new action which our partners have stated will in their opinion raise new and divisive issues. It is not to the point to say that *we* do not think that we are doing anything to compromise the ecumenical dialogue. It is the truly divisive issues which need to be drawn into dialogue and dealt with ecumenically. It is sometimes said that an issue like the ordination of women cannot be solved in this way, and that to commit it to the consent of Roman Catholics and the Orthodox is in effect to delay it indefinitely. The answer is that we cannot know. Certainly the Roman Catholic Church is now meeting the same pressures and some of the turmoil which Anglicans have been experiencing. It could be that the dialogue between Anglicans and what is incontestably the largest and most widely distributed body of Christians could lead to a consensus and decision which would be authoritative for the whole Catholic Church.

Lima on Ministry

1. Neither *Lima* nor ARCIC has an agreed statement on the doctrine of the Church, and the sections devoted to ecclesiology have a tentative and provisional character to them. This must be taken as deliberate policy. Hitherto there has been a natural reluctance to begin ecumenical discussions at the point where disagreement is most obvious and a hope that by dealing first with sacraments, ministry and authority new insights may emerge to temper the ecclesiological assertions which have been so much a part of the history of the various denominations. There is evidence that this hope has been to some extent realised, but the way of proceeding has its disadvantages. A particular church's sacramental practice, understanding of ministry and exercise of authority are almost certainly related to some 'model' or general conception of the Church. In the case of the churches stemming from the Reformation ecclesiastical usage was deliberately altered to conform to a new view of Gospel and Church. The Baptist practice of adult baptism, for example, is closely connected with an ecclesiology: that of the independent, 'gathered' church of spirit-led believers. It is, then, misleading to offer schemes for bringing together ministerial structures when the 'models' of the Church remain unreconciled. The failure of the English Covenant was due not to insufficient will nor to last-minute disagreement over details but to a lack of theological depth and a refusal to face basic ecclesiological issues. Experience in Britain and elsewhere has shown that schemes and

In this paper *Lima* with a paragraph number refers to the statement on Ministry from the World Council of Churches, Faith and Order Paper No. 111, *Baptism, Eucharist and Ministry*. 'ARCIC' with a paragraph number refers to the statement on 'Ministry and Ordination' from the Anglican-Roman Catholic International Commission, *The Final Report*. 'Newbigin' refers to BMU/FO/83/5, Lesslie Newbigin, 'How should we understand Sacraments and Ministry'.

'services of reconciliation' which do not rest on a substantial agreement in faith and order will always encounter the re-emergence, often at a late stage, of the old ecclesiologies.

A. LIMA AND ECCLESIOLOGY

2. Though the Lima statement on Ministry does not offer a systematic treatment of the Church, its importance lies in the fact that it is written by people who are well aware that ecclesiology is at the heart of the ecumenical task. A study of the text reveals a constant concern to identify and reconcile the disparate models of the Church produced by the Reformation era.

3. On the one hand there is the view of the Church which stems from Luther's teaching on justification. Here the stress is on the Word of God which goes forth into the world to create faith in all who 'hear' it. This new relationship with God through trust in his promises in Christ is basic to classical Protestant ecclesiology. The Church is defined as all those whom God has united to himself by the gift of faith; in the world it is an 'invisible' company known only to him, a journeying together of pilgrims who trust in no earthly city. Luther understood that the faithful would need to make use of material things but he regarded all forms and structures as provisional and a matter of expediency. He was prepared to use traditional ecclesiastical institutions but he was equally ready to discard them. His view of ministry was strictly in terms of its functions. A man was a minister *in the act* of preaching or administering the sacraments; when he was not doing so he was a peasant or burgher like other men. In theory any of the faithful could exercise a ministerial function but Luther accepted that it was expedient that the Church should confine public ministry to a special group of persons in order to ensure that things were done decently and in order. He denied,

however, that there was any special or indelible character conferred by ordination or that it differed in kind from installation in office.

4. On the other hand there is the view of the Church which found expression in the decrees of the Council of Trent: that of a historic and visible society, founded by Christ and continuing to act in his name and by his authority. Though its ends are spiritual ones, the Church is constituted and organised in the world as a human institution, and is governed by a priestly hierarchy at the head of which is the Bishop of Rome, successor of Peter. In this model Christ's own ministry as priest, teacher and pastor is present in the Church and exercised through a ministerial priesthood which stands in direct succession from the apostles. Ordination is not a delegation of functions by the Church to some of its members; it is a sacramental action by which a man is 'conformed' to the priesthood of Christ, given the grace for a particular place in the ministerial priesthood, and empowered to perform the functions of his ministry. The grace of holy order remains with the one ordained and imparts to him a permanent or 'indelible' character. [For a modern exposition of the Tridentine teaching, see the Encyclical Letter *Mediator Dei* of 1947.]

B. TOWARDS AN INTEGRATION OF ECCLESIOLOGIES

5. A study of *Lima* shows that it is well aware that these contrasting ecclesiologies retain their power in the thinking of the churches and are entrenched in their formularies. Its principal aim is therefore to develop an ecclesiology upon which all can agree. But it is important that its method be clearly recognised. It does *not* employ the approach of the *via media*: to seek to identify certain elements which both traditions have in common and to build on these while leaving other matters indifferent. This is to invite misunderstanding as to the real meaning

of the elements thought to be common, and may well result in a weakening of the positive character and coherence of each tradition. In fact *Lima* has chosen another method: that found in the documents of Vatican II and particularly in the major restatement of Roman Catholic teaching on the nature of the Church, the Dogmatic Constitution *Lumen Gentium* of 1964. This may usefully be described as the 'method of reintegration'. The authors of the conciliar documents found themselves having to deal with existing formularies dependent on an ecclesiology which stressed the institutional, juridical and hierarchical aspects of the Church. Such a model was already recognised as one-sided and restrictive [see, for example, an earlier attempt at reformulation in the Encyclical Letter *Mystici Corporis* of 1943], and the documents seek to establish a more comprehensive and balanced one. Thus *Lumen Gentium* attempts to hold together the evangelical, prophetic and eschatological dimensions of the Christian community with the visible, sacramental and hierarchical aspects. The Church is at once a 'visible assembly and a spiritual community . . . one complex reality composed of a divine and human element' [*L.G.* I.8.]. In the context of Vatican II the aim was to offer a new and dynamic view of the Church's mission and place in human society by marrying an older ecclesiology with the newer insights of biblical theology. When the method was translated into ecumenical terms in the Decree *Unitatis Redintegratio* (1964) the theory appears to be that the 'Protestant' and 'Catholic' models actually need each other: that they are separated parts of a single ecclesiology, truly Catholic by being comprehensive; and that each by attempting to be complete in itself has become defective. Thus 'Protestantism' has seemed powerless to prevent the multiplication of evangelical sects and 'Catholicism' has tended to identify the Church with a clerical hierarchy. *Lima* is thus to be judged by how far it has succeeded in bringing the positive aspects of the two ecclesiologies together into a dynamic whole.

6. At this point it may be useful to attempt an assessment of 'Newbigin'. It is a learned paper, written with the author's usual force and clarity; it contains valuable biblical insights and useful practical suggestions. But unfortunately it must be considered as an illustration of the ecumenical problem rather than a contribution towards the resolution of it. One may ask how far it is helpful at this stage of the discussion to have an individual's personal exegesis of New Testament material, especially when his mind is so clearly informed by the 'Protestant' model of the Church. In effect Newbigin goes a long way towards rejecting the comprehensive ecclesiology which is at the heart of *Lima*'s work. He stresses the missionary, evangelical and 'discontinuous' aspects of the Church while giving scant treatment to its corporate, organic and historic character. There is little attention to images like 'the Body of Christ' and a cursory and unsatisfactory treatment of the concept of apostolicity. In line with his ecclesiology is his wish to treat ministry primarily as 'leadership' and to define a minister in terms of the functions which he performs [p. 11]. Newbigin's unsympathetic talk about 'pipeline' theories and of Catholics as wishing to introduce an 'ontology' of the ministry reveals a strange lack of understanding of Catholic teaching on ordination. Indeed the reason he gives for the existence of an ordained ministry at all [p. 14] appears to amount to little more than the traditional Protestant desire to ensure that things should be done decently and in order in the church. In effect Newbigin is asking that unity shall be achieved on the basis of the Protestant model of the Church. His contribution may usefully be contrasted with another from the Reformed tradition: Max Thurian's *Our Faith: Basic Christian Belief* (Taizé, 1978). Here, and notably in chapter 19, 'The Church', is an attempt at an integration

143

of ecclesiologies which bears a strong resemblance to that of *Lima*.

C. MINISTRY AND THE PEOPLE OF GOD

7. The crucial test for *Lima*'s method lies in its ability to resolve the dilemma presented by the two apparently contrasting views of the ordained ministry. Agreement in this area is essential if the churches are to move towards visible unity. Yet in one model ministry is seen as derived from the common priesthood of all believers, a delegation of functions which belong to the whole community of the faithful, while in the other model ministry is seen as derived directly from the priesthood of Christ and itself forming a priesthood which is constitutive for the life of the Church. The real difficulty of the problem is shown by the obscure language of ARCIC when dealing with it [ARCIC 13], to which Newbigin has rightly drawn attention. *Lima*'s attempt at a solution is to integrate the two models by restating each within the general concept of 'The Calling of the People of God'. This 'People' is conceived of as a dynamic community called into being and continually sustained by the Gospel and endowed by the Spirit with gifts of ministry for the community and for the world. This master-concept, set out in paragraphs 1–5, is clearly indebted to the first chapter of *Lumen Gentium*, not least for an eloquent exposition of the evangelical, prophetic and charismatic dimensions of the community, and for a vision of the Church as a place where 'diverse and complementary gifts' are exercised for building up the common life and witness to the world. While the image of a People performs much of the same function as the 'koinonia' theology of ARCIC, it is perhaps more effective in indicating the historic dimension of the Church. *Lima* proceeds to use it in a sustained endeavour to hold together the dynamic/evangelical and the historic/corporate.

8. The concept introduces a new way of stating the relationship of the ordained ministry to the community. In a sense the dilemma about the derivation of the ministry is seen as a false one. The People of God has a 'fundamental dependence' on Jesus Christ, and ministry has been from the first moment of the Church's existence constitutive for its life and witness. Both ministry and community depend on Christ and on each other in him. *Lima* is concerned that there should be no over-simple distinction between ministry 'in its broadest sense' [7b] and the specifically ordained ministry, but equally no over-simple equation of the two. The Church is in its very nature built up by diverse and complementary gifts and the comprehensiveness of these is expounded in paragraph 5. Indeed the argument is put succinctly in paragraph 23 in language almost identical with that of chapter II of *Lumen Gentium*: 'The Church as the body of Christ and the eschatological people of God is constituted by the Holy Spirit through a diversity of gifts or ministries.' The ordained ministry must therefore be understood within the context of all the ministries. It must serve them and focus them.

9. This sense of ministry being in and for the community permeates *Lima*'s view of the authority of the ordained ministry. It wishes to dispel any view of a hierarchy separate from the laity and deriving its power to teach and rule from Christ directly: 'the authority of the ordained ministry is not to be understood as the possession of the ordained person but as a gift for the continuing edification of the body in and for which the minister has been ordained' [15]. Ordained ministry is thus a *special* kind of gift for service, and its authority lies in its function continually to present the symbol of the incarnate, crucified and risen Lord [16]. It is authoritative in that the Word of God, set forth in word and sacrament, has the power to engage the acknowledgement and the response of the community. The ministry cannot be exercised without 'the recognition, the support, and

the encouragement of the community' [12]. Their teaching is established as that of the whole community, not by reference to their own status or credentials but by its reception in the life and witness of the community. The condition under which their authority is exercised is that it must conform to the model of Christ's own ministry of service and self-giving [16]. This excludes any notion that ministers can act as 'autocrats or impersonal functionaries'. All this is largely in accord with ARCIC's view [Cf. *Authority in the Church I*, paras. 5 and 6], though there the clarity of the presentation is diminished by a need to accommodate elements of the older hierarchical view which have survived into the documents of Vatican II.

D.   HISTORY AND SUCCESSION

10. The point at which *Lima* becomes less than clear is in its assessment of the 'historic' threefold ministry of bishops, presbyters and deacons. One preliminary point, at least, is made clear: that the question of the historic ministry cannot be determined by a purely historical enquiry. Appeal to the text of the New Testament or to the history of the apostolic age has failed to establish a form of ministry which corresponds to that of any of the modern churches. Paragraph 19 states the situation clearly: 'The New Testament does not provide a single pattern of ministry which might serve as a blueprint or continuing norm for all future ministry in the Church. In the New Testament there appears a variety of forms which existed at different places and times.' This, taken with ARCIC's similar statement [5–6], must be taken as agreement to abandon an appeal to historical scholarship to determine questions of church-order. Both *Lima* and ARCIC, however, appear to lay much stress on the idea that there has been a *development* from this early variety, and that this development has embodied basic characteristics of the Christian community. *Lima* 19 puts it

thus: 'As the Holy Spirit continued to lead the Church in life, worship and mission, certain elements from this early variety were further developed and became settled into a more universal pattern of ministry.' ARCIC likewise sees the development as the working out of 'normative principles governing the purpose and function of the ministry [which were] already present in the New Testament documents' [6].

11. What each text appears to be saying is that the development of the threefold ministry, with a bishop at the head of each local eucharistic community, was under the guidance of the Holy Spirit as a way of exemplifying and building up the basic characteristics of the Church. ARCIC, perhaps because it is a dialogue between two historically-ordered communions, leaves the matter there with the clear implication that it considers that Catholic order has been established. *Lima*, on the other hand, hesitates to commit itself to the proposition that the historic ministry has become obligatory for all. It speaks of 'points of crisis in the history of the Church' when 'the continuing functions of ministry were in some places and communities distributed according to structures other than the predominant threefold pattern'; it insists that 'other forms of the ordained ministry have been blessed with the gifts of the Holy Spirit'; and that 'there have been times when the truth of the gospel could only be preserved through prophetic and charismatic leaders' [19]. The argument is not entirely clear. It seems to be saying that the historic ministry is not essential but it is the norm, departure from which has to be justified by an emergency situation in which the existing ministry actually destroys the essential characteristics of the Church rather than builds them up.

12. This idea that the ordained ministry maintains the Church in its essential characteristics is important in allowing *Lima* to offer an agreed statement on the meaning of 'apostolic succession'. This is not conceived of as primarily succession in ordination. The role of the

apostles was unique and unrepeatable; their relationship to the ordained ministry is that of type and analogy; they 'prefigure both the Church as a whole and the persons within it who are entrusted with the specific authority and responsibility' [10]. The real succession is in the apostolic tradition, and this is 'continuity in the permanent characteristics of the Church of the apostles: witness to the apostolic faith, proclamation and fresh interpretation of the Gospel, celebration of baptism and eucharist, the transmission of ministerial responsibilities, communion in prayer, love, joy and suffering, service to the sick and needy, unity among the local churches and sharing the gifts which the Lord has given to each' [34]. Such a sense of succession in a historic community preserving down the ages its distinctive life of faith and love would have been acceptable to the Tractarians, and is indeed more characteristic of their position than the crude 'pipeline' theory ascribed to them. For them succession in the threefold ministry, and in particular the succession of bishops in sees, was an outward and visible sign of something more fundamental: a local community's fidelity to, and continuity with, the apostles' teaching and fellowship.

13. *Lima* is, however, predictably cautious about episcopal succession. It goes so far as to say that 'under the historical circumstances of the growing Church in the early centuries, the succession of bishops became one of the ways, together with the transmission of the Gospel and the life of the community, in which the apostolic tradition was expressed. This succession was understood as serving, symbolizing and guarding the continuity of the apostolic faith and communion' [36]. This may, of course, be interpreted merely as a statement of historical fact. The text does not say that episcopal succession *assures* continuity in the apostolic tradition, and it is concerned to assert that churches without an episcopal system or succession may have preserved the tradition by other forms of regular ministry. Its doctrine of episcopacy

has, therefore, to rest on the statement that it is 'a sign, though not a guarantee, of the continuity and unity of the Church' [38]. This rather weak view of the *effective* role of episcopacy in the setting forth of doctrine [see the commentary (36)] must consort uneasily with the high doctrine of collective episcopal responsibility for defending and interpreting the apostolic faith found in ARCIC [see *Authority in the Church I*, para. 20.].

E.   UNITY AND DIVERSITY

14. While this must be *Lima*'s formal view, and is in accord with other ecumenical statements like that coming out of the Lutheran-Roman Catholic dialogue, it is in fact countered by another view which appears in a number of other places in the text: that the historic ministry of bishops, presbyters and deacons has a special role in effecting unity out of diversity, a diversity which is moreover both legitimate and lifegiving. This is perhaps *Lima*'s most important teaching on the ordained ministry and, if it is agreed by the churches, could be the most likely basis upon which a reconciliation of ministries is effected. In it the historic ministry is presented as exercising a unitive function at a number of different levels.

(a) It brings together into unity the many kinds of ministry which exist in the Church. *Lima* is committed to the view that 'the community which lives in the power of the Spirit will be characterized by a variety of charisms' [32]. The ordained ministry is included among these but has a special function towards them. It is specially charged with fostering the gifts of all the faithful, and it must not seek to use its function to hinder or repress. But it also has a regulative role: it must bring differing gifts into complementarity and exercise oversight to see that all is done within the apostolic tradition. The historic ministry itself exhibits this unity-in-diversity character.

Bishops, presbyters and deacons have different but complementary functions but find unity under their bishop and in collegiality with each other.

(b) It gives unity to the diversity which must exist in any local community. *Lima* recognises that in all the churches there is uncertainty about the size of what may properly be described as a 'local church', but paragraph 26 seems to indicate that the definition must be an area or population over which one man can exercise a personal ministry of oversight, where he and his fellow-ministers can act in a collegial way, and where the whole community can participate in counsel and decisions. *Lima* clearly sees the historic threefold ministry as best serving the personal, collegial and communal aspects of church-order, with the bishop providing a 'focus of unity' for all, ministers and laity alike. This concept of unity-in-diversity rebukes those who think of the historic ministry entirely in terms of bishops and who imagine that the addition of some persons possessing the rank of 'bishop' makes any kind of church-order episcopal.

(c) It gives the local churches in all their diversity of situation and culture a relationship to the wider or universal Church. In paragraph 29 *Lima* reveals its basic teaching about episcopacy. The bishop of a local church brings all his people, presbyters, deacons and the whole community into communion with the universal Church: he represents them to the wider community and it to them. *Lima* remains silent on the practical arrangements for this and whether there is not need for a ministry in the universal Church which provides a 'focus for unity' and can combine the personal, collegial and communal dimensions at that level. It is to ARCIC that we must look for help in this.

F. TOWARDS A RECONCILIATION OF MINISTRIES

15. *Lima*'s statement on ministry, written from the

perspective of its 'comprehensive' ecclesiology, does not resolve all the outstanding issues. The text leaves open the difficult question whether women can be admitted to the ordained ministry. Yet, if the present denominations can recognise in *Lima* a teaching which accords with their own tradition, there seems no reason why it should not prove a most effective instrument for the growth of the churches into visible unity. Anglicans, in particular, should have little difficulty in receiving it. Some church-men may well wish to say more but the text, as it stands, is surprisingly close to positions adopted by the classical Anglican writers.

16. It may well be foolhardy to suggest what should be done now in the wake of the failure of the proposals for an English Covenant. Perhaps *international* discussions provide the most promising way forward at the present time, but there is no reason why these should not proceed *pari passu* with negotiations at the national level. The following programme is, then, put forward as a way by which the Lima texts might be used to re-invigorate the movement towards visible unity in England.

(a) The churches who wish to take part should resolve by their own procedures that the Lima statements are sufficiently in accord with their own understanding of order and ministry for them to be used as an agreed basis for discussions with other churches.

(b) As a second stage there should be appointed a joint-commission with sufficient theological competence to work out a common pattern of order and ministry to be incorporated into the life of each of the churches. It should be based on a recognition of the comprehensive ecclesiology of *Lima* and endeavour to hold in balance the personal, collegial and communal dimensions of order and ministry. It should allow for a legitimate diversity in spirituality and practice but be such as can eventually serve as a basis for the organic unity of all. If the guidance of *Lima* is followed, it seems likely that these elements will be included. The non-episcopal churches will agree to relate their ministries to the historic threefold ministry of bishops, presbyters and deacons, and establish local communities where a bishop serves as a focus of unity. Those churches which already have the historic threefold ministry will need to recognise that mere possession of it is not enough; it must be properly used within the context of a dynamic view of the Christian community. They will agree to reform their usage in accordance with the principles of *Lima*. For Anglicans this will certainly make necessary a reshaping of their practice of episcopacy and a radical reform of the diaconate. [For a trenchant criticism of Anglican usage with regard to the diaconate, see Newbigin, pp. 12–13.] If the churches can agree to such a 'common pattern', then that may be an appropriate moment for them to 'covenant' with each other that they will effect what they have agreed.

(c) The third stage would be one in which the churches grow together by each reforming itself into the common pattern. Within the promise of the covenant this should be a time of mutual enabling and an increasing interchangeability of members and ministers. At this time there may be a role for a special kind of bishop, perhaps a 'national primate', to be designated by all the churches, who might serve them in the process of growing into unity. There is no reason why this should have to be the Archbishop of Canterbury, though the position which his office has held in the national religious life from the first days of Christianity among us might make this appropriate. Such a 'primate', with the co-operation of bishops from united churches overseas or ministers in episcopal orders at present working in the free churches, could create an episcopate for each of the non-episcopal churches, and they, in their turn, could relate all the existing ministers to the historic threefold ministry. *Lima*'s notion that there is not just ordination to the ministry but gifts of the Spirit appropriate to specific tasks of ministry [39] may be used to provide a way by which the ministry of those already ordained may be renewed and reconsecrated to a specific place in the threefold ministry. A bishop might use a formula of the following kind:

Send down the Holy Spirit upon your servant N to renew and enlarge his ministry, and by this sign to all the world establish him in the office of a Presbyter within the threefold ministry of the Church.

(d) The fourth stage would be reached when the churches decided that the time had come when they wished to bring their episcopates into one and merge their local communities. The complex legislative and constitutional changes involved could be worked out on the basis that what they sought to achieve was already for the churches a living reality.

The Bishop as
Focus of Unity

1. For a Christian the source of all unity is God for he has made all things and in him they have their being and their final end. But in a world fractured by sin, and in which humanity is divided by race, class and gender, Jesus Christ is God's way of reconciling alienated mankind and restoring unity to human society. This work was accomplished once for all on the Cross and in the Resurrection of Christ, and the Holy Spirit is now outpoured to offer women and men forgiveness of their sins and participation in the life of grace. It is this saving work of God, shown forth in the symbol of the Crucified and Risen Lord, which is the way to unity for the whole human race.

2. This gospel is not some abstract or theoretical formula. It is not a 'knowledge' possessed by some individuals which enables them to be members of an invisible and mystical Church. There was not first a gospel message and then the formation of a visible church for the worship and common purposes of Christians. The proclamation of the gospel was by a community of witnesses, already gathered by the Lord, and the effect of the preaching was to draw others into an actual community. Though grace is for individuals its effect is not to create individualism; it is not divided into small parcels of grace. Rather its character is corporate and the very antithesis of individualism and division. It binds the races, classes, cultures and sexes together into one complementary whole. There are many members but grace makes of them one Body. Nor is the 'real' Church mystical and otherworldly, and the Church on earth a pale shadow of it. Christianity is a religion of the

Incarnation in which the divine life became tangible among men and women and effective in the words and actions of Jesus. The human, the ordinary and the vulnerable thus can convey the plenitude of God's presence and activity. It is the teaching of the New Testament, and of Paul in particular, that as Christ is the sacrament of God among us, so the Church is the sacrament of Christ; and it effects what it signifies. It is the real community, tangible and fallible yet Spirit-filled, in which Christ is drawing mankind into unity with God. It follows that all true ministry in the Church must be at the service of this saving and sanctifying work; it must be an outward and visible sign of the ministry of Christ. The unity, then, with which the office and work of a bishop is concerned must be that which flows from the Crucified and Risen Lord and it must serve to keep his Body, the Church, true to its essential nature.

3. This theme of the creation of unity is one which makes some sense of the otherwise confusing early history of the episcopal office. It is difficult now to reconstruct the church-order of the apostolic age; it was clearly a time of diversity, discovery and experiment; and its chief characteristic was that there still existed travelling apostles who could claim a direct commission from the Risen Lord. The evidence of the New Testament itself is fragmentary but it indicates that within the local churches there were ministers who were charged to build up the communities. The texts at least make it clear that this *episkope* was exercised in obedience to a higher authority; it was a charge given by Christ and neither sought nor solicited. It was not given in consideration of human abilities or merits and its exercise was the reversal of the self-centredness which is inherent in worldly power and authority [Luke 22.25–27]. Ministry consists in choice [John 15.16], commission [John 20.21], and gift [John 20.22]. It is significant that from the earliest days the image of the minister was that of the shepherd who guided and preserved the flock of Christ but was subject

himself to the Chief Shepherd whose own work it was [I Peter 5.1–4].

4. While it is impossible to find a uniform church-order in the New Testament, the later writings appear to invisage, alongside the apostles who moved from place to place, a two-fold local ministry of presbyter-bishops and deacons [Phil. 1.1; I Tim. 3.2–3]. At this time and for some generations later the terms 'bishop' and 'presbyter' were interchangeable and referred to the same ministry [Acts 20.17–18; I Pet. 5.1–2; Titus 1.5, 7]. Some churches appear to have had a multiplicity of such ministers, and we hear of bishops at Philippi and elders/presbyters at Miletus; and it may be that in such places the presbyter-bishops acted together as a college. This two-fold pattern persisted until well into the second century. Clement of Rome, writing within the New Testament period, speaks only of the two-fold ministry, as does the Didache, the letters of Polycarp, and the *Shepherd* of Hermas. Only slowly did there emerge a three-fold ministry with one bishop to each local church, assisted by ministers called presbyters and deacons. One important early text, the letters of Ignatius, Bishop of Antioch in Syria, who was martyred *circa* 110, give a clear picture of a three-fold ministry but it has to be said that, apart from Ignatius, there is no unambiguous evidence for it until Irenaeus of Lyons in the last quarter of the second century. It is indeed possible that at Alexandria a college of presbyter-bishops survived into the third quarter of the third century.

5. The likelihood is, however, that for much of the second century a typical local church was served by a single chief pastor, called either bishop or presbyter, and that he was assisted by deacons, the original assistant ministers with important functions in the liturgy, charity and practical administration. The emergence of a second order of ministers, called presbyters, was relatively late and was at first to be found only in large towns like Antioch and Rome where there were many house-

churches and assemblies of Christians in the suburbs and country districts. Such second-order presbyters were regarded as extensions of the ministry of the primary minister, the bishop. In the ordination-prayer of such a presbyter in Rome in the early third century he is compared to the elders in the Old Testament who were appointed by Moses and Aaron because their own ministry had become too much for them to bear [Hippolytus, *Apostolic Tradition*, 8.1.]. In his sub-church the presbyter acted as the bishop and could do everything he could do except ordain, but if the primary minister came to visit he yielded place to him as the eucharistic president. There was then only one ministry and one *episkope* and that was the bishop's, but it was extended throughout the city and its districts through those whom he had ordained presbyter. Their ministry was his and was exercised only in union with him.

6. A bare summary of such developments in church order may leave the impression that the emergence of the episcopate was primarily a matter of pastoral convenience or practical administration. Such a view would, however, seriously understate the theological thinking which lay behind the early Christians' concept of ministry and their strong sense that the outward forms and images of the visible Church were sacramental of the inner life of that invisible and mystical Church where Christ reigned in glory. The Church on earth was the gospel made concrete, active and effective; it was to be a sign and an instrument of communion with God and, in Christ, with all the faithful. It was for the eventual unity of all mankind. It was there to be part of the world, to challenge it and invite it, through the symbol of the Crucified and Risen Lord, to receive forgiveness for sin and a place in the Body. Thus the visible forms are more than just convenient: they will symbolize what they are to effect. They are closely related to the Church's basic message and mission, and part of its 'givenness'. It is therefore perilous to abandon or seek to revise them lest

the dynamic teaching which they embody should be lost or impaired.

7. It is of the nature of the bishop's office that he leads a local church by his setting forth that symbol of Crucifixion and Resurrection which 'makes' the Church. His authority is in no sense a personal possession nor is it to be exercised according to the world's ideas of power or status. He is the servant of Christ and servant of the servants of God. Yet in serving the symbol he becomes part of it, himself a living image of the Lord at the eucharistic celebration. This theology of ministry as setting forth the sacramental signs which keep the community true to its essential nature is eloquently expressed in three early witnesses: Ignatius of Antioch, Irenaeus, Bishop of Lyons who died *circa* 200, and Cyprian, Bishop of Carthage, who died in 258. Writing as they did in the era between the death of the apostles and the 'establishment' of the Christian Church in the fourth century under Constantine, they have usually been taken as providing the classical theology of the episcopate at a time when the early communities were working out in freedom their self-understanding of mission and ministry. It may therefore be useful to summarize their teaching on the bishop as focus of unity.

8. *Ignatius: the bishop as centre of unity for a local church.* Ignatius of Antioch is the earliest witness to the development of the episcopate in the post apostolic age. His letters, written while travelling to Rome to suffer martyrdom, have been of great influence in shaping the Church's theology of ministry. For him the bishop is primarily the one who presides at the Eucharist and so acts as the visible centre of unity for a local church. A church is, for Ignatius, essentially a eucharistic community. In this he is continuing Paul's thought in I Corinthians 10.16–17: 'The bread which we break, is it not a participation in the Body of Christ? Because there is one loaf, we who are many are one body, for we all partake of the same loaf.' Paul is saying that communion

158

in one eucharistic bread is what makes individuals one in a single community. Those who share in the Body of Christ become the Body of Christ. It is the Eucharist which makes the Church one. Unity is not something administrative or numerical nor is it imposed from the outside: it is formed within the community by a common sharing in the sacramental bread which images the Body of Christ.

9. Ignatius's vision of the Church is not some abstract ideal: it is the picture of an actual worshipping community gathered round a table at which a bishop presides. On the table is a loaf of bread and a cup of wine with which the people in union with their bishop make eucharist. In this tangible and visible occasion is signified the very life of heaven and in its sacramental signs Christ himself is present and active in love. There is a direct relationship between things unseen and mystical and the visible and tangible. In Ignatius's thought the bishop becomes the very image or icon of Christ and, as Christ draws believers into *koinonia* with God and with each other, so the bishop becomes the focus of unity for the local church. The *ecclesia* is the people of God called out of the world to be one in making eucharist. In a famous passage Ignatius sums up his essential theme:

Be careful, then, to observe a single Eucharist. For there is one flesh of our Lord, Jesus Christ, and one cup of his blood that makes us one, and one altar, just as there is one bishop along with the presbytery and the deacons, my fellow slaves. *To the Philadelphians* 4.

10. For Ignatius of Antioch, then, the bishop is the focus of the local community's unity in Christ. Indeed the people are seen as personified in their eucharistic minister. Of course, it has to be understood that he was writing at a time when in each city there would have been only one eucharistic assembly. Their bishop was not a distant celebrity or an administrator but the one pastor who

Sunday by Sunday broke the bread at their eucharist, and it was perhaps natural in disputed matters to see following the bishop as the way of following Christ. Ignatius thus writes:

You should all follow the bishop as Jesus Christ did the Father ... Nobody must do anything that has to do with the Church without the bishop's approval. You should regard that Eucharist as valid which is celebrated by the bishop or by someone he authorizes. Where the bishop is present, there let the congregation gather, just as where Jesus Christ is, there is the Catholic Church. *To the Smyrnaeans* 8.

11. It would be a mistake, however, to think that Ignatius was arguing for an episcopal autocrat. If the bishop is to be regarded and followed as the very icon of Christ it is because of the bonds of mutual love which bind Christ and his people. A Christian minister is a servant to build up the church in love and foster it as a community in which love is supreme. The authority of the bishop is not like that of the rulers of this world: it does not depend on status, domination or coercion. Like the authority of Christ it is there by self-sacrificing love to draw out the free response of those whom the bishop has called his friends. There can be no such thing as the imposition of private episcopal opinions on the people. Together, bishop, presbyters and people, will wait on God for his truth to be revealed. Ignatius expresses it thus:

As then the Lord did nothing without the Father (either on his own or by the apostles) because he was at one with him, so you must not do anything without the bishop and presbyters. Do not, moreover, try to convince yourselves that anything done on your own is commendable. Only what you do together is right. Hence you must have one prayer, one petition, one mind, one hope, dominated by love and unsullied joy—that means you must have Christ. *To the Magnesians* 7.

In all the Ignatian letters there is a constant repetition of the word 'one' and this is continually connected with the bishop's ministry. 'Watch over unity' he writes to Polycarp, Bishop of Smyrna, 'for there is nothing more important than this.'

12. The notion that the bishop was primarily a eucharistic president, and that his other roles were closely connected with this, was not peculiar to Ignatius. Indeed it is a constant theme in later writings. In the early part of the third century Hippolytus of Rome in his *Apostolic Tradition* gives a prayer for the consecration of a bishop which calls him a 'high priest' whose task is to 'offer the gifts of thy holy church'. It is interesting that the ordination prayer for a presbyter does not mention the Eucharist but concentrates only on 'government' and administration. It is only indeed in the fourth century that the order is reversed: the bishop becomes an administrator who exercises jurisdiction and the presbyter becomes the usual eucharistic minister. But from Ignatius down to Cyprian in the third century all thought that the office of a bishop was set in the context of that holy mystery where by sacramental means Christ is made known and his work made effective.

13. *Irenaeus: the bishop as link with the apostles.* At the end of the second century Irenaeus, Bishop of Lyons, wrote of the bishop as minister of unity in another sense: as the one who kept a local church in the apostolic or foundation teaching. Though he shared with Ignatius a belief that the bishop was primarily a 'eucharistic person', his conflict with the Gnostics led him to attach importance to the idea that the episcopal office, exercised from a throne or teaching chair at the Eucharist, kept the church firm to its apostolic foundation. The Gnostics claimed to have a secret tradition handed down by their own teachers. Irenaeus replied by affirming that the apostolic tradition was open and public; it was based on the scriptures and taught publicly and continuously in those churches which had been founded by the apostles.

Orthodox doctrine was to be sought in a church which had a continuous succession of bishops teaching the same faith from its chair. Irenaeus thus saw the bishop as the minister who keeps his people in the unity of the Catholic faith. Apostolic succession for him was not merely a succession of bishops ordaining bishops; it was rather a succession of bishops in the chair of a particular church. It is the church which is in the apostolic succession rather than the man. Outward continuity in consecration is only a sign of an inward continuity of teaching. Irenaeus took it for granted that a new bishop would be consecrated by the laying on of hands of other bishops but he is not particularly interested in this as of itself making a man a bishop. It is rather an act of recognition that the person chosen is acceptable by other bishops as legitimately succeeding to the throne of a particular church; it is also a prayer that he may be granted the *charismata* to continue the orthodox and apostolic teaching in which it was founded. No man could be consecrated bishop without a church of which he was eucharistic minister or a throne from which he publicly taught the faith. It follows that Irenaeus's theology of the episcopate could not conceive of titular bishops, suffragan bishops or more than one bishop in one city.

14. *Cyprian: the bishop as link with all the churches.* In the middle of the third century Cyprian, Bishop of Carthage, developed the theology of the episcopate by treating the bishops as a collective body which united the various eucharistic communities and held them in the truth. His contribution lay in exploring the conciliar or collegial character of the universal episcopate and the manner by which the churches could reach a common mind and solve disputes by a meeting of their bishops in synod.

15. Cyprian was well aware that the concept of the Universal or Catholic Church was always in danger of becoming abstract or idealized, and he had no notion that there could be a super-Church or an inclusive world-wide

organisation. Like others of the early writers, for him the 'Church' was something visible and concrete, and he insisted that the Catholic Church in its fulness was to be found in each local church as it was united to its bishop in making eucharist. In a famous sentence he expressed it thus:

The Church is the people united to the priest, the flock clinging to its shepherd. From this you should know that the bishop is in the Church and the Church in the bishop. *Letters* lxvi. 8.

At each Eucharist the whole Christ is present; and each bishop, his icon, has the plenitude of the episcopal *charismata*. When he acts as bishop he is not voicing his own opinion, no matter how learned or clever he may be; it is not his function to propose innovations; to cause division is the very antithesis of the episcopal character. He must speak only of the faith which his church has received and of its implications for the life and mission of his community. He has to 'gather' the witness of the church.

16. It is the faith and experience of a local church which its bishop brings to a council of bishops. The Catholic Church is not a superior level of church organisation; it exists already in the particular churches and they are never swallowed up in some collective identity. In council the bishops represent communities which are complete in themselves but bear a family likeness to each other in spite of their differing situations and outlooks. They meet together to discover a common mind so that each may be strengthened in its Catholicity, made more obedient to Christ and better able to represent him in the world. There are thus individual bishops, each of whom possesses the episcopate in its fulness, and there is also a single episcopate in which all are joined together in unity. This seems to be the meaning of Cyprian's well-known sentence:

Episcopatus unus est, cuius a singulis in solidum pars tenetur.
[There is one episcopate in which each individual bishop has a share and the whole]

Cyprian is saying that though a local church is a microcosm of the whole there is yet a plenitude of episcopal *charismata* when a bishop joins his teaching with that of others in considering what is right doctrine, praying, living and evangelizing. The churches test out their own faith against the faith of others, and none will introduce innovations to which the rest of the bishops of the world cannot give their consent.

17. Cyprian made it clear that he was not concerned with majority opinion in synods: majorities had no right to override minorities or coerce them. The 'common mind' is more than what is fashionable or popular, and truth often exists in holy bishops who stand out against innovators. There has to be a moral unanimity. Together and waiting on the will of God, with Christ present in their midst and the Spirit in their hearts, they will seek a truth which is in the mind of all but greater than that of any. Of course, Cyprian, who had some experience of councils of bishops, knew that there would be insistent majorities and recalcitrant minorities. He was more concerned however that the latter should not be over-riden. Councils were not there to confirm division or suppress it. While disagreement remained unity had to be preserved by patience. The Church is not a political assembly; it is a creation of divine grace and its authority is that of the crucified Lord who did not exercise power like the rulers of this world. Nor was any conciliar decision necessarily the last word; it had to be accepted by the churches. This at least is the implication of Cyprian's dictum that 'the bishop is in the Church and the Church in the bishop'.

18. *A Changed Theology of the Episcopate.* The establishment of Christianity as the official religion of the Roman Empire in the fourth century had momentous

consequences for an understanding of the episcopal office. Bishops became important imperial officials, absorbed in a burdensome work of administration and justice. And with the conversion of the northern tribes a new kind of 'diocese' came into existence. Instead of the small city-dioceses of the Eastern Mediterranean there appeared the large 'tribal' diocese consisting of a whole kingdom. The bishop of such a diocese could not be the eucharistic focus of unity for his flock; he was rather a royal administrator, attempting to govern the whole ecclesiastical system within the area. And it was easy for him to become involved in the feudal arrangements of medieval monarchy as landowner, lord and magistrate.

19. Two important consequences followed from this. With the episcopal office increasingly conceived of in jurisdictional terms, it was the presbyter or priest who became the primary minister of the Eucharist. The idea that it was the Eucharist which 'makes' the Church was succeeded by the notion that grace for individuals was obtained by attendance at Mass. Whereas the second and third centuries had thought of grace as essentially a community experience leading to oneness, it was now thought of as a gift to build up an individual spirituality. Ordination to the priesthood, with the ability to celebrate the Eucharist, was seen as the primary ordination, for the priesthood could do all that a bishop could do except ordain. High medieval thought thus believed that a bishop was only a priest with added jurisdiction. Episcopal consecration was not even thought of as a sacrament in the way that priestly ordination was; it was a commission of power to govern people not to be president of a eucharistic community. Thus in an age of much celebration of Mass there was a separation of Eucharist and Church and a diminishment of the episcopal office into a form of magistracy.

20. The second consequence was a new stress on the Church as a form of universal organisation, centred in the Papacy. The model of the Roman emperor as universal

lawgiver and magistrate had an important influence on ecclesiastical organisation, particularly in the West. From the third century the Roman church had had great prestige. In the capital of the Western Empire and the place of the martyrdom of Peter and Paul it was acknowledged as being pre-eminently a community which stood in the apostolic tradition. It was consulted in disputed matters and occasionally acted as an arbiter. In this it shared a status with certain other metropolitan sees which were, by their antiquity or apostolic foundation, regarded as having the presidency of a group of churches. At a time when churches were being defined territorially a metropolitan, with other bishops, would determine the boundaries of the various 'dioceses' of the area. In this he was not claiming to be other than one bishop among others. But by the twelfth century in the West a different theory had emerged: that of a universal papal monarchy. The papal theorists employed the concepts of Roman law to assert the existence of an ecclesiastical empire which had the Pope as its sovereign lawgiver and supreme magistrate, with the bishops as subordinate magistrates and the ordinary clergy as *ministri*. The result was an increasing centralisation of the Church's administration with the Pope claiming to appoint all bishops as his inferior officers and to interfere in their dioceses by his ordinary jurisdiction. Thus despite the social and political eminence of medieval bishops, their *theological* significance was not great. Though Mass could be celebrated with special episcopal ceremonial, bishops rarely visited their cathedral churches and much of the pastoral work was done by assistant bishops ordained especially to perform the various episcopal functions. At this time the Church's focus of unity was held to be the Pope as supreme head of the ecclesiastical hierarchy, and the test of unity was to be in communion with him as the Universal Bishop.

21. *Modern Roman Catholic Views of the Episcopate.* It is, however, a fact that the most creative modern

theological work on the episcopate has come from Roman Catholic thinkers. *Lumen Gentium,* Vatican II's great document on the Church, was the result of important scholarly research and it has initiated further study. It is not too much to say that the principal thinker behind the document was the French theologian, Henri de Lubac, and particularly his books, *Catholicisme* (1938: English translation as *Catholicism*, 1950) and *Meditation sur L'Eglise* (1953: English translation as *The Splendour of the Church*, 1955). In the years before the summoning of the Council de Lubac wrote with some courage to deny that the Church was to be considered primarily as a jurisdictional entity. It was, he claimed, first and foremost, a eucharistic community. Instead of an individualistic spirituality and external authoritarianism he described the life of grace as essentially corporate. As the Eucharist is celebrated the Church is 'made'; the eucharistic assembly is a microcosm of the whole Church and he who presides at the Eucharist must be the community's leader in life and mission. Authority in the Church must spring from, and be always in accord with, the setting forth of the sacramental symbol of Christ crucified and raised from the dead. Unity 'wells up' from within the community; it is not imposed from the outside. Thus the unity of the Church was expressed in the collegiality of the bishops who actually possessed a diocese within which they resided. The function of the Pope was to be head of the college, its servant, enabler and centre of unity; he is within the college of bishops, not above it or the source of its authority. It is this new ecclesiology, with its return to patristic models, which lies at the heart of the reforms of the post-Vatican II era and which have found expression in the work of the Anglican-Roman Catholic International Commission.

22. *Anglican Episcopacy.* At the Reformation most of the new national churches rejected the medieval episcopacy which they had inherited. Some reformers, like John Calvin, attempted a radical reordering of the constitu-

tions of their churches on what they believed was the primitive model. Indeed Calvin's fourfold ministry of presbyters, doctors, elders and deacons was an attempt to recover the church-order of the New Testament. In England and Sweden where the traditional form of episcopacy was retained many of the features of medievalism were continued. Anglican bishops were recognizably prelates: lords of Parliament, landowners and ecclesiastical magistrates; and it was these characteristics which attracted much Puritan hostility. Because of their political and social importance English bishops were strongly associated with the State. But with their vast dioceses, parliamentary duties and disciplinary function it was hard to see them as the true centre of unity for their dioceses.

23. In many ways the Anglican doctrine of episcopacy did not accord with its practice. From Jewel to Hooker the early Anglican apologists appealed to 'antiquity', the practice of the Early Church over against what they regarded as Popish innovations. Indeed Anglican scholars were leaders in the patristic revival of the seventeenth century and the theology of the episcopate became their particular expertise. It was the achievement of one great Anglican critic, Archbishop Ussher of Armagh, to recover the authentic text of the letters of Ignatius of Antioch and thus reveal the episcopal polity of the second century. These scholars were to claim that the bishops of the Church of England were bishops in the whole Catholic Church, that they held to primitive church-order and they maintained the faith of the ancient and undivided Church. It was Papists and Puritans who had introduced innovations, not they; and they offered in all things to be judged by Ignatius, Irenaeus and Cyprian. In fact, of course, there was more medievalism about the Anglican form of episcopacy than they cared to admit. A church which in the seventeenth and eighteenth centuries celebrated the Eucharist so infrequently had no understanding of the Eucharist-centred ecclesiology of the early

Christians. It is clear, too, that their view of episcopal authority was heavily influenced by the legal forms of the English Establishment. Dioceses were too large for a genuine pastoral episcopacy and, though cathedrals existed as corporate bodies, they were rarely centres of an episcopal ministry. In modern times the burden of diocesan administration on a single bishop has led to the multiplication of 'suffragan' bishops in a diocese instead of the creation of dioceses of an episcopally coherent size.

24. Most problematic, however, is the question of unity in the Anglican Communion. As the Church of England expanded overseas its daughter churches were at first directly dependent on it but now it finds itself but one province in a loose grouping of independent national provinces. Like former colonies the provinces have obtained their independence and have settled all canonical power within their own local constitutions. The Anglican Communion has thus created a system of provincial autonomy based on nationality. And in doing so has based itself on a principle which would not have been recognized in either the Early Church or in the medieval polity. For the Church of the second and third centuries the basic unit was the episcopal community and for the middle ages it was the universal Church under the Supreme Pontiff. Lambeth Conferences have worked valiantly to co-ordinate the doctrine and practice of the Communion but there is clearly an imbalance between the strength of the provinces and weakness at the centre. While they have attempted to emulate the Cyprianic ideal of a synod which seeks moral unanimity, they have in fact relied heavily on their English heritage in divinity and liturgy; and, as the Englishness of the Communion becomes less apparent, there are signs of a certain incoherence, And the question remains of the relationship of this gathering of the bishops of a relatively small communion to the bishops of other episcopal churches. Is it legitimate, even in a divided Church, to act as though the Anglican Communion were the whole Catholic

Church? In an age of ecumenical dialogue and actual agreed statements on doctrine and church-order, is it possible to make decisions without consulting one's fellow-pilgrims in the quest for visible unity? The ecumenical process has moved so far that it begins to look as though the churches are in the preliminary stages of an ecumenical council. It may be that at such a time the Cyprianic principle of patience in disputed matters has much to recommend it.

Ministry and Christian Unity

This paper is a modest attempt to describe the current state of thought about the Christian ministry as this is reflected in some modern ecumenical texts. It has always been recognized that different concepts of the role of the ordained minister lie behind the failure of so many projects for Christian unity, but it seems relatively recently that theologians have placed the question of ministry firmly in the context of the theology of the Church. What emerges is a surprising consensus which challenges entrenched positions, both 'Protestant' and 'Catholic'. In fact the scene changes rapidly and even since the failure of the English Covenant in 1982 there has been significant new work. Behind such texts as the Lima version of *Baptism, Eucharist and Ministry* from the WCC there lies a series of quite radical books and articles which have come from both Protestant and Catholic scholars. On all sides there is a recognition that the debate has been conducted on too narrow a basis. The traditional 'Protestant' view has been that the ordained minister is primarily a functionary: he has a status no differnt from that of any other Christian who shares in the priesthood of all believers; he is simply one authorized by the church to minister the word and sacraments. The traditional 'Catholic' view has been that the church is structured as a hierarchy, that the Catholic ministry of bishops, priests and deacons is that intended by Christ himself, and that the bishops are the lineal successors of the apostles by a continuous chain of ordination. Both views have come under severe criticism from modern biblical and patristic scholarship, and both are seen as dependent of theologies of the Church which are plainly inadequate. So what kind of a consensus is now emerging, and what ways forward does it offer?

Let us look first at modern *New Testament* scholarship. Of course, we know that there is a type of biblical student who simply despairs that the New Testament specialist can shed light on modern church questions. In a recent editorial in *Theology* Leslie Houlden has suggested that the scriptures provide little firm evidence for the words or actions of Jesus. We have only the image of him reflected in the beliefs, expectations and patterns of apologetic of the earliest Christians, and most of these we cannot share. As to church-government there is so much variety within the N.T. documents themselves that no pattern can be regarded as mandatory. This kind of approach can be a veritable *via negativa*, and Leslie Houlden himself comes to the rather despairing conclusion that all that is left is for individuals to select for themselves certain N.T. themes and embody them in a private spirituality. But the most recent ecumenical statements rest upon a more constructive scholarship, and there would seem to be *three* themes to this work.

1. The first is that the church, in the form of the local Christian community, was understood by the first Christians to be ministerial in the sense that it was constituted by a wide but inter-connected series of gifts and charisms. The opening paragraphs of the *Lima* Ministry text reflect a N.T. scholarship which recognizes that the early communities were strongly charismatic. It is clear that there was a pre-eminence given to those called 'apostles' but they themselves partook of a charistmatic character. Even if we do not go as far as Gerd Theissen who describes them as the 'wandering charismatics of the Jesus Movement', it is clear that they were a group wider than that of the original Twelve; they possessed some extraordinary commission which came in some way from the Lord himself; they were authoritative in local churches in a way none of the local Christians were; they did not stay long in any one place; and they had powers of utterance, perhaps miracles and healings, which others did not. Of the other ministers, such as 'prophets' and

'teachers', we know tantalizingly little. The picture of these early charismatic ministries, as they appear in a modern work like Wayne Meeks, *The First Urban Christians* (1983), is of a confusing variety, and it seems clear that the early communities also found them dangerous and divisive. It took a powerful mind like Paul's to assert in the face of dissension and competition that all true ministries contributed to one single ministry or mission. His image of 'the Body' is a valiant attempt to propose the notion of a corporate ministry in which all the baptized share. And it is taken further by the later author of I Peter with his concept of a corporate priesthood, a 'priestly people'. Thus the ecumenical texts like *Lima* begin with the idea of a ministry of the whole people of God in which particular ministries must find their place as part of a coherent whole.

2. The second theme of agreement is that the N.T. writings do not contain any uniform pattern of church-order. If the Pastoral Epistles are the traditional proof-texts for a ministry of presbyter-bishops and deacons, other documents either do not know of these functionaries or actually exhibit hostility to them. The community for which 'Matthew' wrote, perhaps at Antioch in the 80s, had clear ideas how authority was to be exercised; they knew about Christian prophets and 'scribes' [10.41 and 13.52] but not yet about presbyter-bishops and deacons. Especially alert to the danger inherent in admitting any teacher or authority other than the Paraclete himself were the Johannine writers. Of course, many N.T. writers were dealing with immediate controversies and not writing directly about church-order or ministry. There may well have been things which they took for granted, but it has to be said that, taken as a whole, the canonical N.T. does not present us with any coherent pattern or blueprint for ministry. The old sixteenth-century controversies about the scriptural justification for episcopacy or presby-terianism were simply ill-founded.

3. There is, however, a third kind of agreement

173

emerging among the scholars: that there was a development of ideas and practice even within the N.T. itself as
between the earlier and later writings, and there is
congruence between this development and the non-
canonical but very early evidence of the *Didache*, I
Clement, and the letters of Ignatius of Antioch. This kind
of view is well set out by Raymond E. Brown in his recent
book, *The Churches the Apostles Left Behind* (1984). To
put it simply (and perhaps too crudely) the 80s saw
intense threats to the internal unity of many local
churches and to the right transmission of the original
teaching. The passing from the scene by death of the
apostles, the rise of gnosticism, the fall of Jerusalem, and
perhaps the onset of persecution: all these made expedient
a more authoritative order in the local churches and
greater uniformity. Brown and others see the N.T. writers
wrestling with the new situation, and indeed coming up
with various solutions, but increasingly moving towards a
ministry in local 'elders'/bishops assisted by 'youngers'/
deacons. In I Corinthians 12.28 the local church administrator is mentioned quite a way down the list of
ministries; apostles, prophets and teachers are more
important, and the administrators, like of 'rulers of the
synagogues' may well have had their place in a humdrum
world of finances, relief and provision of meeting places.
But by the 80s they are coming to the fore. When Acts
was written Luke is positively anachronistic is putting a
'settling of presbyters in all the churches' back into the
40s but this may well be what was happening in the late
70s. The Pastorals seem to be using Paul's name and
authority to assist a campaign by his followers to
establish presbyter-bishops and deacons in the churches.
When Ignatius was writing *circa* 110 the new pattern of
ministry had taken a decisive hold, and could now be
insisted upon as a way of unity *within* the local
community and *between* the communities. By the later
second century there had emerged the pattern of a single
bishop in each city, acting in collegiality with a body of

presbyters and assisted by deacons. By the third century this was a universal pattern. It is not too much to say that its adoption preserved the Church in its first era of crisis and down to the Reformation (with many variations and in different social and political situations) it remained in both East and West as the distinctive ministry of the Church.

Thus far the *historical description*, but the question remains whether such development has any *prescriptive* character. Does it become *the* order of church and ministry from which there can be no variation? Clearly not every development in the history of the Church is good; some may even be distortions and need eventually to be reformed. There has to be some test of right development. And here the argument moves from pure historical research into the sphere of ecclesiology or the theology of the Church. Interestingly it is here that some of the most constructive theological work is being done, and notably by Roman Catholic scholars in an attempt to get away from the pre-occupation with juridical struc- tures which has characterized their church since the middle ages. It has taken the form of a recovery of a sense of the Church as a *mystery* which was so strong in the patristic age: that is of Christian *community* as the point from which all ecclesiological thought begins. Yves Congar sums up this approach: 'At this period in fact the primal reality in ecclesiology was still the *ecclesia* itself, that is the totality, the continuity, the unity of the faithful . . . Then, in the *ecclesia*, come the *praepositi ecclesiae*, the presidents or heads of the Christian community.' The Church is a mystery, a living communion, and church-order and ministry must serve to exhibit, and maintain it in, its basic characteristics. The structures of the Church are sacramental in the sense that they make visible and effective the inner reality of the community. Even at a time when conscious ecclesiological thought remained rudimentary there was an understanding that ministry was a gift or charism within the community and for the

175

community; and that its work was an active and dynamic one: to maintain in the name of Christ a living community in truth, unity and mission to the world. This is expressed in the very early association of the ministry of the bishop, his presbyters and deacons with the eucharistic assembly. The eucharist encompassed the totality of the life of a local church: it set forth the tradition in word and liturgical action; it drew the whole *ecclesia* into unity with in itself and with all other churches; and it set forth Christ's own ministry to the world. For a believer in the patristic period, then, the ecclesiological problem was not one of theological speculation or about the status or rights of officeholders but the practical task of maintaining communion with the 'catholica'. The test of right development in the emergence in local communities of a uniform ministerial order of bishop, presbyters and deacons was whether such a system maintained the local church in the apostolic tradition, in unity and mission, and the way it became the universally recognized sign of where that tradition, unity and mission were to be found. It is clearly in this sense, and on the basis of such thinking that ARCIC and *Lima* wish to commend this development as under the guidance of the Holy Spirit and a form which may yet serve to signify and effect the unity of the modern denominations. Of course, even to go this far does not exclude the constant need to reform this order and ministry, nor does it necessarily exclude from being churches those ecclesial bodies which have maintained tradition in some other form.

It is this close connection of ministry and local community in modern ecclesiological thought which allows us to look afresh at certain entrenched positions which have proved fatal in recent attempts at Christian reunion.

1. The first and most difficult is the meaning of 'apostolic succession'. It seems generally agreed that the work of the actual apostles in their various missions was

unique and unrepeatable. Their commission was directly from the Lord; it was concerned with witnessing to his Resurrection and teaching; and it was not confined to any one local church. The ministry of presbyter-bishops and later of the single bishop of a city with his presbyteral college lacked such a unique commission and was something which emerged out of the local community. But the new episcopal ministry did secure the unity in one communion of all the scattered local churches and, at a time when unrestrained individual claims to authority were a serious threat, it brought all the ministries within a local church into order. The bishop as president of the eucharist became a symbol of the unity of the community and a sign of the actualization of the universal church in the local. By the latter part of the second century much reference was being made to the apostolic foundation of the churches in the major cities, and it is important to see what this notion of apostolic succession actually meant. It did not mean a tactile succession in ordination; even Ignatius of Antioch does not mention this. Nor is it a succession which is concerned with the bishop alone or is derived from him. It is much more *a succession of the whole community* in the *didache* and *koinonia* of the apostles. Apostolicity is a principle of a church's continuing life, and means that it has its source in constant loyalty to the apostolic witness and ministry. The charism of episcopal office and historical succession in that office is [only] a sign and not of the essence of apostolicity. The fulness of apostolic succession must include a tradition by which a community maintains the rule of faith, the proclamation of the word and the administration of the sacraments, and a mission of service and evangelization to the world. To this may be added the regular transmission of ministerial responsibility within a community. It is in this sense that the succession of bishops within a local church has become the sign and witness to the world that that church is committed to apostolicity.

2. A second difficulty lies in a confusion of episcopacy

and prelacy. We are heirs of a long history in which bishops appear as potentates and temporal lords rather than pastors. The former Roman Catholic pattern of the bishop as master of his diocese and having his clergy at his disposal is one which will die hard. Neither Roman Catholics nor Anglicans can recommend this form of episcopacy without offering it as a ministry capable of reform and renewal. It is here that the *Lima* ministry text has much to offer in presenting some of the more recent theological work in simple form. It speaks helpfully of ministry in the church as having to exhibit the characteristics of being personal, collegial and communal. In the case of the bishop this means that his opinions and his actions can never be those of an individual alone. He is not a man who in exercising his office can be guided entirely by his private opinions. He must listen to his colleagues in the presbyterate and he must carry with him the consent of his whole local community. It is in this sense that the recent Anglican Consultative Council at Lagos requested bishops to 'bring their dioceses' to the Lambeth Conference of 1988. Of course, a bishop does not merely gather the opinions of his own local church. If he represents it to the wider Church on synods and councils, he also represents the wider Church to them. Indeed he brings the living common tradition as voiced by the whole Church into the local situation and the particular emphases of a single church. But perhaps this is sufficient to say that episcopacy is by its very nature collegial and synodical as well as personal.

3. A third difficulty lies in the relationship of the ordained ministry to all the other ministries in the church. It is perhaps summed up in the old Protestant/Catholic dilemma as to whether the ordained ministry is simply a delegation to certain individuals to perform public functions which belong to all Christians or whether the ministry is derived directly from Christ and exercises his priesthood by his authority. Is the ordained ministry derived directly from Christ or from the priesthood of all

believers? *Lima* and ARCIC agree that this is a false dilemma: it is derived from *both*, for the two are inseparable. Indeed if we can reintegrate the doctrine of the ministry into the doctrine of the church, it can be seen as a gift of Christ to his people to bring out and encourage within the church the diverse ministries of all. Ordained ministry thus has a stable and public character, and it allows other kinds of ministry to be integrated into, and find their place in, the life of the church. It is perhaps helpful to think of Ministry under three headings: the Apostolic, the Prophetic and the Teaching. Each is essential, and each represents a different kind of authority. The *Apostolic* represents *episkopé*: the leadership function of those who have been trained, tested and publicly commissioned. It is needful for the public articulation of faith, the co-ordination of mission, the preservation of order. Its function is a service to the whole. The test of its authority is its likeness to the ministry of Christ himself. Without it there will be disintegration and a failure of the corporate character of the community. But it is not the only ministry. There will always be a need for the *Prophetic*: an authority not due to office or academic skills. It does not submit to being bound by rules or proofs; it defies institutionalization; it is needed to discern the signs of the times but it cannot be bound up with any office. It will occasionally be a voice crying in the wilderness, calling the church back to Christ. And then there is the *Teaching* ministry. There is a need for synthesis and criticism, for reasoned argument and informed speculation. It too cannot be institutionalized without destroying its freedom; it is constituted by professional competence rather than by church appointment, and one must take the consequences of that in terms of eccentricity and partiality. It is important that none of the ministries seeks to usurp the function of the others or seeks to repress them, but only the Apostolic has that element of permanence and continuity which allows the others to work profitably to the church. It

179

alone has that place in the visible structures and known public order which allows it to serve all the other ministries and bring all into coherence and pastoral fruitfulness. Of course, it is as capable of distortion as they are but it has greater resources for stability and change. The ordained ministry is not over against the ministry of all believers nor is it identical with it. It is a special charism and gift to make the whole church more effective in ministry.

What practical outcome is there for such convergences, and how can they assist us in our search for the visible unity of the modern denominations?

1. Much can be built on the notion, now widely accepted, that apostolic succession in a church is a more comprehensive thing than mere tactile succession in episcopal ordination. In the Lutheran-Anglican, Lutheran-Roman and Anglican-Reformed joint-statements there is a recognition that ministerial succession is only one element in 'apostolic succession'. John Meyendorff in his recent book, *Catholicity and the Church* (1983), speaking from an Orthodox standpoint, stresses that the other elements are of equal importance: agreement in the content of faith, in the sacramental life of the church, and in a church-order which can be a recognized sign of the unity of the local church and its participation in the unity of all the churches. He criticizes Anglicans for isolating the element of a mechanical succession in episcopal ordination. Mere succession means nothing if the other elements are not present. If they are, the question of the mutual recognition or validation of ministries ought to become a relatively minor matter.

2. There is much to be built on the notion that the basic unit of Christian society is a local church united under its bishop. What is meant by *local* in this context is still not clear, though the Anglican-Reformed report has some wise things to say on this. And it is interesting that the ARCIC Final Report makes the point that the unity of the church is built up *from below* and not imposed from

above. In its essence the Church is not a monarchy nor a bureaucracy but a communion of communions. National churches, denominations, even world councils of like-minded Christians, are all secondary to the local community.

Such convergences have hope but they contain certain cautions for the framers of future covenants or unity schemes.

1. A scheme or a set of proposals solve nothing by proposing some formula for the recognition or mutual validation of ministries, if this is seen as an operation isolated from ecclesiology. It is no use recognizing ministries if these are bound up with two very different, even discordant, concepts of church-order or the local community. If, for example, Anglicans and Methodists are to covenant, it is insufficient to ordain the secretary or annual president of the Conference or the heads of the various departments as bishops, no matter how influential they may be. This is to make episcopacy a rank, a position of power in a hierarchy and not as (what alone makes sense) the chief pastor of a local community.

2. Before a union can take place there must be a growing together of separated churches, so that their faith and order are one in their basic characteristics, allowing for a legitimate diversity of language, spirituality and pastoral practice. Not to ensure certain agreements in essentials is to create obstacles to mission and unity in the future.

What immediate way forward is there? I would say that in the light of the Anglican-Lutheran and the Anglican-Reformed joint-statements and in the light of the former Anglican-Methodist scheme there is sufficient basis for a new attempt at visible unity in Britain. We can acknowledge each other as having in our divisions preserved the substantial elements of apostolic succession. We need now to work on a common statement of the content of faith and we need to explore how our church-orders can be brought to embody that 'reformed

Catholicism' to which *Lima* points. If we can thus agree in faith, order and sacraments, no Anglican ought to stand on the question of the re-ordination or conditional ordination of ministers who have not been episcopally ordained. Perhaps the idea of *incorporation* of ministers who have not been episcopally ordained into the historic pattern will serve. There should be no suggestion that any reflection is cast on the reality of any previous ministry nor that Anglicans are asking Free Churchmen to be incorporated into the *Anglican* ministry. We should all be concerned to share in a ministry which can be an outward and visible sign of the unity of all Christians in the one great Church which is more complete than any of our separated denominations.

Ecumenism and Catholic Concerns

It is sad that those who profess to stand in the 'Catholic' tradition of the Church of England often appear to their Anglican brethren to be negative in their attitude towards proposals for Christian unity. There would seem to be two reasons for this. One is an admitted theological failure among Anglo-Catholics which has led them to fix on certain details which they dislike in unity schemes and fail to set out any positive theology of the Church which might convince others that their objections were more than party fixations. But another reason must lie in the nature of the proposals which similarly seem to lack a coherent ecclesiology and often appear to be concerned primarily with securing an inter-changeability of ministries between the existing denominations. There has been on all sides an unwillingness to do the patient theological groundwork which will lift all the participants above their entrenched denominational patterns of thought and practice to a sense of being renewed by being conformed to the One Church which is more complete than any of its fragmented parts. That is why for Anglican Catholics the *Lima* and ARCIC texts are important events: both in liberating our own minds from past narrowness and in showing other Anglicans that there is a wider ecumenical movement which takes traditional Catholic theology and church-order seriously and sees it, in a renewed and contemporary form, as a foundation of faith and order upon which to build.

At the heart of that Catholic theology is an affirmation that the Church, in the sense of the visible, ordered Christian community, is itself a sacrament of Christ's continuing presence and ministry among us. It is more than a convenient assembly of the faithful for religious exercises; it is (as the great Calvin himself asserted) an instrument used by the Spirit to accomplish the purposes of God. Indeed when God communicates himself to men he does so in a mystery by which things ineffable and unutterable become known in the familiar and the tangible and we are addressed through the things of our ordinary human society and relationships. The gospel of God's mighty acts in Jesus Christ did not at any time exist in a void; it was, and is, a tradition preserved and set forth in an actual historic community. Jesus did not himself write anything but established a *community* of disciples, chosen by him and entrusted with the ministry of being his witnesses. And the gospel which they preached had the effect of drawing men and women into the life of that community. To have saving faith was not to possess a set of opinions or even to have the right theological formulae (that would limit salvation to a kind of gnosticism) but it was rather a turning of the whole personality to Christ. And that was conceived of as a *social* experience in which an individual was given his place in a spirit-filled community, centred in the eucharistic action and commissioned to evangelize the world. It is this kind of ecclesiology which is at the heart of *Lima*, and it is not difficult to see that it comes from the important role which Roman Catholic and Orthodox theologians played in the writing of the texts.

What, then, Catholic-minded Anglicans now wish to contribute to our local ecumenical discussions is nothing which is particularly local. As the church-unity scene becomes wider, we become more concerned that what we do in Britain should not be too influenced by our past history and ancient deadlocks. Any scheme for uniting the churches in Britain must be congruent with the emerging ecumenical consensus to which *Lima* and ARCIC witness. If, in the future, we should be forced to oppose any British proposals (and I pray we shall not) it will be only because they are inconsistent with or contravene what has already been achieved. To avoid that I would direct attention to three important elements in the new consensus.

1. There must be *substantial agreement in the content of faith before there can be institutional unity*. As Henry Chadwick has warned us repeatedly, this is the area in which our Roman, Orthodox and Evangelical Protestant brethren regard Anglicans with deep suspicion. It is perhaps a product of our history that we tend to minimize our doctrinal requirements and allow individuals a considerable latitude in interpreting what is required. Even the Doctrine Commission finds it easier to talk about the mode of believing than about the actual content of faith. To many of our ecumenical partners this seems simply feeble and they suspect that the only kind of unity of which we are at present capable is of Liberal Protestant with Liberal Protestant, based on a weak version of the gospel and an indifference to any kind of church-order. Yet in the ecumenical movement at large there is a decisive turning away from this kind of unity by understatement. The *Lima* texts in particular reflect a new belief that there must be a genuine convergence of doctrine, ecclesiology and understanding of the sacraments; there is no doubt that they represent a raising of the theological profile of ecumenism beyond a level which many Anglicans find comfortable. But Catholics in the Church of England will welcome this to the extent that we shall expect any new proposals for unity in Britain to be preceded by serious theological discussions and a formal statement of doctrinal agreement. And may I say how much I welcome the recent report of the Anglican-Reformed discussions, which seems in this respect to be distinctly better than other similar reports?

2. It now seems generally agreed that any new unity scheme must be based on *the principles of church-order which characterized the patristic age. Lima* makes it clear that this is not a proposal to reproduce the details of the church life of the age of Ignatius, Irenaeus or Cyprian; and it is similarly clear that by the sixteenth century that order had suffered distortion and corruption. Even today in churches which retain the historic pattern there is

evident need for reform. But what is the character of this reformed Catholicism which Lima puts before the churches? Perhaps in view of some evident misunderstanding in the General Synod, it is necessary to explain. It is not claimed that this order is explicit in the New Testament. The epistles and gospels show a variety of ministries and indeed differing concepts of authority and church-government: the apostolic and the charistmatic as well as the local administrative. But it also seems clear that this variety proved confusing and even divisive for the first Christians. To preserve the integrity of the apostolic teaching and the essential characteristics of Christian community there was a move towards greater definition and uniformity in church-order. By about 110 the writings of Ignatius of Antioch show that a development had taken place and by about the middle of the second century there was established a universal pattern in each local community of a single bishop, acting in collegiality with a body of presbyters and assisted by deacons. Ignatius already sees this pattern of ministry as the outward and public sign that here was to be found an authentic tradition of teaching as distinguished from that of sects or opinionated individuals. And at the end of the century Irenaeus of Lyons completed the picture. If each local church under its bishop was the whole Catholic Church in its local manifestation so there was also the 'catholica', an agreement in faith and order in which all the churches shared, even when there was legitimate local diversity and particularity. Loyalty to that *common* tradition was an important part of the whole concept of catholicity. *Lima* clearly wishes to recommend this patristic pattern to the modern denominations, and it is one which Anglican Catholics would gladly endorse. And not least because it makes clear that the real unit for ecumenical attention is the local community. It is important to reconcile denominations, national churches and international communions but the essential thing is to find a common pattern of order for the local church and *Lima* proposes in as many words that this should be based on a collegial ministry of a bishop, presbyters and deacons as a sign, well-known and already accepted by the majority of Christians, that here is the Catholic Church in that place, a church in unity with the other churches of God. And here there must be a note of warning. A scheme for unity or for a covenant does not solve anything by proposing some formula for the 'recognition' or general validation of ministries if these ministries are bound up with two different concepts of church-order. If, for example, Anglicans and Methodists are to covenant, it is wholly insufficient to ordain the secretary or the annual president of the Conference or the heads of the various departments as bishops, no matter how influential they may be. This is to make episcopacy a rank and to take it out of the context in which alone it makes sense: that of the chief pastor of a local church who exercises his ministry within the ordered life of a community.

3. There remains the question of the status of the ministers of those denominations which either by necessity or by deliberate choice have adopted some other system of church-order. I want here to speak as clearly as I can for the Anglican Catholic position on this has been grievously misrepresented. Catholics believe that the historic pattern of ministry of which I have been speaking has been and continues to be a sign of and a means towards the unity which we all seek; they do not wish to depart from it and they do not intend to do so; but they do not thereby dismiss or seek to belittle the ministers of great and historic denominations like the Lutherans, the Reformed, or the Methodists. Apostolic succession is much more than merely tactile succession in episcopal ordination. John Meyendorff in his recent book, *Catholicity and the Church* (1983), writing from an Orthodox standpoint, stresses that other elements of apostolicity are equally important: transmission of the apostolic faith, church-order, and sacramental life. He criticizes Anglicans

for isolating overmuch the element of mechanical succession in ordination and suggests that *if the other elements are present* the question of the validation of ministries ought to be a minor one. Indeed, so it should be. We can gladly recognize the reality of those ministers of churches where there has been loyalty to the apostolic teaching, an ordered church-life, and a regular transmission of ministerial responsibility. What Anglican Catholics call for is not ordination, re-ordination or conditional ordination but an *incorporation* of those ministers into the historic pattern of order, that they and we may be signs and representatives of the unity of the Church of God. It seems appropriate that this should be done by some clear and sacramental action. I hope that it does not need to be said that there can be no suggestion of incorporating them into an *Anglican* ministry. With *Lima* one can only say that such an action should imply no reflection on anyone's former ministry; it would be a positive move into the future and a sign to all the world of the coming in of the one, great Church.

Preface to Crockford's Clerical Directory 1987/88

In the Church of England things are not always what they seem to be. Indeed the public perception of its character rarely corresponds to the reality of its working. To the religious affairs correspondents of national newspapers the Church is essentially a part of the English establishment and is usually dealt with in terms of its relationship with the monarchy, the Prime Minister or Parliament. Such a view is supported by images which the media project: royal weddings, archbishops in purple at state banquets, and bishops orating in the House of Lords. And there is shock, almost amounting to a sense of treasonable activity, if the Church is seen criticising Government policy, abandoning the old Prayer Book or making ancient parish churches redundant. Yet, contrasting with this view, is that of many ordinary churchgoers, involved perhaps marginally in the business of 'Synodical Government'. To them the Church appears as committed to an experiment in popular democracy. Elections are held and energetically contested, votes are taken in deanery and diocesan synods, and reports come down of critical debates in the General Synod. It is easy to conclude that, for the first time, policy is being made at the grassroots. A little knowledge, however, of the way the Church of England actually works makes it clear that both these perceptions are false. Ancient and complex institutions have a way of disguising who it is that exercises influence within them and sometimes even those who are closely involved in their business cannot see the wood for the trees. These are critical times for Anglicanism, and now more than ever there is need of an informed and critical account of the state of the Anglican Communion in general and the Church of England in particular. It is not easy for any individual churchman to write such an independent survey in his own name for inevitably it will point to matters which are not for our comfort and it must extend to deal with personalities. It is therefore a fortunate circumstance that there exists a longstanding custom that each edition of Crockford's directory should have an anonymous Preface in which Anglican affairs are subjected to the scrutiny of a writer who is given complete independence. And now that the routine events of the year are dealt with by that urbane voice of the ecclesiastical establishment, the writer of the Preface to *The Church of England Year Book*, there is scope in Crockford for something wider-ranging and more trenchant.

In search of
Anglicanism

In the summer of 1988 the Lambeth Conference, the ten-yearly gathering of the bishops of the Anglican Communion, will meet in Canterbury. It will work in four sections devoted to 'Mission and Ministry', 'Dogmatic and Pastoral Matters', 'Ecumenical Relations', and 'Christianity and the Social Order'; and it will doubtless issue predictable and wholly unmemorable statements on all these topics. But overshadowing all its other concerns will be a larger question about the nature and future of Anglicanism itself. Normally this is a subject which the bishops would seek to avoid or dispose of with the usual platitudes about 'unity-in-diversity' and 'mutual responsibility and interdependence' but this time it will not go away so easily. The action of certain provinces in ordaining women to the priesthood and the likelihood that they will soon consecrate a woman to the episcopate will force a closer definition of what kind of ecclesial communion Anglicanism is and what kind of authority it claims to exercise.

The truth is, however, that Anglicans have never been happy with questions which require them to set out a coherent doctrine of the Church. At their Reformation in the sixteenth century they were distnguished not so much by a doctrinal confession or an ecclesiology as by a strong adherence to the notion of national independence. When the two English provinces of the Latin Church of the West assumed a separate existence this was effected by giving to the secular ruler a supreme jurisdiction in ecclesiastical affairs. Indeed a defence of this Royal Supremacy became the mark of the first apologists for the Church of England and a true ecclesiology was somewhat slow in developing. When it did emerge, principally in the writings of John Jewel and Richard Hooker, it had a distinctive character: it sought to avoid mere Erastianism and Popery or sectarianism by finding its authority in scripture as this was interpreted in the life and practice of the undivided Church of the first four centuries of the Christian era. Such a conservative ecclesiology, with its great stress on the institution of episcopacy and the independence of the local church, came to be recognised by other Christian denominations as a distinctive Anglican position, and there was wide respect for the achievement of Anglican scholars in their chosen field of patristic studies. It is such an ecclesiology which still underlies Anglican public statements and which has become the basis on which ecumenical discussions, such as those of the Anglican-Roman Catholic International Commission, proceed.

Yet it may be honestly questioned whether such an ecclesiology is understood or even accepted by most Anglicans today. Perhaps it never was. The various traditions or parties in the Church of England have always lived in a quite remarkable intellectual isolation from each other and it is on the doctrine of the Church that there has been the least meeting of minds. Anglican Evangelicals have, for example, paid little attention to ecclesiology, except to deny the assertions of others. So what in the past has kept the Church of England together, with its clergy and members even establishing a reputation for the way in which different traditions of churchmanship can coexist? There seem to have been four factors at work. Pre-eminent has been the state-establishment. Whether there is any justification for the state to exercise control over the Church, it has at least allowed men and women of differing ecclesiologies to live within an authoritative system. Governments have been concerned to avoid partisanship in religious affairs and they have usually worked to prevent any one group from dominating the national Church. Secondly, there has been the uniting effect of the Book of Common Prayer, a liturgy of considerable literary power. Though it was possible to have different theological interpretations of the texts there was a common liturgical language which became part of the cultural heritage of all Anglicans. Thirdly, there was a common ministry and ordination in the practice of which all joined. Its claim that it represented primitive usage could be accepted by all the traditions. But perhaps most important of all the factors was the conservative theological tradition of the English universities with their strong links with the Church of England. Even into the mid-twentieth century it was received opinion among continental Protestant theologian that Anglican academics lived in a world of their own and set up a firm resistance to the kind of biblical criticism which was commonplace in European theological faculties. English scholars tended to do their theology through a study of church history and it was hard to deny that most of their work was done within the usual Anglican assumptions about the authority of Scripture and the normative character of patristic usage.

An English descent It is not sufficiently realised how far the Anglican Communion is heir not to any particular doctrine or ecclesiology but to past practicalities of life in the Church of England. Indeed in its origins it was simply the Church of England as it followed the movement of English people overseas. When great empires fade as political powers they leave their images behind in churches which preserve their cultural ethos and mark the extent of their expansion. Thus the story of Anglicanism is closely paralleled by that of the British Empire. At first there were chaplaincies on the American continent and in the West Indies but soon a vast growth as the Church followed the flag into Asia, Africa and the Pacific. All were under the direct authority of the mother-church. It was only with the formation of the Protestant Episcopal Church in the United States in 1784 that Anglicanism took a new departure. It allowed the creation of a new national Anglican church which took to itself supreme authority to order its own doctrine, ministry and liturgy. At first the implications for Anglican ecclesiology were scarcely recognised. The new church remained heavily dependent on English usage and its members were thought of as a repository of Englishness amid the rapidly changing America of the nineteenth century. Gradually other churches in other former colonies followed the American way of independence and by the 1930s an Anglican Communion had come into existence as a family of independent churches. But what, apart from their English descent, did hold together these autonomous bodies, each of which had assumed full power to alter its doctrinal formularies, change its practice of ministry and, if it chose, unite itself with some non-Anglican church?

It is this question of authority within the Anglican Communion which has exercised the mind of virtually every Lambeth Conference since the first one in 1867, and their repeated attempts to define an answer are a measure of the uncertainty which existed and still exists. In the early days of the conferences it was usual to draw up lists of 'fundamentals' from which no church could vary if it wished to remain in communion with the others. The most celebrated of these lists was the so-called Chicago-Lambeth Quadrilateral of 1886 and 1888: the use of the canonical Scriptures and the historic Catholic creeds, the threefold ministry of bishops, priests and deacons, and the sacraments of Baptism and the Eucharist. Yet by the mid-twentieth century there was a growing realisation that such statements of fundamentals were wholly inadequate as a way of defining the terms of communion. Not only were they capable of a wide variety of interpretation but most threats to Anglican unity stemmed from disagreement about the meaning of the fundamentals themselves. The point was well illus-

By what authority?

193

trated by Professor Stephen Sykes's important (but ultimately unsuccessful) book *The Integrity of Anglicanism* (1978). In emphasising many different sources for Anglicanism he became the leading exponent of the notion of 'dispersed authority'. Sykes welcomed the fact that the Communion no longer had a specific confessional identity and that it exhibited a wide variety of opinion and usage. In a modern up-date of the old formula *lex orandi lex credendi* he sought to find the essence of Anglican unity in a common tradition of worship based on the Book of Common Prayer. The function of the consultative bodies of the Anglican Communion he thought of in terms of a complex process of gathering the many and various sources of authority to discover a common mind. Yet despite the great influence which it has had, Sykes's extensive theorising about the nature of Anglican authority is unconvincing. The liturgical tradition to which he points and on which he bases so much is fading as fast as the Cheshire Cat's smile and he utterly fails to deal with the concrete reality of having to reach decisions in a divided and troubled communion. At least his book illustrates well the reluctance of Anglicans to admit that authority has any location and their refusal to allow any central authority, whether primate or synod, to encroach on the absolute independence of the national churches. His book had the valuable function of throwing the problem into sharp relief; it did little to provide any answers to it.

Lambeth 1978: an unimpressive conference   Perhaps the signal example of the failure of Anglicans to deal with the question of authority was that of the Lambeth Conference of 1978. It is now generally admitted that it was poorly prepared for, indifferently led, and heavily under the influence of consultants who had not themselves thought through the ecclesiological implications of the advice which they gave. The least satisfactory performance of the whole conference was that of the section chaired by Bishop Patrick Rodger and concerned with 'The Anglican Communion and the Worldwide Church'. Clearly influenced by the work of

Professor Sykes, it attempted to identify various factors in the maintenance of Anglican unity but in fact did little more than rely on the old 'fundamentals', and in particular the standard of worship in the prayer-books and the use of the threefold ministry. In practical terms it had nothing to say beyond recommending a loyal relationship to the Archbishop of Canterbury as 'the freely recognized focus of unity' and respect for the statements of past Lambeth Conferences. Such a feeble effort was trenchantly criticised by the Board for Mission and Unity of the General Synod in January 1983. They drew attention to the unhappy fact that virtually all the factors which the 'Rodger' statement cited as making for unity were in fact the very matters on which Anglicans were divided. With such poverty in ecclesiological thinking the conference fell back on the usual platitudes about living with diversity until Professor John Macquarrie came to their rescue with the notion of a 'hierarchy of truths' and the need to draw a distinction between those matters which 'made' the Church and those matters which could 'unmake' the Church. This was, in fact, nothing more than a reintroduction of the idea of 'fundamentals' under different language, and still offered no adequate test of what was to be accounted fundamental and what not. When the fathers of Vatican II had used the same phrase they had made it clear that the hierarchy of which they spoke existed within the total context of the Church's faith and order, and was not an invitation to regard any parts of the Church's traditional teaching or practice as disposable. But Professor Macquarrie's suggestion was eagerly seized upon by a conference faced with the accomplished fact that some Anglican provinces, acting on their own authority, had admitted women to the priesthood. The bishops could not be unaware that this break with the universal tradition of both East and West and the teaching of all the sixteenth-century Reformers had placed at risk the relationship of full communion between the provinces and was likely severely to compromise ecumenical dialogue with the Roman Catholic and Eastern Orthodox churches. But, given the *fait accompli* and on the basis of there being a hierarchy of truths, they decided to make no decision at all. They burked the ecclesiological issue and fixed their minds on the legal right of each province to act according to its own canons; they contented themselves with lofty exhortations that each side in the dispute over women-priests should respect the convictions of the other. Yet in one respect they had made a decision, and one which was to affect the very nature of Anglicanism. They had consecrated the notion of an ever-increasing Anglican diversity and the obligation of all provinces to 'accept', at least in the sense of co-operating with, anything decided by a particular province. It now remains to be seen whether there will emerge any determinable parameters to Anglican diversity. The substantial failure of the conference was exemplified in the closing address of Archbishop Coggan. In an extraordinary manner he dismissed the notion that there could be any authority in the Anglican Communion which could speak for all the provinces. He rejected the idea that the Archbishop of Canterbury might be an Anglican patriarch; he rejected the Lambeth Conference, the Anglican Consultative Council and even a Doctrine Commission as able to exercise any authority within the Communion. Indeed he had no positive suggestions at all and contented himself with remarking that Anglicans did not like rigid definition and that some good might come out of disagreement. And so on this unhelpful note but amid expressions of mutual regard the conference ended. It had never faced the possibility that a notion of authority so obscure in conception and so imprecise in its exercise might in fact be no authority at all.

The unimpressive performance of the Lambeth Conference of 1978 could well be attributed to lack of preparation and an urge to hasty compromise in the face of serious disagreement but it can also be seen as a sign of a more fundamental malaise in Anglicanism, for it cannot be denied that the last thirty years have seen a significant erosion of those very factors which once created unity within such a diverse communion.

It must be clear to all that the 'Englishness' of the Communion is not what it was. It is easy now to forget how recently the English diocesan bishops dominated the proceedings of Lambeth conferences, and even in 1968 it was apparent enough to provoke some mild protests from other bishops. Until the Second World War American Episcopalians deliberately affected English ecclesiastical styles and their seminaries were staffed with a high proportion of English academics. Indeed Anglican theology was done for the most part in English universities, and notably at Oxford and Cambridge. Generations of priests throughout the Communion were brought up on the textbooks of English theologians and their theological colleges were closely modelled on Cuddesdon, Mirfield, Ridley and Westcott House. Many African dioceses were ruled by expatriates who looked to the mother-church for guidance in doctrine and churchmanship. But the post-war era has seen a rapid decline in this English predominance. The fading of Britain's power in the world, together with the poor record of the Church of England in pastoral matters, has had its effect. With the spread of American influence and the natural desire of African and Asian dioceses to break with their colonial past and develop their own indigenous styles, there has been an undeniable shift away from 'Englishness'. Now there is even suspicion of the Church of England and talk that it wants to 'own' the Anglican Communion and that it is unwilling to accept its status as just one national church among others. Yet the hard question remains: without its English style what does keep the Communion together?

Stands England where it did?

No change in Anglicanism during the last thirty years has been more remarkable than the virtual disuse of the prayer books based on the English Book of Common Prayer. Perhaps some of the national churches had a parallel tradition based on the Scottish liturgy but even here the same considerations apply. In England within a

The case of the disappearing book

197

generation the Book of Common Prayer has been virtually eliminated by services which are in theory only permissible alternatives to it. It may well be that there were good and valid reasons for all the churches to produce modern liturgies, and many of them are by no means as bad as their detractors would suggest. Certainly in Africa there was real need to have a liturgy which was truly indigenous. But nothing is more apparent than Anglicanism's break with its liturgical past, and any attempt to define Anglicanism by reference to its tradition of worship is now on very insecure ground. It is sometimes said that the new Anglican services have a 'family resemblance' but this may be only a reflection of the common forms of the ecumenical liturgical movement. Certainly it does not take a very close examination to detect that the liturgies have distinct doctrinal differences from each other. This would indicate that they are not so much a factor for unity as a sign of increasing diversity.

Focus of unity? In a denomination the ecclesiology of which has been so uncertain there has been a basis for confidence in the existence of an episcopal ministry which claimed to be identical with that of the ancient and undivided Church. And, distinct from matters of theory and interpretation, episcopacy has the advantage of being a practical, working system. Indeed in describing the denomination as 'Episcopal' or 'Episcopalian' other churches have rightly detected that the Anglican understanding of unity is closely related to the ministry of their bishops. It is true that episcopacy has been variously understood by the different traditions of Anglican churchmanship but all ministers have submitted to its authority and received an ordination which was acknowledged in all parts of the Communion. It is a cause of real grief to Anglicans that Roman Catholics have in the past refused to recognise the validity of their orders. They regard the reasons given for this refusal as unsound and they welcome signs that Rome is reconsidering its position and may be ready to accept that Anglicans have a place among those churches which have retained the historic ministry. Thus, to propose a variation from the traditional practice of episcopacy is always to strike at the heart of Anglican self-understanding and to create deep divisions. Discussions of the nature of episcopacy are ones which Anglicans find difficult to handle in a theological way. At once basic d.fferences in ecclesiology emerge and it would seem that the matter can only be resolved by the victory of one side over the other. Yet the last twenty-five years have seen repeated attempts to modify the Communion's traditional practice. For this plausible reasons are given. To insist strictly on episcopal ordination will inhibit schemes for union with non-episcopal churches and seem like raising matters of church order above agreement in matters of faith and mission. To confine the episcopate to males only, as has been the invariable practice in all the episcopal churches, is to have discrimination at the heart of a ministry which should be one of reconciliation and should represent the unity of all humankind in Christ. And so the episcopal ministry, which we are repeatedly told is the focus of ecclesial unity, has become a focus for Anglican disunity. The consecration of a woman to the episcopate would thus bring to the surface the divisions which are always latent in Anglicanism and call in question the one institution which hitherto all have been able to acknowledge.

Perhaps, however, the most significant change is the decline of a distinctive Anglican theological method. in a magisterial study of the great divines of the seventeenth century H. R. McAdoo identified this as giving attention to Scripture, Tradition and Reason to establish doctrine. The context of such theological study was the corporate life of the Church and the end was to deepen its spirituality and forward its mission. Such a view of theology still appears in official Anglican reports and in archiepiscopal addresses. But the last real exponent of classical Anglican divinity was Archbishop Michael Ramsey whose many scholarly studies represent a last stand before the citadel fell to the repeated assaults of a

A theology in retreat

199

younger generation of academics. The essential characteristic of the new theologians lies in their unease in
combining the role of theologian and churchman, and
their wish to study both scripture and the patristic age
without reference to the apologetic patterns of later
Christianity. None will dispute that this is a legitimate
aim for an academic who wishes his specialty to take its
place alongside others in a modern secular university, but
it is important to recognise the gap which has opened up
between the method of modern academic theology and
that of the classical Anglican search for an authority in
the sources of faith. Increasingly theologians are expres-
sing doubt as to how far either Scripture or the teaching
of the patristic writers can be used to prescribe modern
doctrine or church practice. Here the work of Professor
D. E. Nineham has been of great influence. In his
numerous writings he has stressed the distance between
the world of thought in which the New Testament was
written and that of our own day, and he finds that first-
century Christians had views about the universe, history
and literary forms which we cannot share and which
cannot be translated into our own situation. And in
similar style Professor M. F. Wiles has questioned the
relevance of the doctrinal formularies of the first four
centuries for the modern Church. In their apprehension of
the mystery of God the patristic writers were men of their
own day and their definitions cannot be prescriptive for
those of us who have to live in an entirely different world
of thought where quite new questions are being asked of
Christians. In particular the modern theologians are ready
to open up for discussion the doctrine of the Person of
Christ. Such a distancing of the modern Church from
what had been regarded as its prescriptive sources clearly
has serious consequences for Anglican ecclesiology, and
this has been helpfully set out in Mr J. L. Houlden's book
Connections (1986). Here he quite specifically rejects the
notion of 'living in a tradition'. It would seem that
modern man must live amid the ruins of past doctrinal
and ecclesiastical systems, looking to the Scriptures only

for themes and apprehensions which may inform his individual exploration of the mystery of God.

It is doubtful whether such views, explicitly stated, are acceptable to most modern Anglicans. In 1976 the Doctrine Commission, under the chairmanship of Professor Wiles, produced a report in which some of its members advanced such ideas. Archbishop Coggan, who had nothing if not a good political sense, judged that it would be divisive and unacceptable to the General Synod. The document was never debated and the commission was reconstituted with a new membership. Yet the movement in theology which it represented was not thus to be set aside. English faculties of theology are now part of an international scholarly enterprise which has moved steadily apart from the churches. Even where theological scholars are priests or ministers there is a tendency to bridge the gap between their work on early Christianity and their participation in the present life of the Church by a downgrading of the value of Christian tradition. The most notable casualty has been the study of ecclesiastical history which appears now to have a low priority on the agenda of theological faculties. If Anglicans once did their theology through a study of the historical experience of the Christian community that seems no longer to be the case, and the notion is in eclipse that the spirituality or the teaching of the era from the Fathers to the Reformation has anything to offer the modern Church. What is most definitely discouraged is any form of denominational history. While such a tendency is understandable in theological faculties in modern universities, its effect is most notable in Anglican theological colleges which have now trained a whole generation of priests with a minimal knowledge of classical Anglican divinity or its methods. Clergy without a sense of there being some authority in the historic experience of the Church may well come to think that theology is the latest fashionable theory of theologians.

It is now clear that this weakening of the distinctive character of Anglicanism is beginning to have its effect on

The Church and the theologians

The Provinces and the Communion

201

the coherence of the Communion. Though it is usual to speak of the Anglican 'provinces' this is to give the false impression that there is a single Church of which the provinces are sub-divisions. The real fact is that there is a loose association of independent national churches with some weak consultative bodies which attempt to ensure agreement in faith and order and advise on common action. Seasoned observers at meetings of the Anglican Consultative Council know that the level of theological and ecclesiological discussion is not high and their most notable characteristic is the way in which the representatives of the churches come with opinions already formed. It is usual for such meetings to issue statements insisting that their authority is only moral and persuasive, and this is indeed necessary since the churches are accustomed to take as little notice of what is decided as they do of the recommendations of Lambeth Conferences. Anglican provinces, increasingly lacking a common mind, tend to look inwards for the formation of opinion and to the concerns generated within their own societies. Having full canonical power to make changes they develop a strong disposition to put into effect what a local majority wishes and then expect the rest of the Communion to follow suit. The issues of the ordination of women to the priesthood provides a cogent illustration of this point. When it was first proposed to the ACC meeting at Limuru in 1971 it was in terms of allowing the small diocese of Hong Kong in special circumstances to be allowed a dispensation from the usual practice. But a plea for tolerance easily passes into a demand that others should conform, and as certain provinces from the prosperous First World began to ordain women it was not long before the Church of England in particular came under attack because it did not receive the ministrations of these women priests. In 1983 this culminated in an imperious speech from Archbishop 'Ted' Scott of Canada before the General Synod of the Church of England in which he soundly berated it for not accepting a decision in which it had not been consulted and to which it had not given its consent.

And since that time the Archbishop of Canterbury has been receiving the usual expressions of 'pain' and 'hurt' that the Church of England has not yet conformed to the action of these provinces.

At the seventh meeting of the ACC in Singapore in April 1987 the delegates sought to grapple with what they perceived to be the failure of the consultative bodies of the Communion, and they considered the office of the Archbishop of Canterbury, the Primates' Meeting, and the Consultative Council itself. They did this in the light of the high probability that certain provinces were at the point of consecrating a woman to the episcopate with all the consequences that this would have for the unity of the Communion and the future of ecumenical dialogue. In true Anglican style the Singapore meeting was much better at analysing the problems than offering solutions. They were right to point to the affection with which the holder of the office of Archbishop of Canterbury is held but less than realistic to ignore his actual powerlessness. He has no right to intervene in any province's internal affairs; he can advise and warn but his worldwide journeys have the disadvantage that everywhere he goes he is an honoured guest. It is easy to see what he is shown and to hear only the opinions of the predominant party. There is even a danger that a pleasing personality like Dr Robert Runcie may give an impression of approbation for a local church's stances which is positively misleading. The council's criticisms of the Lambeth Conference were particularly cogent. It is too large and costly; its meetings are infrequent; and it has a disproportionately large number of bishops coming from certain countries. It has acquired a reputation for being badly prepared for and serviced, and its recommendations are increasingly disregarded. The Primates' Meeting is useful for an exchange of information but its members lack the authority to make major recommendations in matters of faith and order. It thus becomes clear that if there is to be a 'central body' with a clear responsibility for Anglican coherence it will have to be a reconstituted Consultative Council; it

(margin note) Holding the Churches in unity

203

will have to meet more frequently, have an adequate secretariat and the assistance of theologians and other experts. It seems probable that there will have to be some self-denying ordinance by which the provinces agree that certain matters shall not be decided locally but only after a common mind has been established among the churches. Finding a constitution for a new kind of Council will not be easy but it is perhaps not too much to say that the future of Anglicanism in the world Christian community depends on its being achieved.

The American
Church: a
study in change

The problems of modern Anglicanism are highlighted by the case of the Episcopal Church in the United States. Among the American churches it is a very small denomination but it has a prestige beyond its size because of the social standing of its membership. To become an Episcopalian has traditionally been a sign of upward mobility in American society. In the 1950s English visitors were impressed by the vigour of the Episcopal Church which seemed to reflect its nation's new confidence as a world power. It had full congregations and its members were generous in their financial contributions. Certainly there were weaknesses. Many of its bishops seemed to have been chosen as administrators and pastoral activists and few of them had any particular qualification as theologians. Indeed the church often gave the impression of being spiritually shallow with much of its preaching devoted to the propagation of 'American' values. It was thus a body which proved highly vulnerable to the rapid liberalisation of middle-class opinion in the 1960s, and many of its younger clergy and seminarians were deeply affected by the radical ideology of the universities of that era. Within a short time the Episcopal Church acquired a strong party for liberal causes, among them a movement for the ordination of women. It was an issue which conservatives found difficult to handle, given the untheological character of Episcopalians and the strength of current opinion about civil rights and sexual equality. Faced by a vociferous campaign, a cautious Presiding Bishop tried to set the debate within the wider context of the unity of the Anglican Communion but in 1974 he found himself confronted with a deliberate act of defiance when three retired bishops ordained certain women to the priesthood in a service which was clearly uncanonical and irregular. The uncertainty with which the House of Bishops handled the situation led to a critical vote in the General Convention at Minneapolis in 1976 when a motion that women should be eligible for all three orders of ministry was passed by a very slender majority. If six votes had been cast differently it would have failed. But by 1978 over 90 women had been ordained as priests. The Episcopal Church thus acted unilaterally with less than a two-thirds majority in its House of Bishops and a bare majority in its House of Deputies.

The consequences for American Anglicanism were momentous, and have not been sufficiently understood in the Communion at large. At the Consultative Council at Singapore in 1987 the American delegates sought to present a reassuring picture of the state of their church. It was said that the issue of the ordination of women was no longer causing serious difficulty; only twelve dioceses did not have women-priests; and the numbers in the breakaway Anglican churches were very small. Unfortunately they did not tell of the methods by which this effect had been achieved or the change in the character of their church which they had involved. It is clear that the major casualty has been the comprehensiveness of the Episcopal Church. In 1977 the House of Bishops issued a 'Statement of Conscience' which affirmed the wide tolerance of Anglicanism and promised that none should be coerced or penalised for conscientious objection to the General Convention's decision. It is, however, apparent that this statement was given a minimal interpretation. Many bishops, including even some who had at first been cautious, exerted great pressure on dissenting clergy to conform, while some liberal bishops acted in ways which were not only in total breach of the spirit of the statement but seemed to be aimed at driving conservatives

The making of liberal ascendancy

205

out of the church. Except in a few dioceses dissenting clergy were denied diocesan office and vetoed for the episcopate. Within a short time the commanding heights of the church were occupied by the liberal party. And the result is obvious to those who have spent some time in the United States, though it may not be readily appreciated by senior English bishops on carefully arranged short visits. The liberal ascendancy has transformed the younger clergy of the Episcopal Church into a national force for radical secular causes. The number of ordinands from the Catholic and Evangelical traditions of Anglicanism has diminished and been replaced by men and women of a remarkable uniformity of outlook. The Episcopal seminaries are centres of a liberalising theology which bears little or no resemblance to traditional Anglicanism; training in the spiritual life is widely discounted and few seminaries have any daily corporate prayer; the sexual mores of both staff and students appear to have broken with the standards usually associated with the Christian ministry. It is significant that Evangelicals have for the first time felt it necessary to establish a separate seminary for their own ordinands.

This liberal ascendancy among the bishops and influential clergy has undoubtedly caused severe tension in the Episcopal community. It has produced styles of leadership and a content of preaching which are deeply unwelcome to the traditional laity, and there has been withdrawal of financial contributions. It has led to the marriage discipline of the church being relaxed to the point where the American pattern of divorce and remarriage is the norm for both clergy and laity. The Episcopal Church has a rapidly changing membership with conservatives withdrawing and liberals from other denominations, notably from the Roman Catholic Church, joining. Perhaps the most difficult position has been that of the traditional clergy. Many felt a great loyalty to Anglicanism as they had understood it: they had no desire to join a schismatic church nor did they wish to become Roman Catholics; many had some sympathy for the ordination of women if it could have been established with ecumenical consent or at least by a consensus within the Anglican Communion. Most have endeavoured to keep their heads down and make their parishes enclaves of an older kind of Anglicanism. Indeed the real strength of the American church today lies in the fine achievement of certain of its great parishes rather than in the quality of its leadership. Significant was the election in 1985 of Bishop Edmond Lee Browning of Hawaii to succeed the deeply respected John M. Allin as Presiding Bishop. Though Bishop Browning has the reputation of a pastoral man who would like to allay tension in his church his early addresses leave no doubt that the primacy of the American Church has now come to a deeply committed libral who may well be expected to press on with the consecration of a woman to the episcopate no matter what the consequences for the Anglican Communion. Indeed there is even a possibility that a woman may well be elected before the Lambeth Conference of 1988 under a special procedure which allows consent to be obtained at a meeting of the General Convention.

It now remains to be seen how the Lambeth Conference of 1988 will deal with an issue which threatens to have such critical implications for the future of Anglicanism. Not only would women-bishops make the episcopate itself a cause of disunity but those whom they ordained, men as well as women, would be unacceptable to many. At a time when the Anglican-Roman Catholic International Commission is making such encouraging progress towards a reconciliation of the two communions there is no doubt that this new question about Anglican orders would be a setback which some would regard as irretrievable. Pope John Paul II in a frank correspondence with the Archbishop of Canterbury has warned against the raising of new obstacles. Doubtless there will be some from the provinces which have already ordained women who will see these disadvantages as a necessary consequence of the pursuit of an important principle and who will refuse to be restrained by the objections of non-

Lambeth 1988: dealing with crisis

Anglican churches. Those of us who are regular readers of the writings of Bishop John S. Spong of Newark will be aware of the type of mind which sets no store by tradition and has scant regard for the ecumenical process. Bishop Spong's interpretation of Anglican comprehensiveness is that everyone should do what seems right to him in conscience and that everyone else should accept it. It is not hard to describe his views as ecclesiologically simplistic and basically sectarian and a recipe for the destruction of Anglicanism as a meaningful communion. On the other hand there will be those like the Bishop of London who would regard the consecration of a woman-bishop without a wider ecumenical consent as so serious a breach of Catholic order that it would dissolve the terms of communion. Bishop Graham Leonard has recently been severely criticised for offering to take into his episcopal care a priest and congregation which had been excluded from the Episcopal Church. It is not necessary here to go into the rights and wrongs of that particular case. What is important is the larger question which it raises: how far can a province go in changing its practice unilaterally while still demanding that other churches and other bishops should observe the strict rules of episcopal collegiality? In Dr Leonard's view the Episcopal Church's treatment of its minority who held to the traditional practice of American Anglicanism justified his action. His colleagues in the English House of Bishops disagreed with him almost to a man, and in this they demonstrated the determination of the bishops of the Communion to maintain episcopal collegiality no matter what the cost in terms of theological and ecclesiological coherence. The statements issued by the ACC meeting at Singapore in 1987 would seem to indicate the manner in which the ordination of women issue will be handled. Behind a screen of talk about unity-in-diversity there will be an attempt to secure a general recognition of women-priests throughout the Communion but there will be counsels of caution and pastoral sensitivity on the issue of women-bishops. It may be, of course, that by the summer of 1988 the consecration of a woman will already have taken place. But no one should underestimate the capacity of a Lambeth Conference to take its real decisions by doing nothing. It is clear that this important meeting ought to be supported by the prayers of Anglicans.

One may well feel great sympathy for the man whose office gives him responsibility for guiding the affairs both of the Anglican Communion and the Church of England. Robert Runcie has been Archbishop of Canterbury since 1980 and has already established himself as a notable holder of the primacy. He has intelligence, personal warmth and a formidable capacity for hard work. He listens well and has built up a range of personal contacts among clergy and laity far wider than that of any of his predecessors. His speeches and addresses are thoughtful, witty and persuasive. In the General Synod he has an ability to influence the course of debate which can be decisive for the success or failure of a motion. In spite of the lack of an adequate staff at Lambeth he has survived the work-load remarkably well with only occasional periods of exhaustion. In what must be the latter part of his primacy he has travelled extensively and has established himself as the friend and confidant of most of the leaders of world-Anglicanism. His influence is now probably at its height. It would therefore be good to be assured that he actually knew what he was doing and had a clear basis for his policies other than taking the line of least resistance on each issue. He has a major disadvantage in not having been trained as a theologian, and though he makes extensive use of academics as advisers and speechwriters, his own position is often unclear. He had the disadvantage of the intelligent pragmatist: the desire to put off all questions until someone else makes a decision. One recalls a lapidary phrase of Mr Frank Field that the archbishop is usually to be found nailing his colours to the fence. All this makes Dr Runcie peculiarly vulnerable to pressure-groups. In a rare synodical moment of self-revelation he once described himself as 'an

An Archbishop in toils

209

unconvinced Anglo-Catholic' though it is the latter part
of that description which should not be taken too
seriously. His effective background is the elitist liberalism
of Westcott House in the immediate post-war years and
this he shares with Dr John Habgood, the Archbishop of
York. In particular it gives him a distaste for those who
are so unstylish as to inhabit the clerical ghettoes of
Evangelicalism and Anglo-Catholicism, and he certainly
tends to underestimate their influence in the spiritual life
and mission of the Church. His clear preference is for men
of liberal disposition with a moderately Catholic style
which is not taken to the point of having firm principles.
If in addition they have a good appearance and are articulate over the media he is prepared to overlook a certain
theological deficiency. Dr Runcie and his closest associates
are men who have nothing to prevent them following
what they think is the wish of the majority of the moment.

The Church of
England: the
problems of
decline

It was unfortunate for Archbishop Runcie that his
going to Canterbury coincided with a period in which
many of the tensions within the Church of England began
to come to the surface. Soon he found himself having to
deal with the challenge of the new theology to the
traditional doctrinal formulations of the Church, with a
scheme for a Covenant with the Free Churches which
recreated old controversies about ecclesiology, and with
persistent demands that there should be a liberalisation of
the stances on divorce, homosexuality and abortion. Basic
to all these pressures was a belief in clergy and laity that
some new departures were needed to arrest a decline in
the influence of the Church which none could fail to
recognise. Between 1960 and 1982 the rate of infant
baptisms for each 1000 of the population fell from 554 to
347. Easter communicants fell from 2,339,000 to
1,674,000 and the annual number of confirmations from
190,713 to 84,566. It would thus appear that fewer than
5 per cent of the English population could be regarded as
Anglican churchgoers and that there was a declining
number even in that vestigial relationship which led them
to use the Established Church for their 'rites of passage'.

It could be reliably estimated that the usual Sunday attendance at all services was under one million and was probably exceeded by attendance at Roman Catholic worship. While prosperous suburban parishes were holding up well there was low morale in the countryside and in the old urban areas. In particular the Church of England was becoming more and more a middle-class community. This was to be seen not only in the character of those recruited to its ministry but in those who were selected to its synods. It has become a Church which reflects the attitudes of the bourgeoisie, both in its constant propensity to guilt and in its highly selective forms of liberalism. The gibe that the Church of England is now the SDP at prayer has enough truth in it to be uncomfortable. Though it remains the Established Church and keeps some of the trappings of its former position few of its leaders, either clergy or laity, have attained eminence in public life; they are too narrowly the products of the system itself. A denomination with such great privileges and substantial endowments which has been so marginalised needs to do something more than entrench itself even more firmly into the attitudes of its remaining constituency.

It may seem to outside observers that the General Synod is at the centre of the government of the Church of England and that the struggles which occur in every group of sessions are to determine the Church's policy. Much of the criticism directed against the Synod is that it has monopolised power which was once better exercised by others. In a recent book *The Synod of Westminster: Do We Need It?* Peter Moore and others dealt caustically with the General Synod as part of a verbose and bureaucratic system which, so far from forwarding the Church's mission, actually wasted its resources and fractured its unity by continually introducing contentious issues. The authors noted a widespread hostility to a body which was dubiously representative of either clergy or laity but which undertook to govern the Church on their behalf. But what the criticism failed to understand is that

Synodical Government?

211

for the most part the Synod is virtually powerless and consistently ineffective. Its strings are pulled from elsewhere. At least the members of the House of Commons have a Government which in extreme circumstances they can vote out of office and the daily operations of which they can influence. The General Synod, by contrast, finds itself faced with a government of the Church which is almost wholly independent of it. The irritation which many bishops feel at having to spend so much time at synod meetings, and their desultory contribution to its debates, is founded on their knowledge that nothing the Synod does has much effect on them, the administration of their diocese or the work of the leadership group within it. Most of the debates are for show. They are set-pieces on reports from the various boards or commissions which have appended to them motions which, whether passed or amended, lead to no action at all. They provide the membership of the Houses of Clergy and Laity with opportunities for speeches and they are then forgotten or passed down to the diocesan synods 'for study'. In theory the Synod has considerable powers over the budget but the details of this are beyond the grasp of everyone except for a few financial experts who can usually be dealt with firmly by the official spokesmen. For a body which meets three times a year for periods of up to five days on each occasion and has a heavy weight of agenda papers, it is disturbing that so very little is actually done. There is a thin stream of Measures, dealing mostly with minor administrative changes, and there are occasionally the excitements of proposed liturgical change. In fact during the seventeen years of the Synod's existence there have been few moments when the future of the Church hung in the balance.

Voices signifying very little

The ineffectiveness of the Synod is shown at every level of its operation. It is usual, for example, at its meeting for elaborate respect to be expressed for the contribution and opinions of the House of Laity. That House has a high sense of its dignity in representing the great majority of practising Anglicans, and it is an unwise clerical speaker

212

who indicates that he thinks the laity less expert in theological matters than the clergy. Certain episcopal speakers, notably the Archbishop of Canterbury, are skilled in appropriating this lay conviction of their own wide experience. Yet behind the courtesies, what is the reality? The House of Laity is a set of men and women who are dubiously representative of anybody. They are not elected by all the people on electoral rolls but by the lay members of deanery synods. They have to be the kind of person with the time and disposition to serve on deanery synod, diocesan synod and General Synod and do the committee work involved in all these. They must be able to spend almost three weeks in the year in London or York. And the result is what might be expected. The members of the House of Laity are rarely in regular employment; they are professional people, the self-employed or retired; and many women among them are widows or clergy-wives. It is a system which makes it almost impossible for young people, working-class men and women, or those bearing responsible positions in business or public life, to participate. When such do become members of the Synod it is at great cost to themselves. The over-all result is a House which is not very impressive. It relies heavily on a few excellent speakers and its formidable small contingent of lay academics. In particular the laity's belief that they can deal with theological matters as competently as the clergy is grievously mistaken and often embarrassing. Certainly most members of the House find themselves overwhelmed by the mass of papers and reports sent to them and there is evidence in speeches that they have not been able to digest the matter adequately. It is evident that the Laity are essentially a reactive body; they respond not so much to argument as to appeals; and they have a disposition to vote for that which is recommended by the public leadership of the Church.

The least persuadable part of the General Synod is the House of Clergy. Over the past seventeen years it has consistently refused its consent to measures which would have changed the character of the Church; and it has thereby become an object of some irritation to the establishment. There are regular campaigns to remove the requirement of a two-thirds majority in each House when alterations are proposed in the doctrine or liturgy of the Church or in its relations with other ecclesiastical bodies. Yet it can hardly be doubted that the clergy would be even more troublesome to the liberal ascendancy if the House were more representative of the parochial clergy. It is true that every diocesan clergyman has a vote directly for the General Synod but these elected proctors account for only 180 members of the House against a total of 250. Apart from six elected university proctors and two members of religious orders the rest come from 'constituencies', the members of which are appointed by bishops or by the Crown. No fewer than 43 members of the House are archdeacons, there by a system which allows the archdeacons in each diocese to nominate one of their own number. The fifteen Deans and Provosts are generally taken to be an assured bloc of votes for liberal causes. From 1987 there will be a new 'constituency' to represent women-deacons. Without these 'fancy franchises' the diocesan clergy would provide an even larger body of resistance. These are priests who bear major responsibility for local pastoral care and who may perhaps be said to speak for their laity as much as any indirectly chosen lay member of the Synod. It will be upon their shoulders that the immediate impact of divisive change will fall. Their convictions, their hopes and fears deserve better than to be dismissed by bishops and laity as mere conservatism.

The Standing Committee of the General Synod   If then the Synod itself is so ineffective, who does direct it and decide when its authority shall be used to further a particular policy? It might be thought that the real power of initiative lies with its Standing Committee, which prepares the agenda, makes appointments to boards and committees, and possesses in its Policy Sub-Committee a set of persons specifically charged to advise on the direction and priorities of the Synod's work. A widespread belief in the importance of the Standing Committee is attested by the vigorous competition which goes into the election of its eight members from the House of Clergy and its eight members from the House of Laity. Yet these elected members report their almost complete powerlessness. Over against them is a solid bloc of ex-officio members: the two archbishops who act as chairmen, two church estates commissioners, and four chairmen of boards, usually bishops. In theory the elected members, with the two prolocutors and the chairman of the House of Laity, ought to be able to determine the business of the committee, but this is emphatically not so. The meeting is large and the proceedings formal; the room is filled with officials and observers of various kinds. It is never made clear who decides on the items of the agenda but these are so crowded and directed to matters of detail that discussion of policy is impossible. Business comes from the various boards and their reports have to be passed on to the Synod no matter what their quality or usefulness. It is said that the first principle of good government is to separate policy decisions from routine business. The emasculation of the Standing Committee lies in the consistent breach of this principle and the control exercised over its business by its chairmen, its officers and the staff of the various boards. Like the ordinary members of the Synod their elected representatives on the Standing Committee are largely reduced to the position of having to react to other people's initiatives. This effect is most clearly seen in the case of the Policy Sub-Committee. The body which is given responsibility for discussing policy in fact never does so. We hear reports that even at their residential meetings the members are faced with papers so loaded with detail that they find themselves being treated as a working-party preparatory to the main committee. When the permanent officials are unable to summon up sufficient dense matter, the practice is for the archiepiscopal chairman to cancel the meeting.

It is a belief almost universally embraced by members

A case of
Yes, Minister?

215

of the Synod that the real power lies with the Church House bureaucracy and in particular with Mr W. D. Pattinson, the Secretary-General. Yet devoted viewers of the television programme *Yes, Minister* will know that senior civil servants have aims which are not the same as those of ministers or politicians. Mr Pattinson is a ubiquitous figure in the Church of England. He is seen in his black jacket and striped trousers at virtually every service or ceremony or meeting. His knowledge of what is going on at every board, committee or cabal does nothing to dispel the notion that he is 'a man of secrets'. Yet the fact is that he is not so much a power-broker as an immensely dedicated and hardworking civil servant, and he presides over a group of administrators who are equally diligent and often hard-pressed. Much of Mr Pattinson's time is spent in attempting to see that complex business is carried through as expeditiously as possible with the limited resources available to him. It is doubtful whether he and his senior colleagues are personally sympathetic to the policies of the liberal establishment but they have to work with all parties and like good civil servants they have a healthy respect for those who exercise real power. Mr Pattinson's influence is thus not on the formation of policy but on the manner of its execution. He is adept at advising on procedures, suggesting names, and outmanoeuvring troublesome groups or dissident individuals. His presence at most committees, his often decisive contribution to discussions, and the air of conspiracy with which he imparts perfectly well-known information have given him the reputation of a wire-puller which is not wholly merited. If anything his fault lies the other way: in allowing the Synod to become bogged down in the complexity of its business and thereby preventing it from doing the things which it was originally intended to do.

The House of Bishops If then synodical government is so ineffective, where does influence lie? The reality is that beside the system of synods, with their elections, debates and votes, there exists another system of episcopal executive authority, the characteristics of which are deference, patronage and self-recruitment. It is the influence of the House of Bishops which over the last five years has increased and is now increasing. Though the diocesan bishops often give the impression of being harassed and overworked men, oppressed by their engagement diaries and their piles of correspondence, their actual power and patronage are recognised by all their clergy. In most dioceses, behind the facade of Bishop's Council, synod, boards and committees, there exists a wholly unelected group, usually called 'the staff meeting', which actually runs the diocese. It consists of the diocesan, the suffragans, the archdeacons and other officials, and it unifies executive action. While a new bishop may find himself working with people appointed by his predecessor, he will nominate all new members of the group, and with them will make all major decisions and exercise most patronage. The elaborate system of episcopal references which governs appointments in the Church of England is in fact operated by such groups. Only the existence of private patronage prevents them having a monopoly in determining the work which shall be given to the clergy. It was once a laudable custom that a bishop would seek to preserve among his senior colleagues a balance between the various churchmanships but this is now increasingly disregarded and bishops appoint suffragans of opinions like their own. A long episcopate will thus leave behind a leadership group in a diocese which will have considerable influence in the appointment of his successor. It is not difficult for a reasonably determined bishop to mould the character of his diocese, and it is an obserable fact that there is a correlation between the way a diocesan synod votes and the views of its bishop. It is sometimes said that in the Church of England there is a 'creative tension' between synodical authority and episcopal authority but the notion severely over-rates the role of a body as occasional as a synod and under-rates the effectiveness of the groups which actually administer the affairs of the dioceses.

The Crown Appointments Commission

With episcopal influence on the increase it becomes all the more important that the Church of England should possess an adequate way of appointing its bishops. The summer of 1987 will see the tenth anniversary of the coming into operation of the Crown Appointments Commission, and those interested in the location of power in the Church must give careful attention to a body which has virtually created the present diocesan episcopate. With it things are most certainly not what they purport to be. In 1977 by an agreement with the then Prime Minister, Mr James Callaghan, a commission of members of the General Synod was set up to propose names for appointment to diocesan bishoprics. This followed a period of agitation for the Church to be given 'a decisive voice' in such appointments. It was known that Archbishop Coggan was uneasy at what he feared would be a diminution of the Archbishop of Canterbury's position as the Prime Minister's chief adviser, and the composition of the new commission was carefully devised. The two archbishops were to be members ex officio and each was to act as chairman when a vacancy in his own province was under consideration. Three members were to be elected by the House of Clergy and three from the House of Laity. On each occasion they would be joined by four persons elected by the Vacancy-in-See committee of the diocese concerned. Special arrangements were to apply when an appointment was to be made to one of the archbishoprics. The Commission was to be serviced by the Archbishops' Patronage Secretary and the Prime Minister's Patronage Secretary and its meetings were to be strictly confidential. It was agreed that it should propose two names in a preferred order to the Prime Minister who could either choose one of them or call for further names.

Choosing bishops

It is this system which by the summer of 1987 has chosen for all but eight of the forty-three sees which come within its competence, and it may now be useful to examine its working. It is not at all easy for an outsider (or even an ordinary Synod member) to know what goes on in it. Its business is kept elaborately secret and its members are required to take precautions to see that the day and place of their meeting is not known. Its annual report is presented by Professor J. D. McClean with that air of judicial impartiality and deliberate lack of information which has made him the leading lay figure in the new liberal ascendancy. The impression is given of a dispassionate body, working confidentially to eliminate any embarrassment to those being considered, seeking men whom they may promote on ability alone, and gathering information by diligent consultation. Much is made of the welcome which the permanent members offer to the diocesan representatives. In 1986 a group of 'three wise men', Lord Blanch, Professor Henry Chadwick and Mr Oswald Clark, were asked to comment on the working of the system. Their report is a synodical masterpiece and a case study in the failure of even very distinguished members of the General Synod to see the wood for the trees. They concentrated on the minutiae of procedure and wholly failed to ask the real questions. Who in fact does manage the system and what kind of an episcopate has it created? For it is clear to the members themselves that behind the secrecy, the mandarin officials, and the elaborate consultations, a complex power-game is being played out with momentous consequences for the future of the Church of England.

The meetings of the Commission take place over two days. On the first two patronage secretaries produce dossiers of persons, usually as many as fifteen, who are to be considered. The names have been suggested by a variety of sources, the archbishops, other bishops, members of the commission and (more recently) by the dioceses themselves. The secretaries will have visited the vacancy-in-see committee and made their own soundings in the locality from people whom they think influential. It quickly becomes apparent what great power rests with the secretaries: they compile the list of candidates, they report on the result of their soundings, and they produce extracts from reports on the men being considered. Until recently they did not divulge the sources of their information. The secretaries have a privileged position. To question whether their assessments are fair or adequate is 'bad form' and at once countered from the chair. It is never made clear how the list of names has been arrived at nor how far it has previously been discussed with the archbishops. Much of this first day is spent in 'discarding' names, and for some there is such sparse information that this was their inevitable fate from the beginning. It is on the second day, when only four or five candidates remain, that the dynamics of the group come into operation. The role of the archbishops is now crucial. Their status, the authority which comes from their wide knowledge of the work of individuals, and their professed concern for issues wider than those of a single diocese give them a decisive influence in directing discussion, though they are careful not to declare their preference at too early a stage. Much of the debate is carried on by the elected members. In the commission of 1982–7 the three clergy and three laity appeared to have been elected to represent the three traditional parties of Catholic, Evangelical and Liberal, but the significant fact was that the 'Evangelical' members sided consistently with the Liberal ones to prevent the appointment of Catholic-minded bishops. It is, in fact, easy to veto candidates. The negative opinion of a majority of the elected members is enough to lead to a name being discarded and even the strongly voiced objection of a single person can lead to the same effect. The commission of 1982–7 was unfortunate in possessing one member who indulged in destructive character assessments of individuals who displeased him and who affected close knowledge of diocesan opinion though this rested on little which could be called impartial. He should not have been allowed the influence which he undoubtedly exercised. It is sometimes said that the decisive voice is that of the diocesan representatives, and it is true that if they combine to refuse a man he has no chance of further consideration. But since the recommendation is that a diocese should be represented by men and women of differing viewpoints it is usually not difficult for a chairman to steer enough of their votes in the right direction. The main problem with diocesan members is their predilection for someone who already has episcopal experience and thus for a suffragan bishop, himself once the appointee of a diocesan bishop.

The reality of the Crown Appointments Commission has been, at least over the past five years, a predominant influence of the two archbishops, exercised with the aid of the Liberal and 'Evangelical' members. With the arrival of Dr Runcie and Dr Habgood at Canterbury and York there were in the two archbishoprics men who shared the same basic outlook and worked closely together to create a new kind of episcopate. The result has been a virtual exclusion of Anglo-Catholics from episcopal office and a serious under-representation of Evangelicals. There have been Evangelical appointments, though often from the more liberal wing of the movement. In the past it was thought the way of wisdom in a comprehensive Church to have the leading clergy of the different traditions of churchmanship among the bishops. Even in the days of Evangelical or Anglo-Catholic predominance there was no policy of marginalising those of different opinions. The present discrimination is sometimes explained as a policy of appointing 'central' candidates rather than 'party' men but it must be a matter of legitimate doubt whether Liberals are so central to the life and spirituality of the Church of England or whether they are foremost in its mission. One thing cannot be doubted: the personal connection of so many appointed with the Archbishop of Canterbury himself. A brief biographical study will reveal the remarkable manner in which the careers of so many bishops have crossed the career of Dr Runcie: as students or colleagues at Westcott House and Cuddesdon, as incumbents or suffragans in the dioceses of St Albans or Canterbury, or as persons working in religious broadcasting at a time when he was chairman of the Central Religious Advisory Committee of the BBC and IBA.

What kind of bishops?

221

There is indeed no more fertile recruiting ground for the new establishment than Broadcasting House. Though one may accept that an archbishop should have an influence on appointments, it is clearly unacceptable that so many are the protegés of one man and reflect his own ecclesiastical outlook. Those who speak so glibly of the Crown Appointments Commission as designed to allow 'the Church' to have a decisive voice in appointments should ask themselves some pertinent questions as to whose voice the commission does actually represent.

The Prime Minister and the bishops

There has recently been much speculation in the Press, aided by some inspired leaks from members of the Crown Appointments Commission, about the role of the Prime Minister in the appointment of bishops. The fact is that Mrs Thatcher has always acted in complete conformity with the terms on which the Commission was set up. If anything, her office has been over-ready to co-operate with the archbishops and disinclined to challenge the names proposed even in the face of constant complaints that the system was producing an unbalanced episcopate. Only in a few instances where the Commission over-reached itself and would have brought into the House of Bishops one of the shriller exponents of the opinions of Dr Spacely-Trellis had the second name proposed been preferred. Indeed the degree to which 10 Downing Street has come under the influence of Lambeth Palace is shown in the curious case of the appointment of Deans, which has not yet come under the aegis of a synodical commission. There is no more consistent body of liberal stalwarts than the inhabitants of deaneries, though some of them are of the old 'Church and State' variety. They are largely recruited from former members of the staff of Church House and Broadcasting House with the addition of some archdeacons who have come up through their local diocesan establishments. One does not doubt that they were selected after the usual consultations and after advice was sought from the diocesan bishop and Lambeth. Indeed it cannot be said that most, or even many, deans are obviously the kind of people whom the present Prime Minister would choose. One can only offer some advice to the patronage secretary at 10 Downing Street by suggesting that too much reliance on the opinions of the local establishment may well lead to the vetoing of men who would be well qualified for a cathedral ministry. It could be a justification of Crown patronage in the present circumstances that it worked to preserve a comprehensive Church rather than placed yet more power in the hands of those who already have too much.

The appointments of the last ten years are now beginning to have their effect in the formation of the Church's policy. Synod-watchers have begun to take it for granted that there will be a wide gap between the voting pattern of the bishops and that of the clergy with large majorities among the former for liberal causes. Whereas in the early days of the Synod the House of Bishops played a relatively minor role, now as its character has become more consolidated it has begun to take initiatives and even put pressure on the Synod to adopt particular courses. Inded the Archbishop of Canterbury has warned us to expect a much higher profile from the House. Notable was their attempt to obtain a new marriage discipline with the bishops giving permission for the re-marriage of divorced persons. More recently they procured the withdrawal of the 'McClean' report suggesting ways of dealing with the conscientious objections of those who could not accept the ministrations of women-priests. Increasingly the Bishops are asserting their rights as the guardians of the doctrinal formularies of the Church, though few of them perhaps could be regarded as eminent theologians. A sign of the times is the increasing isolation of the diminishing number of Anglo-Catholic bishops. Many of them are now older men moving towards retirement and their resistance to the liberalisation of the Church is becoming somewhat weary. Most exposed of all is Dr Graham Leonard, the Bishop of London, whom the Press love to portray as the Archbishop Lefebvre of the Anglican Communion. He

The Liberal Establishment feels its strength

223

has not always been particularly adroit in the presentation of his case and he has a predilection for popish ecclesiastical outfits but all this should not obscure the simple fact that his ideas on faith and order place him securely in the mainstream of Anglicanism. A series of small books which seek to offer a modern spirituality based on a traditional theology makes him one of the few bishops able to speak to those who feel the spiritual emptiness of so many Church publications. More precarious is the position of the group of Evangelical bishops. They represent a growing constituency in the Church with many strong parishes and an increasing proportion of ordination candidates. Their unease with the theological liberalism of many of their colleagues is manifest but they hesitate publicly to distance themselves from them. It could be wished that some of the really able men among them such as Bishop Michael Baughen of Chester and Bishop John Taylor of St Albans would exhibit a stronger Evangelical presence. The majority of the present episcopate is not strident in its policies and many are genuinely pastoral men. They have indeed been considerably irritated by the pastoral insensitivity and intemperate partisanship of Bishop David Jenkins of Durham, and many of them have come to see that the appointment of a man of such imprecision of mind and expression under the guise of being a theologian was a minor Anglican disaster. The controversies which he has initiated have revealed the highly ambiguous position which many bishops hold on central matters of doctrine, and this they would prefer to avoid. The report by the House of Bishops in 1986, *The Nature of Christian Belief*, was a highly self-conscious and ambiguous document, designed to defend their orthodoxy and yet revealing the latitude which some bishops expected for themselves. Most diocesans are, of course, not concerned with such abstruse matters. Their liberalism is in practical matters and they give the impression of having stumbled into it rather than having thought it through; they are going along with what they think is majority opinion. Of

course when the controversies become rough and prospect of schism comes into view there is much backtrack-
ing. But deep in the liberal mind is a conviction that with
a little procrastination and an application of pastoral
'sensitivity' the changes which they propose can be forced
through. That there may be issues of fundamental
principle at stake is not a notion readily understood. It is
continually discounted by Archbishop Habgood, the
leading theological relativist among the bishops. It thus
seems likely that the time is near when the House of
Bishops will throw its full weight behind the movement
for the ordination of women to the priesthood. Opposition to this among the bishops has now been marginalised
and the House can now proceed with the assurance that
only a few (and that a diminishing number) will refuse to
co-operate. It begins to look as though the Archbishop of
Canterbury has now overcome his fear that there might
be a substantial withdrawal of clergy. His clear change of
stance would indicate that he now thinks the damage can
be contained and that it is necessary in the interests of the
Anglican Communion at large and to satisfy what he
conceives of as majority opinion in the Church of
England.

It is, of course, possible that a preoccupation with The real
particular issues may obscure the Church's real needs in agenda
an increasingly difficult situation. The times are perhaps
hard for the communication of the Christian Gospel and
there is clearly no simple formula for winning the English
people back to the faith of Christ but there are certainly
areas of the Church's life which need urgent consideration. They are matters on which all Anglicans can be
united rather than divided.

The Rural Mission. Perhaps the most serious problem
of all is the future of the Church of England in the
countryside. A hundred years ago the heart of the
pastoral work was in the rural communities where in
virtually every village there was a parish church and a
church school with a priest resident among the people.
The life of the local church was an important contribu-

tion towards the identity of the community. Now, at a time when most other denominations have largely withdrawn from the rural scene, the Church's ministry is beginning to struggle badly. The English countryside is a place quite different from what it was only twenty-five years ago. There are fewer people working on the land and village schools, shops and bus services are under constant threat. By a misguided policy, based on the so-called 'Sheffield Report', the Church has progressively stripped its manpower from the countryside, and now a few priests are spread thinly over the parishes. In a diocese like Lincoln the number of villages which have to be cared for by one man represent an impossible task if a real pastoral ministry is envisaged. Houses and glebe have been disposed of and teams of clergy work valiantly each Sunday to provide services for small congregations. Yet the closure of an ancient parish church, when so much else has been withdrawn, would be a serious moral blow to the village, and there is ample evidence of the value to a rural community of a caring and spiritually minded pastor. At a time when there is so much discussion of a ministry to the inner cities there is urgent need for new thinking about the rural ministry and new encouragement for the clergy and lay people involved in it.

Problems in the City. Of course, like the nation at large, the Church does have to face the dereliction of the older urban areas with their high unemployment, poor housing and a population largely alienated from that other Britain which is prosperous and secure. It is a sign of hope that Anglicans have produced a report as challenging and informative as *Faith in the City*. Yet it has little for our comfort. The Anglican presence in the inner cities is relatively small and weak, and the fine and sacrificial work done by the clergy there is with only a few in a vast, unchurched population. If there is a Christian presence it is often mainly represented by the Roman Catholic Church, and it is in co-operation with them that we have to plan any strategy. The work in Liverpool of its two bishops is an earnest of what can be achieved. The Church of England's Urban Fund has now been established and it should soon have a substantial endowment not only from the Church Commissioners but from dioceses, parishes and private contributions. It is important that this money be properly used. Many will be concerned that it should not be spent on projects which simply duplicate the government's provision of social services, nor must it become the modern equivalent of charity by which well-meaning outsiders come into the city to do things for its inhabitants. It must be used to draw out a sense of local community and to encourage local leadership and self-help. It is understood that the Church must care for the whole man or woman and cannot confine its mission to the purely evangelistic but it may be that a sense of Christian community is not the least gift which the Church can bring. It must certainly try to evolve new forms of worship and ministry appropriate to those in considerable personal and economic deprivation.

Black People in the Church. One important result of *Faith in the City* has been a new concern for Black people in the life of the Christian communities. Many citizens of African or Caribbean origin have a background in countries with a strong Anglican presence, and it is a deeply disturbing fact that some do not believe themselves to have been made welcome in English parishes. There has been a rapid increase in the number of independent local churches which are Black-led and which reflect in their worship the style and preferences of the Black communities. But in the case of many young people there has been a progressive alienation from any kind of religious practice. In a recent debate in the General Synod the members listened with dismay to stories of neglect and perceived rejection at the hands of white congregations. An unwise decision of the Standing Committee not to set up a Commission for Black Anglican Concerns, as had been recommended by *Faith in the City*, was greeted with outraged protests by Black opinion. It would, however, be over-simple to ascribe this uneasy relationship merely to white racism in the churches, and such accusations cause real distress. The majority of white Anglicans are not racists; they are middle-class men and women who do not find it all that easy to understand or mix with working-class people, whatever their colour. Most churches have a style of worship and a content of preaching which quite unconsciously reflect white, middle-class attitudes and concerns. The differences are not so much ones of colour as of class and culture, and the real problem is to increase common understanding. One side needs to abandon suspicion and a tendency to instant accusation and the other side needs to exercise its imagination. It is greatly to be hoped that the new sub-committee of the Standing Committee will work on some constructive suggestions, to eliminate any kind of discrimination, whether conscious or unconscious, and to point to ways by which Black and White people can be one in Christian love and fellowship; they must be more than a body for the detection and articulation of grievance. There is certainly an urgent need for a quite new deal for Black people in the Church, for new styles of worship and for the fostering of Black vocations to the ministry. And it is possible that in such new approaches we may take the first steps towards rescuing the Church of England from its present suburban captivity and making it once again a Church for the English people.

Ascensiontide 1987

THREE SERMONS

The Grace of Humility

A University Sermon preached at Oxford, 16 February 1969
Galatians 5.26: 'We must stop being conceited, provocative and envious'

The Reverend William Master founded this sermon 'on the grace of humility' in 1684. He was a country clergyman and a moralist; and he deeply disapproved of the things which went on in Restoration Oxford. To his mind, accustomed to the rural simplicities of Preston, near Cirencester, the young of his old university appeared extravagantly dressed; they talked with an unheard-of freedom in sexual matters; and they appeared to relish political excitement more than application to their books. Their elders were factious and assertive, and concerned more with the even tenor of their ways than with urgent reformation. What better gift than a sermon in which on the Sunday before Lent the assembled university of Oxford should be given some unvarnished admonition on the subject of humility?

Now it is quite clear what Mr Master thought humility was. The preacher of this sermon has to choose his text from a prescribed set of thirteen scripture passages all of a severely hortatory character; and these thirteen texts plus a little research reveal the secret. They are all to be found in the sixth chapter of the 17th century devotional classic known as *The Whole Duty of Man*; and that chapter (you will not be surprised to learn) is on 'the grace of humility'. As we read those faded but eloquent pages we learn what picture of humility was presented to the tens of thousands whose spiritual life was formed by this immensely popular book. It was conceived of in terms of self-abnegation and self-control. The *Whole Duty of Man* was the precursor of a whole *genre* of pietistic literature which was to become immensely influential in Victorian England: whose object was to drive men to virtue by the path of fear. The method is perhaps worthy of note. Some vanity or vainglory is set before us; and a cool, prudential, insistent voice begins to speak. We are shown the transitory character of our human existence: withered beauty, fading · strength, vanished glory, the worm in the skull. There is even an anticipation of the modern advertisement. Are we quite sure that other people are not laughing at us? The voice goes on to suggest that perhaps we are not just falling into folly—but even into danger. The author never actually *mentions* hell—but he has a subtle way of indicating that he can smell burning. So what must we do? His advice is urgent. We must 'conquer ourselves, overcome our unruly passions, which of all victories is the greatest and most noble'. And we must strive to imitate the humility of Christ. With some intense pathos he expounds the character of Jesus in terms of Matthew 11.29: 'Learn of me, for I am gentle and humble in heart'. Our Lord is represented as gentle, placid, and inoffensive; thinking well of everybody, accepting all insults and offences. And at the end of the book there is an unnerving list of questions for self-examination. *Are* we humble enough? Do we have 'a mean and low opinion of ourselves'; are we 'content that others should have so of us'?

Self-control, conformity to an idealised portrait of a placid Christ: one wonders what damage this kind of spirituality has done. It has certainly worked deeply into the English religious mind the notion that a real Christian is good-natured, but somehow weak and ineffective. Those golden-haired sweet Jesuses of Victorian illustrated prayer-books are part of a continuing tradition. In English literature and drama clergymen are either intelligent, and thereby not quite respectable, or well-meaning but unworldly and inconsequential. Dean Swift once remarked in his sharp manner that the English would forgive their clergy anything but wit and intelligence. And so what view of man has been presented for popular admiration? Among others the insipid Arthur in Thomas Hughes's otherwise muscular *Tom Brown's Schooldays* or even the preposterous Eric in Dean Farrar's *Eric or Little by Little*. Such a vision of man has been a stumbling-block to many who have had some notion of the inner depths of our human nature. One thinks of Swinburne's bitter lines:

'Thou hast conquer'd, O pale Galilean,
The World has grown grey from thy breath';

or of Edward Gibbon's vehement protest at his own early religious upbringing. Virtually the whole of the *Decline and Fall* is an attack on the unnatural suppression of normal vigour in favour of a foolish insipidity of character. He continually contrasts classical paganism with its 'love of pleasure and love of action' with the servile qualities admired by the early Christians:

an insensible and inactive disposition . . . would be rejected, by the common consent of mankind, as utterly incapable of procuring any happiness to the individual or any public benefit to the world. But it was not in *this* world that the primitive Christians were desirous of making themselves either agreeable or useful.

This is a point with which most modern psychologists (and indeed anthropologists) would readily agree. It *is* highly doubtful whether humility in the sense of suppression of natural vigour is the path to health or mental balance. Self-effacement, meekness, a yielding to others are more likely to be a mark of those who are in some measure *ill*. On the contrary it would seem that *aggression*, an impulse to dominate and subdue, is a more genuinely normal attitude to the world around us. There are some psychologists, notably Americans, who would dispute this. They hold that man is not by nature aggressive, and that he has no *inner need* to act thus; his aggression is only a response to an unsatisfactory environment. Remove the pressures, and you may discover again a basically peaceable being. The view may *appear* to be optimistic, and it fits in well with the assumptions of social improvers; but it would not seem to commend itself much to psychologists in general. They see aggressiveness as an essential part of the make-up of a normal man. Primitive man was a hunter and a builder; and his aggression was not just for survival but for the purpose of subduing his environment and creating a better life. From this impulse to explore, to master the world of things, and to secure his independence from them, has come some of his most significant achievements: his science and his art, his defences against poverty and sickness. Such aggression is necessary, too, for our mental health. It is necessary if we are to break the bonds of infantile dependence and make our way to our own separate, autonomous existence. Human beings have an extraordinarily prolonged childhood; and in this lengthy dependence on our parents lies great danger. To submit to someone else is to feel yourself in their power, and to be insecure. Unless at the right moment we have the personal force to assert our individuality all kinds of retardation disorders may come. The real peril lies in having our natural aggression suppressed or frustrated. *Then* it may well break out in disguise, in illness or irrational anger. And so a healthy child will not be passive and placid, as the Victorians seemed to expect, but will take quite naturally to games of simulated aggression. Whether we like it or not, children *love* plays and stories with violence in them; and we, if we are honest, will admit that we enjoy boxing matches and war-films. And, of course, all of us know how deeply satisfying we find a bit of anger, if only we can persuade ourselves that it is righteous. The fact is that while we profess to admire placidity and meekness, most of us would find an unmixed diet of it tedious beyond all endurance.

But all this is not to deny that the aggressive side of our nature is deadly dangerous. If it lies behind our achievements, there is the stark fact that we are (in Dr. Anthony Storr's words) 'the cruellest and most ruthless species that has ever walked the face of the earth'. Animals kill for food, and they do so without hatred; they practically never kill animals of their own kind. Only man does this: kill his own kind unnecessarily and with hatred. This is our dilemma. How shall we reconcile our natural creative drive with the need that we shall not be perverted into hatred and self-destruction? In its way civilization tries to solve the problem: it attempts to unite us for positive objects while letting us work out our competitiveness in harmless ways, in games and competitions and politics, where nobody is actually killed or maimed—at least not usually. But the examples are abundant where this kind of civilized remedy has broken down into war and violence.

It is tempting to say that the answer must lie in the sphere of education, and in the training of individuals in self-restraint. But here we need to be careful. Say I do have this old-fashioned view of humility and peaceableness, and following some ideal (perhaps Jesus himself) I strive to hold myself in restraint, to suppress within myself all this aggressiveness, this urge to handle other people violently. I put on a show of meekness and humility. But it is *an act*. I am trying to be something which I am not. On the outside, there is this carefully constructed picture of a man, placid, gentle and yielding, but inside there is the real me, wanting to dominate. In this state it is doubtful whether we shall have much in the way of peace and joy to go with our humility. And if I forbid my aggression to appear on the surface, it will certainly escape my guard and appear in disguise. It is a fact which you may have noticed that the life of groups which make heavy moral demands on their members is marked by internal disputes, schisms and persecutions, the Christian Church not least among them. And the most earnest and virulent disputants have been the men who treated themselves most severely by discipline and self-control. A church historian may be permitted the reflection that much of what has passed as dispute on high doctrinal principle has, in fact, been only a desire in disguise to impose oneself on others. Certainly much insistence on *moral* principle is based on a will to bend other people's lives to one's own. Even our admiration for the virtue of humility itself is often self-deception; and this indeed was clearly the case with *The Whole Duty of Man*. Its popularity lay not with the children, servants and employees who had to read it, but with the parents, masters and employers who thought that humility *in others* was a treasure beyond price. But the cool fact remains, that you cannot manufacture humility; and if you try to you will not in the long run be very convincing. Men will quickly detect the unease and violence which lies beneath, and you will fail to win them or their love.

How subtly this was shown in that excellent post-war film, *The Prisoner*, in which Alec Guinness played the role of a cardinal, leader of the Roman Catholic community in a Communist country. At first he appears as a strong man of principle: calm, moderate, and courteous, but utterly devoted to the religious liberties of his people. He is arrested in his cathedral while celebrating Mass, and taken to prison to be interrogated. And here in the person of the head of the secret police he is confronted with a mind as keen as his own, and more subtle. Like an analyst the interrogator probes; he reveals past history: the ambition and ruthlessness which had led the young priest up the ladder of preferment; the poverty-stricken spiritual life; the anxiety which went into keeping up the appearance of being a humble pastor of the flock; and the facade of humility which covered so much self-dramatisation. In the process of this dreadful revelation the cardinal is reduced to self-despair, and the interrogator believes that he has the game in his hand; there will be a public trial and an abject confession. But the result is *not* quite that. In discovering himself the priest is able to discover as well a new meaning of the loving mercy of God. And in this he finds a strength greater than his former strength.

And so what is an alternative view of 'the grace of humility'? That is, if it is still to be considered as a fundamental ingredient of Christian character? If it cannot be manufactured, from whence does it come?

It comes from an ability first of all *to accept ourselves as we are*. If I understand the meaning of the gospels aright they do not *primarily* present Jesus as an example or an ideal to be followed. As in his encounter with the Rich Young Ruler, Our Lord was well aware of the danger of a religion which presented itself primarily in terms of rules, or standards, or indeed ideal persons to be imitated. He clearly did not present himself in that light; and we must take care not to construct some portrait of what we *suppose* his character to have been, and then impose it upon our lives as mandatory. The ideal or the standard will always be there to persecute us, and our idea of Christian spirituality will be that of a candidate in an examination-room or a prisoner in the dock. Against such a view of life and religion Jesus uttered his strongest protest; from such a view he promised freedom. 'Come unto me all ye who labour or are heavy laden' is addressed not to those wearied by physical labour, but those who have made their own lives a thing of self-concern and anxiety. Real Christianity begins with *the grace of a humble acceptance of the truth about ourselves*. Jesus's encounters with individuals were surely directly to this end. By a deft surgery of probing questions he removes the layers of self-justification and illusion which we build up about ourselves: whether the unreality of pride in our own excellence OR an equally false conviction of our own worthlessness.

But *how* do we accept ourselves? How do we have the courage to be ourselves, to accept what we are? Our ability to do so can only come when we have the assurance established in us that *God* has accepted us *just as we are*. This is the ground of our humility: that gracious word of God penetrating through our fog of fear and illusion, anxiety and self-concern, to tell us that we, even we, are accepted. Is not this Jesus's own method? To lead men to the truth about themselves, and yet *at the very same time* to declare to them that, no matter how imperfect they may be, God is forgiving and that he accepts?

From this assurance then will flow *two kinds of humility*.

The first is humility *with regard to myself*. I can be humble in the sense that, being what I am without fear, I can be gentle with myself. Shall I continue to be harsh with myself, condemning my failures, anxious about what I shall become? 'It is God who justifies. Who is he that condemns?' Certainly not we ourselves. So if I accept this quintessence of the gospel, then I have no need for an apparatus of despotism over myself. I can dismantle it, and be simply myself, warts and all: 'just as I am without one plea'. My humility stems from the fact, not that I am frightened into virtue but that I am called to a creative freedom. My old position was based on an underlying weakness and sense of failure; my new one is based on a position of strength. It is based on the absolute strength of Almighty God and the word of his gospel.

The second kind of humility is humility *towards others*. So much of our harshness and uncharity to others stems from our inner insecurity. Usually it is that some aspect of their character or conduct seems to represent a threat to our own personalities and position. I am, for example, lustful—but by an effort of self-control I suppress this and convince myself and the world around that I am the model of chastity. And then there comes along some young man who is successful with all the girls and who flirts with them outrageously. I find myself unreasonably hostile to him and bitterly censorious. But if by grace I can admit all the things I am, and perceive God's acceptance of me, then perhaps I shall be able to accept that young man as he really is, without putting upon him a caricature which comes from my own fears and frustrations. I can look upon other people in a new and compassionate light, knowing that both they and I are in the same boat: we both depend upon the mercy which God wills to have upon all men.

And so if humility is based on the security which springs from the gospel, and if it allows us to face the truth about ourselves and others: then it is of vital importance for those aggressive impulses of ours. My aggression will not be distorted by illusion and fear and turned to other men's destruction. Rather the creative drive will be directed, as it can be, to the problems and obstacles which still stand between men and their human fulfillment. But this is only a way of saying that we shall have discovered the true nature of the grace of humility: that it flows not from ourselves but from God. Human beings come to their full stature not by their own contrivance but by responding to his love by faith in him through Jesus Christ Our Lord

To whom with the Father and the Holy Spirit
be all glory and praise.

The Oxford Movement, 1833–1983

A sermon preached in Manchester Cathedral on 14 July 1983
2 Pet. 3.13: 'We wait for new heavens and a new earth
where righteousness dwells.'

The church of God has an extraordinary power to renew itself. Just when it seems that all vision has failed, the springs of spirituality have run dry and mission has ceased, then there is a sudden surge of new life and expectancy. Certainly in 1833 the Church of England seemed almost dead. Indeed the famous Dr Arnold of Rugby said publicly that there was no human power which could save her as she was then. Serious misuse of resources, an almost total lack of pastoral provision for the new industrial cities of the North, and a general hostility throughout the country: all this added up to a church in real trouble. And the worst thing was that she seemed incapable of doing anything about it herself. More and more, people were looking to the Government, the secular politicians, to legislate to reform the Church, but in 1833 neither Parliament nor public office was confined to Anglicans or even Christians.

Yet this was to be a moment of renewal, and one which began in a place which seemed the very citadel of old Church of England privilege: the University of Oxford. It began with a group of young clergymen, each in his way brilliant, fresh and visionary. They were members of Oriel College because to be elected a Fellow there was, at that time, a token that a man was one of the ablest of his generation. They looked to John Keble as their leader because he was rather older than the rest and the chief tutor of the college. Nothing can diminish Keble's spiritual stature. He was academically brilliant yet a man

240

of deep humility, simplicity of heart and transparent goodness. He had no greater ambition than to be a parish priest, and the greater part of his ministry was to be spent at Hursley, near Winchester. What was perhaps characteristic of him was that he was a poet, and in his poet's way he could look at the Church and see through all its dullness, cynicism, careerism and lack of real faith, to what was within, to what it could be; he could understand what riches of prayer and worship and overflowing grace it had in store, if only it could bring them out of its treasury.

Keble's pupil, John Henry Newman, always dated the beginning of the Oxford Movement precisely, to 14 July 1833, when Keble preached in St. Mary's, Oxford, his famous sermon before the Assize Judge on 'National Apostacy'. At first view it seems like a vehement attack on the Whig Government of the day for passing an act to reduce the number of bishoprics in Ireland, but as you read on you see that it is more than that. He is asking a critical question: 'What is the *real* nature of the Church? In what does its very being consist: its inner glory, freshness and power? What makes it different from being part of the English constitution, or a historical museum, or an agency for social welfare or the agitation of moral causes?' Keble's answer was clear. The Church had one end: to make Christ, the Crucified and Risen Lord, known. In spite of all its sin and failure, this community is still his Catholic Church: an extension of the Incarnation, the place where He is today present, drawing men and women to Himself by the bands of love and reconciling them to their God. It is His Church, one, holy, Catholic and apostolic, where men and women who live in a sinful world are being called into a distinctive community of faith and love.

The Oxford Movement was, then, a Catholic revival in the sense that it re-affirmed that a Christian was not just one who believed certain things but one who belonged to a divine society. Indeed for Keble, Newman and Pusey it was always the Church which was the teacher of divine truth. They had a deep suspicion of the solitary intellectual who (all on his own) thought that he could discover all that there was to be known about Christianity. They saw the Church as possessing a holy Tradition, a wisdom of long experience of turning theology into prayer and vocation and service. In the common life of the community religious ideas were tested and proven by seeing whether they led on to love, unity and mission. When, as Vicar of St Mary's, Newman listened to the sermons of the Regius Professor of Divinity, R. D. Hampden, he experienced a kind of despair. Here was a learned and clever man, but all this stress on evidence and proof, all this assertion of the latest fashionable intellectual theories, all this contempt for what he called 'magic and mystery': you would think that he discovered nothing in his prayer, never knew God the more clearly in humble penitence or in a moment of sheer joy and praise. How different it was with Dr Pusey, also a Regius Professor! He felt that he could not begin to be a theologian except by following the rhythm of the Church's prayer and receiving the grace of the sacraments. Keble himself rejoiced that so much of Anglican teaching was to be found in a Prayer Book, a rule of Prayer and sacrament which went right back to the Early Church in a continuous succession of believing and praying Christians. The Oxford Fathers laid so much stress on the historic ministry, the succession of bishops, continuity in liturgy, because these were the outward and visible signs of a holy community living down the ages in the apostles' teaching and fellowship.

But one does not understand the movement without realising its passionate concern for holiness of life. They looked for nothing less than the transformation of man by the grace of God. And by grace they meant the Holy Spirit putting into our minds and hearts the image of Christ. As by grace they received the impress of His perfect humanity, so they became more like Him and they became one with the Eternal Father. Pusey used language which might seem almost extreme. Christ, he said, took our human nature and transfigured it; He raised it up to God and *deified* it. This is humanism in the true Christian sense of the word, and it is full of hope: a conviction that sanctifying grace can transform the sinful, weak and inadequate into *saints*. It led on to a new sense of oneness with the great saints of the Church, and an awareness of their ministry of intercession. It set on foot a revival of the religious life in the Church of England. It restored the Eucharist to a central place in the Church's worship. But not least it revived for many a priest and ordinand a new sense of vocation: that by God's calling and the enabling of His grace a man might share in the bitter-sweet mystery which lets a poor, sinful creature become a channel of grace for others.

One thing the Oxford Movement Fathers were not afraid of was *change*. Because they had a vision of what the Church *could be*, they longed to reform it and make it more effective. Though men like Keble and Pusey loved the Church of England, they were well aware of her faults. We sometimes forget just how innovative they were, and how much of the transformation of the Church was due to their impetus. They advocated a massive sharing-out of the historic endowments; they developed a new kind of ministry to the urban poor, to the slums and society's outcasts; they transformed worship by introducing colour, movement and music; they were leaders in a vast missionary movement which has carried their vision to much of the Anglican Communion. But above all they were pioneers in Christian Unity. Looking today at Pusey's writings, one sees how much of the modern ecumenical movement he had anticipated. And it was Newman, who went to Rome, who took into the thinking of that great communion many of the distinctive ideas of the movement he had left behind, and in this generation they are bearing fruit in the thought of the Second Vatican Council.

Perhaps that is the note for this celebration of this 150th anniversay: that this was (and by God's grace still is) a movement of life because it is rooted in the life which comes from our Lord Himself and is a perpetual source of renewal for us.

'If I only had one sermon to preach . . .'

A sermon preached as a Lenten Address,
Liverpool Parish Church, 1987

If I had only one sermon to preach, it would of course have to be about the love and free mercy of God to sinners, for that is the essence of the Gospel of Christ. It should be the Church's constant theme because it is something which the world desperately needs and which no one else can offer. One of the sad things about much modern Christianity is the way its spokesmen are continually moralising, exhorting, and condemning. To listen to some of our leaders it would be easy to get the impression that the Church thought of itself as being expert in economics, industrial policy, or politics. But I suspect that the world takes much of this with a pinch of salt. They know that Christians *as Christians* are no more expert or informed about these things than a well-meaning unbeliever is. And over-much moralising, criticism and telling people how to conduct their lives is quite counter-productive; and what is more it lacks the authentic note of the Gospel of Christ.

A few years ago I drove all the way across the United States, from coast to coast. It was a great experience not just because the scenery was so magnificent but because one came to realise the vigour and the activism of America and its people. But perhaps the biggest shock was the impact of American popular religion. Right across the country my car radio brought me the voices of preachers, and in the evening in my motel bedroom there was a choice of TV religious shows, lavishly produced with large choirs, preachers as handsome as film-stars,

245

and mass audience participation. The media evangelists are national figures with immense influence. They are the leaders of the so-called 'Moral Majority' and their denunciation of evils in American society now has real political effect. And I must say I was much interested one evening when one very prominent TV preacher announced to us that he was going to preach on the parable of the Pharisee and the Publican. In fact, he was magnificent. The Pharisee became the symbol of all that was mean, grudging and hypocritical in American life: it was a splendid, resounding piece of denunciation. Afterwards one of his associates led us in prayer. 'Let us thank God', he said, 'that we in this church are not like that Pharisee in the story'.

So, who then *is* the Pharisee, and what does the parable mean? Like most of Jesus's stories this one has no element of denunciation; it is not about types of people; it is about basic religious attitudes. It is about men and women in the presence of God. Jesus was certainly not against Pharisees as such; they were a religious set of men, patriotic, serious about their religious duties, and generous in good works. There was nothing wrong in being a Pharisee in itself, and clearly many of Jesus's early followers came from this group. I suppose that Pharisees, like any religious person, were in danger of missing the wood for the trees: to think that knowing about religion was the same as relating to God; to think that having all the right ideas and doing all the correct things was the same as being religious. The story is then about a religious man who did not have the heart of the matter; he had fallen out of his relationship with God. His mind had become fixed on the details of religion, but mostly it had become fixed on himself, and his reputation, and his good works. He was the victim of the *sin of pride*. Pride is when we trust in ourselves that we are righteous and despise others; pride is when we try to give ourselves value because we have no confidence that there is anyone else who values us. Pride is the sin of the insecure, when we must seek to re-assure ourselves by congratulating ourselves on our excellencies and achievements. We want other people to praise us. Pride is known by an interior compulsion to criticise other people, to diminish them, and take away the regard which other people have for them. It is a lonely business, always in danger of falling back into the faithlessness from which it comes. And it is not only religious people who fall into it. Young secular people seem its particular victims: at least when it comes to valuing oneself by one's good looks, vigour, popularity or correct, fashionable opinions. And some modern causes seem to involve a real despising of others. But it is true that religious men and women are not immune, at least in pride's most subtle form: to believe that one is a sensitive and fair-minded person much valued by other people for always being on the right side of a good cause. The root of all these illusions, and their basic ungenerosity to others, is a lonely human will, seeking approval, defending itself, drawing attention to itself, because it has nowhere else to put its trust but in itself.

Of course, it cannot be said that Jesus was much in favour of publicans or tax-collectors *as a type*. They were quislings, usually rich on extortion from their fellow-countrymen; and the gospels indicate that they were made painfully aware of the hatred they attracted, their rejected and despised status in the eyes of right-thinking Jews. And that is why it is such an effective dramatic device for Jesus to make a tax-collector the one who exhibits a genuine religious attitude, who stands in the presence of God and utters a true prayer without pride or false self-confidence. In a moment the usual categories go upside down, Pharisee and Publican, righteous and sinner, the good and the bad; and we get to the heart of the matter: the basic religious attitude.

True religion, says Jesus, is simple dependence on God for what he gives. It is not to be always caught up in self-concern and self-assertion for these destroy our simplicity in God's presence. The teaching of Jesus is clear: that

God comes to us as pure gift: he raises up and gives life to those who put themselves into his hands in trust. If we are full of self-confidence, sure of our right opinions, convinced of our moral status, it is likely that God will remain obscure and unreal to us, for we have no need of him. Indeed it may require some shock, some shattering of our world, before we are ready to turn to him. In his gentle way Jesus himself often administered just such a shock to individuals: to stop them in their tracks, make them see themselves in a different light, and turn in simple trust to the One who is Creator, Redeemer, and Giver of Life. It was to stop the struggle for self-justification and discover the loving purpose and will of God for us. The Publican discovered God as gift, as the One who brings forgiveness, a new beginning, and a new spirit of trust in God for what he gives day by day.

'Thy will be done'. In the Lord's Prayer Jesus goes to the heart of the matter and gives his followers the basis of his own life and relation to others. It is a pattern into which he seeks to draw them. Fundamental to all else is belief in a loving Father who is to be trusted as the source of all true life. And that is surely the meaning of the Cross. Our humanity, usually so full of pride and self-concern, in Jesus comes into the Father's presence in trust for what God can and will do when we have nothing of our own in which we trust. Jesus on the Cross was naked, stripped of all possessions, deprived of all reputation, and abandoned by all the powers, parties and causes of his own day. All he had left was his trust in God, his deep belief that the Father gives a resurrection and an interior gift of his spirit which will be sufficient for us. That God did indeed give such a Resurrection is the Gospel.

It is full of hope—but no-one would pretend that to pray that prayer and be drawn into it is entirely a comfortable experience. Perhaps I am not very good at prayer but my own experience is that the thought of trusting myself into God's hands actually produces in me some struggle, confusion and resistance. There are only occasional moments when I break through to some surrender to the will of God, and stop thinking of myself. The trouble is that one is having to come to terms with the kind of sacrificial love which was in Christ. 'Thy will be done' is not to be repeated parrot-fashion like some Christian mantra; it is a prayer to be made one's own amid the hard experience of life with its constant temptation to faithless self-concern. But, then, it is not a prayer for those who think they know all the answers or who have such a moral status that they can condemn others. Rather, it is the prayer of those who know that they are empty and would be filled, who know that they are sinners and would be forgiven, who already have some small experience of what grace can do in a human life and who want to be more at the disposal of God's indwelling love.

I think that this one sermon of mine has become a plea for a church which has the Gospel as its chief and only treasure. It is for a humble community of those who know that they have been given a great gift which was quite undeserved. They are not placed in the world to condemn it, moralise to it, or advise it but to love and serve it: to be alongside those who are in trouble, despised or neglected. In other words, their vocation and their joy is to show the mercy which has been shown to them.

EPILOGUE

In Memoriam
Gareth Vaughan Bennett

Address by the Revd Dr Geoffrey Rowell,
Chaplain and Fellow, Keble College
New College Chapel, Oxford, 15 December 1987

In the silence of death, and of a death we mourn, so sudden and so tragic, the only word that is creative is the life-giving Word of God. And so I take three texts—the first from the psalms (a cry of the human heart), the others from Revelation (the vision of the End).

'Enter not into judgment with thy servant, O Lord: for in thy sight shall no man living be justified.' (Psalm 143.2).

'He who has an ear, let him hear what the Spirit says to the churches.' (Revelation 2.9).

'God will wipe away every tear from their eyes, and death shall be no more, neither shall there be mourning, nor crying, nor pain any more, for the former things have passed away.' (Revelation 21.4).

Those words, as all words spoken today, are spoken for love and out of love. They are spoken out of our love for Garry, whom we commend today into the keeping of God. They are spoken out of love for a church, sinful and divided, yet constantly recalled by her Lord to be faithful, to live by the way of love and of mercy as a sign of reconciliation to the world. They are spoken out of the love of God, whose very gift to us is his own life, the love which comes down to the very lowest part of our need. That love of God is the fundamental reality. It is by that love, and with such love that all of us are judged. St John of the Cross, whose feast we kept yesterday, said of that judgement: 'At the end He will examine thee in love.' Love is the one thing needful, and the one reality by which we are both judged and healed.

The Christian faith, which Garry professed, and by which he lived, is at its heart a simple response of faith and trust in the God who in love gave us and all things being. It is faith in that same love reaching out to us in our darkness and pain, our sin and despair, with the promise of redemption and forgiveness, and the hope of eternal life. It is an *incarnational* faith, a faith in the God who emptied himself to be as and where we are. It is a *redemptive* faith in the one who came among us knowing human suffering and the ambiguities of our human life. It is faith in the Son of God who entered into the experience of death which comes to us all, meeting death in isolation, abandonment and betrayal. He descended into the dark hell of rejection, and in his cry of dereliction, that his Father had seemingly abandoned him, came to the darkest point of the human spirit. Yet above all the Christian faith is a *Resurrection* faith, a faith in the mercy of God who out of despair gives hopes, and in the place of death brings forth his new creation. By doing this we proclaim our Easter faith, a faith which gives us hope in the face of this darkness and this pain.

God created Garry, our friend and brother, in his image and likeness. He gave him gifts of deep and simple faith and sharp intellect, of historical perception, of sensitivity combined with firmness, of love felt if not always easily shown, of wit and of wisdom—and for these we give thanks. When pain and darkness drove him to a hell of despair, the God we trust who met him there was the God who in Christ crucified went down into the darkness. To that God we now commend him. This breaking of bread, this eucharist (thanksgiving) for the love of God, is a sacrament and pledge of that life which God gives, through which the resurrection life of his Kingdom is established in us, and we abide in him. It is a prophetic sign of the brokenness of the Lord upon the Cross, where we know the length and breadth and depth and height of the Divine compassion meeting our broken lives with healing. Only in this place, in this way, can we discern meaning and renew our hope. Here we are caught out of our pain and grief into the very offering of Christ himself, and pray the one prayer of his loving purpose for Garry, and for ourselves, and for the whole Church of God.

There are many pains and griefs here today—pains 'counter and keen'—of loss, of anger, of guilt; the pain of one alone, bearing accusations and striving to know what was right; the pain he felt in belonging to a church which could seem ruled by trend and not the tradition handed on; the pain he felt and shared with others in the church that apostolic faith, and ministry, and sacraments, were threatened, not so much by changes in ministry, about which there may be debate, but by the way those changes were pursued, and by the lack of concern for the bonds of ecumenical friendship and the character of historic Anglicanism by those who pressed for them, come what may, and sure that they were right. There are other pains also which others feel, but these are ones felt here and now. All this pain must be recognised and acknowledged and brought before God in our prayer today and in the church in the months ahead.

'Enter not into judgement with thy servant O Lord: for in thy sight can no man living be justified.' Indeed, all are under judgement, whether they be friend, or Fellow, or bishop, or journalist—and you and I and all of us here need no less and no more than that same mercy and forgiveness of God, to whom we pray for our brother Garry. And in all of this we ask for the healing light of the Spirit that we may indeed have ears to hear in the words written and the death to which in the end they lead, what is said to the churches.

One place which Garry loved and cared for was Pusey

House, and so it is fitting for words of Edward Pusey to speak to us today, words from a sermon entitled, 'God's Presence in Loneliness':

'It is only afar off that the wilderness looks a waste, and terrible, and dry. Was it not there that man did eat Angel's Food, and water gushed out of the hard rock, and bitter waters were made sweet . . .? There shalt thou speak to God "face to face", and "hear what the Lord thy God will speak in thee . . ." There shall he renew thy soul, hear thy prayer and answer it, shed hope around thee, kindle thy half-choked love, give thee some taste out of His Own Boundless Love, give thee longing to pass out of all besides, out of thy decayed self, gathered upward unto Him, Who came down hither to our misery, to bear us up unto Himself, and make us one spirit with him.'

Or, as the poet Henry Vaughan puts it:

> But a twin'd wreath of *grief* and *praise*,
> Praise soil'd with tears, and tears again
> Shining with joy, like dewy days,
> This day I bring for all thy pain,
> Thy causeless pain! and sad as death;
> Which sadness breeds in the most vain,
> (O not in vain!) now beg thy breath;
> Thy quickning breath, which gladly bears
> Through saddest clouds to that glad place,
> Where cloudless Quires sing without tears,
> Sing thy just praise, and see thy face.